Order this book online at www.trafford.com/07-2324
or email orders@trafford.com

Most Trafford titles are also available at major online book retailers.

Note for Librarians: A cataloguing record for this book is available from Library
and Archives Canada at www.collectionscanada.ca/amicus/index-e.html

Printed in Victoria, BC, Canada.

ISBN: 978-1-4251-5279-6

*We at Trafford believe that it is the responsibility of us all, as both individuals and corporations,
to make choices that are environmentally and socially sound. You, in turn, are supporting this
responsible conduct each time you purchase a Trafford book, or make use of our publishing services.
To find out how you are helping, please visit www.trafford.com/responsiblepublishing.html*

*Our mission is to efficiently provide the world's finest, most comprehensive book publishing
service, enabling every author to experience success. To find out how to publish your book, your
way, and have it available worldwide, visit us online at www.trafford.com/10510*

 www.trafford.com

North America & international
toll-free: 1 888 232 4444 (USA & Canada)
phone: 250 383 6864 ♦ fax: 250 383 6804 ♦ email: info@trafford.com

The United Kingdom & Europe
phone: +44 (0)1865 487 395 ♦ local rate: 0845 230 9601
facsimile: +44 (0)1865 481 507 ♦ email: info.uk@trafford.com

10 9 8 7 6 5 4 3

UNITED STATES MARINE CORPS

SEMPER FIDELIS

WE
BURIED
OUR
BUDDIES
&
My Stories

by charles Wysocki, Jr

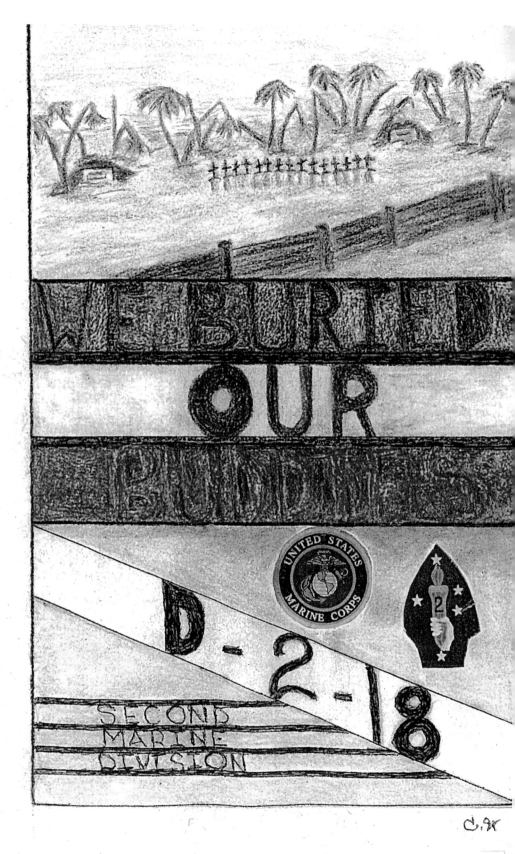

GUADALCANAL · TULAGI · TARAWA · SAIPAN

WE BURIED OUR BUDDIES

UNITED STATES MARINE CORPS

D-2-8

SECOND MARINE DIVISION

TINIAN — WORLD WAR TWO

1

This page was drawn by the author

To my wife, Bernice, my children, Patricia, my Daughter, and Paul, my Son,— "Thanks", for the encouragement you gave me to write this book of my experiences in World War Two.

INDEX

There are no Chapters in this book, - but I will list some the articles, I have written, that might be of special interest to the readers —

3

P.F.C. Charles Wysocki, Jr. - 1945, Age 23.
United States Marine Corps. - 1942-1945,
Tulagi - Tarawa - Saipan - Tinian -
Wounded on Saipan.

Bernice P. Gaszak
Milwaukee, Wisc. - 1945.
We were married on February 15, 1947.

The Road to War
Asia and the Pacific

World War Two was fought across the entire globe, but it actually began as two separate and unrelated conflicts that were oceans apart. Fighting began in the Pacific in early 1937 and evolved into full-scale war in Asia between China and Japan within a short period.

In Europe, another war started on September 1, 1939 when Germany invaded Poland with Britain and France then coming to Poland's aid. World War Two officially begins at this time.

The Second World War was the costliest and largest conflict ever fought in all of human history. While this chronology is about the Pacific portion of that war, a few figures of the immensity of World War Two overall are provided to enable the reader to better understand its impact.

Every man, woman, and child alive today has been affected in some manner by that war and its aftermath.

More than 60 million people were killed. It was the first total war. Twice as many civilians died than did uniformed soldiers, sailors, airmen and marines. Over 85 million men and women served as combatants and survived. Well in excess of 2 trillion dollars is a conservative estimate of the economic cost of World War Two.

How did the war in the Pacific start? What were the causes? The road to the war in Asia and the Pacific was a long one, filled with sidebars and potholes. America saw it coming, so why wasn't the U.S. military ready at Pearl Harbor? Because America underestimated Japan's ability even though their military possessed the capability.

Why did Japan attack a nation that was considerably more powerful and very capable of a sustained conflict that would defeat Japan? Japan greatly underestimated American will and determination. They considered the U.S. to be soft, comparable to Russia in 1905, lacking in the stamina and spirit that made Japan strong and capable of overcoming superior odds.

This chronology, as complex as it may be, is provided to better understand why.

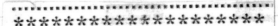

****

"The willingness with which our young people are likely to serve in any war, no matter how justified, shall be directly proportional to how they perceive veterans of earlier wars were treated and appreciated by our nation."
Quote from George Washington submitted by Jim Nixon (LTC, USArmy, Ret.) Life Member DAV

DEDICATION

This book is dedicated to the Marines of, — Co. "D", 2nd Batt, 18th Marines, (formerly the 2nd Pioneer Battalion), 2nd Marine Division, — both the living and the dead. These men did their duty for, "God and Country", to the fullest. They died protecting the freedoms we now enjoy, — they are the, "Heroes".

Those of us who were lucky and returned must always remind everyone of the sacrifices made by the men of our Armed Forces around the world.

"Remember, — Freedom Is Not Free!!

year 2007

HONORING THE GREATEST FIGHTING FORCE IN THE WORLD

THE FEW, THE PROUD, THE MARINES

"PREFACE"

The stories you are about to read are all true, written by one who was there, - the Author, Charles Wysocki, Jr. I was a member of, - Co. "D", 2nd Batt., 18th Marines, (formerly the 2nd Pionee Battalion), 2nd Marine Division. We were used as Infantry,* Beach Party and Combat Engineers. The stories will cover the years, - Feb. 1942 through April 1945 and will include the Battles for Tulagi, (Guadalcanal Campaign), British Solomon Islands, Aug. 7th, 1942, - the Bloody Battle for Tarawa, Gilbert Islands, Nov. 20th, 1943, - and the Battles for Saipan and Tinian, Marianas Islands, June 15th through the 9th of Aug. 1944. These stories are basic- ly about Co. "D" and the part they played in the conquest of the Japanese in the above mentioned campaigns, of which I was very much a part of. What was accomplished was due to our training, discipline, dedication, and the love of Country and family

    My experience in World War Two gave me the opportunity to meet many people, both in the Military and Civilian life. What I learned about life and war, I believe I became a better person and a better human being today.

*Beach Party, - the name given to the those who went in with the Assault Troops to clear the beaches of the enemy and then direct the supply boats to their stations. They would also help to -

~ evacuate those who were wounded. In other words our job on the beach was to keep the traffic moving off the beach.

WORLD WAR II

World War II was the greatest military conflict in the history of the world. It was the first war that engulfed every continent on earth and inflicted more death and destruction on people and nations than any other recorded event.

However, the most notable result of World War II, and the very thing that has been ignored by historians and scholars is that the victors, the nations forced into war by the aggressors Germany and Japan, in the most compassionate and humanitarian action in history, rebuilt the devastated economies and their political and social structures of their defeated enemies thus enabling them to become the powerful democracies they are today.

It should be noted that following all previous wars, the victors ravaged their defeated enemies, taking all their wealth and property, holding executions and enslaving their population as "the spoils of victory"!

The American people took no spoils or reparations in *1945;* but rather assumed a great and heavy burden to insure that nothing like World War II would ever happen again.

—Jack Bernabucci, 1997

Join us, as we journey back in time, and travel through our history, to touch the aircraft and the people who made that history.

These are the men of - D-2-18, (Pioneers). →
Left to right -
1st Row - Lt. Barney Boos - Bill Ralph - ? - ? - Rawlings - ? -
        Kleber - ? - Marsten - Crelia - Wetternach - ? -
2nd Row - ? - ? - ? - Singer - ? - ? - ? - ? - Perry - ? - Wysocki -
3rd Row - Sgt. Wesley C. Worthington - ? - ? - ? - Ellis -
        Smith - Stoffer - "Buger Red" Anderson - ? -
        Duffy - ? - ? -
4th Row - Lt. Sayler - Sgt. Mike Matkovich (Masters) - ? -
        Green - ? - Snelling - ? - ? - Scholl - ? - ? -
        Rice, Corpman - Sgt. Bass -

18th Marines

Top Row - Frye - Woods - Schouviller - Robinson - Duffy -
        Harrison - Middle Row - Jackman - Tomaszewski -
Bottom Row - Baron - Curcio - Drake - Costa -

(Pioneers)   The "Good Guys" 1S-2-/8th Marines, (Island of Tulagi, British Solomon's) P.F.C. Charles Wysocki, Jr.-X

" My Life

If Anyone Is Interested "

    I, Charles Wysocki, Jr, was brought into this world on January 10th, 1923 in the city of Milwaukee, Wisconsin. I was born into the family of Charles, Sr. and Emma Wysocki who already had two children, — my brother, Robert, the oldest, and my sister, Lorraine. After me two more girls would join the family, — Grace, a very pretty girl, who became very ill at the age of five, — doctors at first were puzzled by her sickness and weren't sure what it was she had. She became crippled and sometimes she would have a spell, falling down and hurting herself, — this went on until she died at the age of forty. We were all born about two years apart, except for the last born, my sister, Mary Ann, who was about six years younger than Grace. We were all born at home and Mary Ann would have had a twin brother, but he didn't make it. He was born in a sack, — which was to be broken, — but nobody knew what to do, so he suffocated. There were two others, a boy, Joseph and a girl, Mary, — both died shortly after birth. I remember their funerals which were held in the Sun Parlor of our home.

    We lived in an area called, — "Polish Town", near St. Cazmiers Catholic Church, where we went to Church. It was a beautiful Church.

    I remember some of the streets names, Bremen St. where we lived until we moved to North Pierce St, and Locust St. where my Mother's folks lived in their own home, a flat. Her sister, Polly, lived upstairs and down the road, on Locust St., my Mother's family had a, "butcher shop", and some-times Mom would take me into the basement where she taught me how to, "candle eggs". While I was doing that, Mom, would be Killing and dressing chickens and drawing blood from the geese for that Polish "delicacy", - "Blood Soup"!!

I remember the first house we lived in, - it wasn't very much, - no basement, an iron wood stove for heating and cooking, two bedrooms and a round tub for taking baths. We wern't very old or very big, - we fit in the tub, perfectly! This was on Bremen St., Then we moved to a lower flat on North Pierce St., where I remember, in the summer time, while sitting on the front porch steps, my Dad would give me a bucket, about a pint, and tell me to go across the street to the local Saloon and "get a pint." I liked doing that because at the Saloon there would be a bar full of cold cuts, cheese, pickles, olives and breads, - and I could eat all I wanted, - until the bucket got filled, - and they didn't hurry. I'd carefully take the bucket of beer to my Dad and for a reward I'd get to sip off some of the foam, - mm, mm, good. Oh, for the good ol days!

There was a park, not to far from where we lived and I remember going there many, many times with my Mother, Brothers, Sisters, Cousins and Aunts, - we would have a ball! Gordon Park was located on the Milwaukee River and Locust Street. It would become a meeting place for all of us, - for picnics, get togethers and just plain fun. In the

winter we would go there to ice skate, play
hockey and slide down the hill. I remember
one time I borrowed my Cousin Gene's skies
and tried to ski down the ski hill at the Park, - I
almost killed myself, - I never tried it again.
It was a great park for year-round activities, -
I'll always remember the good times we had
there

    When I was about six or seven years old, -
in the middle 1930's, - my Dad had our future
home built on the North side of Milwaukee, -
North 21st and Olive Streets, - near Rufus King
High School and it was a beautiful house. There
was room for everyone, - three bedrooms, but only
one bathroom, which proved to be a big problem at
times.

    My brother and I had the upstairs bedroom,
the only room on the second floor besides the attic,
which was for storage. It had two windows that
we could open for fresh air, - they were on the
South side of the room so we could get a lot of sun-
shine into the room. The only bad thing about the
room was that in the winter time we couldn't get
much heat to come up to our room, - but we could
always throw another blanket on the bed. We would
survive!

    After we moved to our new home there
was a lot of work to be done around the house,
especialy getting the grounds ready for grass
seeding and the flower beds ready so my Dad
could plant his array of beautiful flowers. My
Dad looked & found a vacant lot, a couple of

blocks away from home, which contained a lot of real nice black soil, ideal for the yard. My brother, Bob, and I got the job of digging and hauling the black ground back to the house and spreading it around the front and back yards. We did this for weeks and weeks with a coaster, two bushels, a shovel and a grub-ax. We would do this after school, on weekends, until it got to dark to see what we were doing. It was worth all the hard work, — the grass came up to a beautiful lawn and my Dad had the most beautiful flower-beds in the neighborhood. He was very proud of his gardens and every year he would prepare the grounds for a new batch of plants, — he must of had a "green thumb", he never had a failure. Then I got the job of keeping the lawn clear of dande-lions, — sometimes I'd dig for hours, but I did it, even though I'd get so frustrated because I had to sit there and dig weeds when everyone else was having fun playing games. The lawn looked real good, so my work was worthwhile.

A while later I developed a problem which would last for several years; — I became a bed-wetter. In those days I don't think parents knew much about what caused bed-wetting, — at least my Dad didn't. He used to treat me like you would a dog, — if you rubbed a dog's nose in it's mess you could train it not to do again. It didn't work with me and I told him many times; — I couldn't help it, but he would say, I was just lazy. I was lucky; — my brother saw what my Dad did to me, — so he thought he could do the same thing, and he did.

Eventualy my problem went away, but I was to encounter others. Yes, I had problems growing up, - but I also had some good times. I loved sports, mostly baseball and football and I was always wanted on someones team. Once when I was playing hardball, - I was an outfielder, we were being scouted by a White Sox Scout. After the game he asked if I would be interested in playing for them in the minor league. Believe me, - I was excited and I told the Scout, - I'd love to, but you would have to talk to my Dad first, - which he did, - with a negative answer, - NO!! My Dad didn't want me exposed to other dangerous attractions, - like wild women and booze, - at the age of seventeen. Well, that opportunity went down the drain!!

I loved sports, more than girls, - at that time and my first date with a female would take place in New Zealand, City of Wellington in 1943, during World War Two.

When I was around 12 and for a few years before, I was having a lot of trouble with my older sister, Lorraine, who I think, at that time was my Dad's favorite and anything she told him about me he believed. It seemed I was the one getting blamed for most everything that was happening in and around the house. My Dad had a variety of weapons he used for punishment, - besides his hand and I was to be the recepient of all of them. I was no angel, I probably deserved some of the punishment I received. He had a barbers strap that was cut into strips, about 3/4 of the way up and when you were hit with it, - boy it stung.

Mom used it once in awhile on all of us. Then he had a siphening hose, about 4 or 5 feet long, that he would whip you with and it hurt bad and leave welts all over your body. Then he had the grandaddy of them all, — a piece of garden hose, again about 4 feet long with a buckle, (a hose attachment), on the end of it. I had many bumps, welts and bruises from that one, — but I would never let him know that he was hurting me. That wasn't all he had, — in the basement of our house there were two rooms, one was called the, "Fruit Cellar", and the other I called it the "Dark Room", because that's what it was, — so DARK you couldn't see your hand in front of your face. The room contained mostly his garden tools, a garden hose coiled on the floor and there was no light or window in the room. Sometimes, Dad, would lock me in the, "Dark Room", and leave me there for hours. Mom would sneak down once in awhile to give me some food and drink, — but never to let me out for fear of my Dad. He could get kind of crazy once in awhile. He'd leave me out when he was good and ready, and he never showed any signs of remorse for what he did to me, — that I could see. When I came home from World War Two, I went to him, — he was sitting in his favorite chair in the living room and I knelt down along side him, — I "Thanked" him for his descipline. I feel very strong that the descipline I received, as a kid, was very helpful in getting me through the War. I think that if anyone was desciplined today the way I was, when I was a kid, that person would probably be in jail. There are two things missing in our society, today, descipline and obedience, this must be corrected.

My problem with my sister, Lorrain, was getting to a point where somthing had to be done about her snitching and lieing about me. One day at the supper table she started telling my Dad that I had done somthing I wasn't supposed to do, - which was not true. At this point I had had it, - I got up and leaned across the table; - I belted her a good one!! I left the table and went up to my room expecting my Dad to follow me and punish me, - but nothing happened and nothing was said, - there were no more problems.

Mom, - she was the most wonderful person in the world, - she was always there for us, - in the morning before we went to school, - always had our lunch bags ready for us, - she was there when we came home from school, - she was there when we were doing our homework, - whenever we needed her, she was there, she was the homemaker and much, much more. I remember when Mom and I would do the dishes, - we'd sing our favorite song, "Home On The Range", and we were pretty good. Mom, taught me a lot about life and "God", and I "Thank" her for the knowledge she passed on to us. Mom and Dad never finished grade school but their knowledge was unbeleivable. The last time I saw my Mom after I enlisted in the Corps was that same day, - Feb. 5th, when I was leaving to catch the train to San Diego and the Marine Corps Recruit Depot. Next to our house was an empty corner lot & from

the kitcen window, of our house, you could see
the street corner and on up the street. I had said,
"Goodbye", to Mom and my sisters earlier in the day
and my brother, Bob, was already in the Army, - the
32nd "Red Arrow," Division. As I left the house, to catch
a streetcar a couple of blocks away, I turned
around to have a last look and there was, Mom,
waving to me in the kitcen window. There was a
lump in my throat as I waved back and then continued on. That picture of, Mom, would stay with
me forever

    My Dad, was really a pretty good guy even
though he would have his mean streaks. He was
a good provider, - he worked hard for the Railway
Express Co. and always provided, Mom, with enough money to run the house and pay the bills.
We all helped out doing odd jobs in the neighborhood such as, - baby-sitting, grass cutting,
shoveling snow and selling the, "Saturday Evening
Post" and "The Ladies Home Journal". My brother
had a paper route, - The Milwaukee Journal and
I helped him until I got my own route. I also
had a paper corner where I'd sell the Milwaukee
Sentinel in the morning and the Milwaukee Journal in the evening. I was also a jumper for the
Sentinel District Manager. I'd get up about 4: A.M. &
the Manager would come by to pick me up and
we'd proceed to cover the District, filling the corner
paper boxes, dropping papers off at the local business places, - then I'd go to my corner to sell papers.
About 6:30 A.M. I'd go home have my breakfast
and go to school, - St. Agnes Catholic Grade School.

—later, Rufus King High School. So we were able to contribut to the family income, but we were allowed to keep some of the earnings for our own use.

I was a student at Rufus King High and in Grade 10B when my Dad decided, I should learn a "trade". He took me out of school and enrolled me in the Milwaukee Vocational School to learn the Machinest Trade,—not my choice and I was never to use the trade.

Another time, when I was around 15, I was out with my friends and one of them said, "Gee, it would be nice if we had a car so we could go for a ride",—and I said, "We had a car and I could get the keys. I snuck into our house took the keys off the hook and we went down the alley to where my Dad had rented a garage,—one of the guys said he knew how to drive, (sorry, but I don't remember their names), but he backed the car out and we went for a ride. What I didn't know was that my brother, Bob, had brought the car home earlier because he was having trouble with it,—shortly we would find out. I think there were four of us and we were crusing up and down Capitol Drive when all of a sudden the car conked out and it wouldn't start up again. What do we do now!! We decided to leave the car, wipe it clean of fingerprints, promised each other we would say nothing about what we did. The next morning, Sunday, my Dad and my Brother went to the garage to look at the car,—but there was no car. Dad called the Cops and the determined it was,—"an inside 'job". The police asked who I had been with last night, - I told them and felt safe that no one would say anything. The police left and within an hour they were back, - the first friend they went to see, - "spilled the beans". The police rounded us up and took us to the Juvenile Detention Center where we were booked and fingerprinted. Eventualy everyone was released to their parents, - except me. My Dad had told the police to keep me in detention until I had learned my lesson, - which I did. When they released me there was no one there to pick me up, - so I had to walk home, - about 15 miles. When I finally got home I was expecting to be punished, - but nothing happened, except that my Dad didn't talk to me for a long time. Being in that Detention Center, - mixed in with some of the toughest kids you'd ever want to meet was a lesson I'd never forget. It was always a reminder to me, - "Don't Screw Up!!"

I was always interested in music and when I went to work for Decca Records, (pre-war), it was the start of a long hobby of record collecting, - 78's, 33's and 45's. Up to about five years ago I had 3,000 records in my collection and then I sold a majority of them, donated some and kept about 50 special records. My hobby now is collecting Military DVD's, - to date I have about 500 videos.

Getting back to my interest in music; - in grade school I was in the Church Youth Choir which I enjoyed very much. When I went to High School I checked in with the Music Dept. to see what they had to offer. All that was available was a French Horn, - which I didn't know anything about, but I thought I'd give it a try. I told the teacher I'd have to take it home to get my Dad's approval, - that was a big mistake!! When I showed him the French Horn and told him I was going to learn how to play it and be in the school band, - he said, "Oh no your not going to play that thing in this house and besides you won't have the time". That was the end of that career, - I took it back the next day. In the meantime my brother, Bob, got to take lessons to play the Banjo, - he did well. My sister, Lorraine, got to take piano lessons and toe dance lessons, - she did well also. When I asked my Dad if I could take piano lessons or the accordian, - he said, "He wasn't going to waste anymore money on music lessons", and yet when my sister, Mary Ann, wanted to take piano lessons, it was OK. We had a real nice piano, in the living room, that my Dad would play the only song he knew when asked to play. I used to sit down and play, making up my own tunes, which I thought were pretty good, - but that did not influence my Dad to give me a chance.

It was the summer of my 18th birthday, 1940, and I had completed my required schooling, got a job at Blatz Brewing Company and I was doing very well. At this time in my life there woud be a big change, - a war would come along. My life after the war years will continue later in the book.

Now the War years - - - -

"How I Became A Marine"

It was the summer of my 18th birthday, 1940, & it was a Sunday afternoon and two of my friends, also 18, were visiting me, - we were laying on the living room floor looking at a map of the U.S.A. with ideas of doing some traveling around this beautiful Country of ours. We were all out of school, had no jobs at this time and looking for something to do. We never considered how we would pay for a trip to anywhere, - we had no money. While we were talking my Dad, sitting in his favorite chair & reading the Sunday paper, was listening to us at the same time, - he put the paper to one side and looking around the edge said, - "If you want to travel to see the world, why don't you join the Navy!!" We looked at each other and the consensus was, - why not. We talked it over and the next day, Monday, we went to the Federal Building in downtown Milwaukee, Wisc. where all the Military Recruiting Offices were. The Recruiter on duty welcomed us and asked what he could do for us & in unison we said, "We want to join the Navy". From that point on we started the sign-up procedure and when we got to the physical examination, - I didn't make it!! I was told I had a Hernia that would have to be taken care of before I could enlist. My friends made it and were to be sent to the Great Lakes Naval Training Station, - near Chicago. I wished my friends, "Good Luck", - went home to tell my Mother what had happened. Arraingments were made for me to have the operation and after the recuperation period, - which was a lot different and longer than it is today, - "Pearl Harbor" happened, - Dec. 7th, 1941. As soon after, as I could, I went to join up again; but when I got there every Recruiting Office had a line of people that looked like they were a mile long. I wasn't going to wait in line, - so I looked around and there it was, - "The United States Marine Corps Recruiting Office", with only a few guys in line. I said to myself, - "That's for me", and I got in line to wait my turn. I passed the examination & was ordered to report to the Northwestern Railroad Depot at 6:P.M. that same night, Feb. 5th, 1942. I went home to get whatever I was going to take with me and to say, "Good Bye", to my Mom and sisters, - my Dad was still at work and he would meet me at the Station, - my brother was already in the Army, - the 32nd, "Red Arrow", Division. At about 5:30 P.M. that evening I met my Dad at the Station, - we talked a bit and at 6:P.M. I boarded the train with other recruits and we were on our way to San Diego and the Marine Corps.. I wouldn't see my family again for about, 3 years, 3 months & 12 days.

The "bill" for my Hernia operation wouldn't be paid until I got back from the War, 1945.

Now you know how I became a "Marine".

·USMC·

"Day of Infamy"

It was Sunday morning and the Wysocki family was getting dressed to go to Church at St. Agnes Catholic School & Church. As always we were dressed in our, "Sunday Best", - we were going to, "God's House", and that is what we were brought up to do. After Church we would go home and Mom would start preparing the, "noon lunch", - Dad would settle in his favorite chair to read the Sunday paper. Us Kids would help Mom or we would fight for the, "Comics", after Dad was through with them. But on this particular day we were all doing what we usually did and Dad was about to turn on the Radio to listen to one of his favorite programs, the "Father Caughlin Hour". What he got was not his favorite program, - it was an, "Emergency News Broadcast", - the Japanese had, "attacked Pearl Harbor", - it was December 7th, 1941, - "A Day of Infamy!!" We looked at each other and wondered, - "Where's Pearl Harbor". Shortly after the announcer mentioned the Hawaiian Islands, - then we had an idea of where it was, but we still got out the maps and Geography books to pin-point where the Islands were located. On the World Maps the Hawaiian Is.'s were just dots on the maps.

We knew that this cowardly attack by the Japanese would mean an all out war by the U.S.A. against the Japs and their Axis friends.

I turned 19 on January 10th, 1942 but it wouldn't be until February 5th, 1942 that I felt well enough and strong enough to try joining up again, - & I did.

Day
of
Infamy

DECEMBER 7, 1941
PEARL HARBOR

The sinking of the U.S.S. Arizona

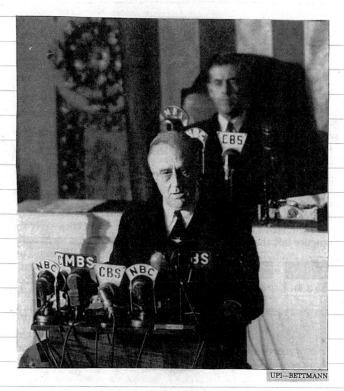

UPI—BETTMANN

"A Date That Will Live In Infamy," President Roosevelt asks a special session of Congress to declare war against Japan.

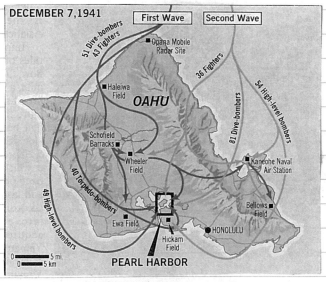

DECEMBER 7,1941

First Wave   Second Wave

51 Dive-bombers
43 Fighters

■ Opana Mobile
Radar Site

36 Fighters

54 High-level bombers

■ Haleiwa
Field

OAHU

81 Dive-bombers

Schofield
Barracks ■

■ Kaneohe Naval
Air Station

Wheeler
Field ■

40 Torpedo-bombers

49 High-level bombers

Ewa Field ■

Bellows ■
Field

■ HONOLULU

Hickam
Field ■

0 ——— 5 mi.
0 ——— 5 km

PEARL HARBOR

"The Attack"

27

"The Target"

"Boot Camp"

Three days after leaving Milwaukee, on Feb. 5th, 1942, we arrived in San Diego, Calif. and the Marine Corps Recruit Depot. Until this day I have never seen or been on a military base, but when I saw the Marine Emblem above the main entrance to the base it was "Awsome". In the next few weeks I would get to know that base inside and out, - including the "boondocks", (fields, openspaces). First we were issued all of our "GI" equipment and clothing, then we had to send our civilian clothing back home. I hated to do that because I had a beautiful sweater that I didn't want to part with, - but rules are rules and it was sent home and I was never to see it again. Next we were assigned to a "Boot Platoon", and introduced to our "DI's", - who seemed like pretty good guys, (drill instructors). All the preliminaries were taken care of and now it was time to start learning how to become a Marine. We had close order drills, day after day, bayonet practice, hand grenade drills, hand to hand fighting drills and the first time we had extended drills in the "boondocks", - running as hard and as fast as you can and then hitting the dirt in a firing position I felt a sharp pain, where I had the Hernia operation, - I guess it didn't heal completly. I didn't report it, - I just hoped it would take care of it self, - and it did. Finaly "boot camp" was over, -- and we were ready to be assigned to a line company. One day we were called out for a "General Assembly", on the "Parade Grounds", where an Officer proceeded to tell us about a new unit that was being organized called the, "Pioneers". He didn't tell us what the duties would be but said,- "In due time the operations of the new unit would be explained to us." He then asked for volunteers. Usually one doesn't volunteer for anything,- especially in the, "Corps",- but a bunch of us did. I guess, "curiosity", got the best of us and we were anxious to find out what the new unit was going to be like,- we would find out shortly!!

"Pioneers"

Once I and the others had volunteered for the, "Pioneers", we officialy became part of the, "Second Marine Division". My unit would become,-"Company D, 2nd Battalion, 18th Marines.

Our training would pick-up in ernest but first we were billited on the far side of the,

"Parade Grounds", in what we called, "Tent City", made up of eight man tents. We were located next to the, "2nd Raider Battalion", - this kind of made us wonder, - were we to be anything like the, "Raiders"!! In our ongoing training we would find out that we could be used in several different ways, - as Infantry, Combat Engineers and Shore Party. We would be sent wherever needed and in future assaults against the Japanese held islands all of our training would be applied.

Our advance training for combat consisted mostly of ship-to-shore operations, - which lasted for weeks. Over and over again we would go over the side of the ship, down the, "Cargo Nets", into the landing craft that was bobbing all over the place, - so you had to be very careful of when you would let go of the, "Cargo Net", and drop into the, "Higgens", boat. Sadly, it did happen when one would let go at the wrong time and miss the boat. We always trained with full combat gear, - so if you missed the boat, - you didn't have a chance! We also practiced hitting the, "beach", driving inland and putting up, "beach markers", which would indicate where the supply boats with, - ammo, water, food, and medical supplies should come in and be unloaded. We were getting pretty damned good at this job, - but that was our own opinion! Training would never stop, we were aiming for perfection.

One day when we woke up in the morning & went top-side to get some fresh air, - and there was plenty of it, because during the night our ships had up-anchored, destination unknown!!

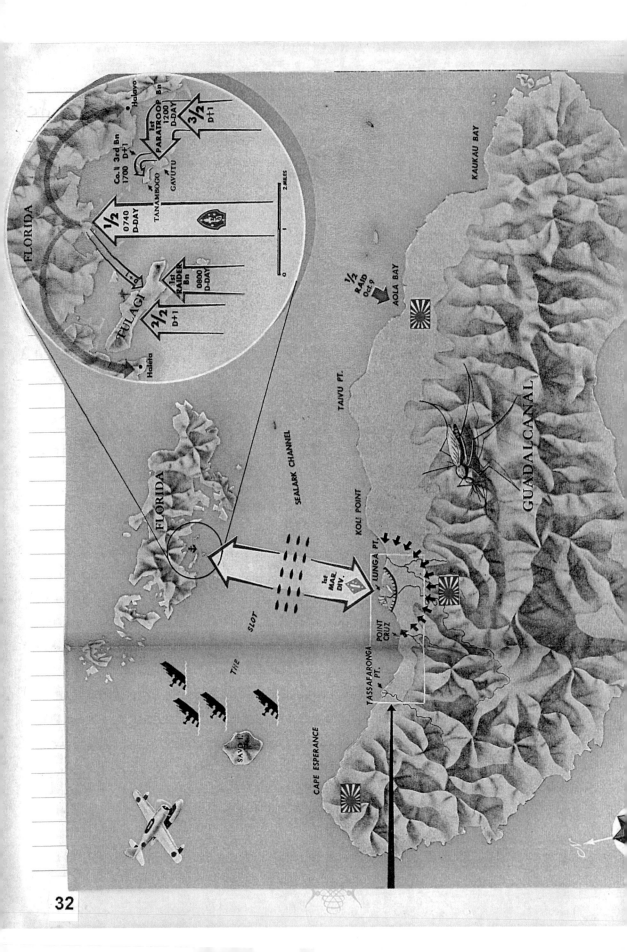

FLORIDA

Haleyo

1st
PARATROOP Bn
1200
D-DAY

3/2
D+1

Co.1 3rd Bn
1700 D+1

TANAMBOGO

GAVUTU

1/2
0740
D-DAY

1st
RAIDER
Bn
0800
D-DAY

2/2
D+1

TULAGI

Haleta

2 MILES

0

FLORIDA

SEALARK CHANNEL

KOLI POINT

TAIVU PT.

KAUKAU BAY

1/2
RAID
Oct 9

AOLA BAY

1st
MAR.
DIV.

LUNGA PT.

POINT
CRUZ

TASSAFARONGA
PT.

GUADALCANAL

THE
SLOT

SAVO I.

CAPE ESPERANCE

GUADALCANAL
FLORIDA · TULAGI · GAVUTU · TANAMBOGO

Over the side we go, down the cargo nets into the bobbing Higgins boats for the long, wet ride to our designated beach, and the attack. This operation would take place many times in the "Pacific Theater." For me it would be four times, plus all the practice ones. Also, one at night while the ship was moving, that was a scary one.

FLORIDA ISLAND

MAKAMBO

TANAMBOGO-GAVUTU

TULAGI

I landed here, *, on Tulagi

"Guadalcanal – Tulagi"

We were on our way, to where, we did not know!! In the meantime aboard our ships, known as the, "Unholy Four", we got a bunch of shots in our arms, on both sides, at the same time. Boy, did we have some sore arms for a few days. We would exercise every day, write letters home, check and clean our gear, watch the Dolphins and Flying Fish that were along side our ship, it was fun watching them and it helped kill the time.

The four ships that were assigned to us were, the U.S.S. President Hayes, my ship, President Jackson, President Adams and the Cresent City. We would travel as fast as the slowest ship and the Cresent City was the slowest, and we'd get a kick out of watching it come out of the water with it's screws spinning like crazy and the ship would shutter until it dropped back into the sea. One day we ran into a storm that lasted for three days, what a wild ride that was!! One minute we'd be riding the crest of a wave then we'd drop into the hollow of it with water all around us, it was very scary and awsome. We rode the storm out O.K., but we heard we lost a couple of persons who were washed overboard on some of the other ships.

After a few days at sea we were called top-side for a meeting, this is when we would find out what our destination was to be. Maps were spread out on the deck and an Officer began, "Men, today we are preparing for the first offensive assault of the war against the Japanese. The place would be Guadalcanal, in the Solomon, Is's. Where the heck are the Solomons; never heard of them! The Officer proceeded to point out where they were on the map and the main objective was to be the, "Canal". Other Islands in the group were Florida, Tulagi, Gavutu and Tanambogo Islands. The date was, - Aug. 7th, 1942

On the way we stopped at the Tonga, Is's, for a break, and that's all it was. We left the ship walked around the main square, waved to all the natives including the Queen, who was a very big woman. Once around and we went back aboard ship to continue our journey. That was the shortest "sight-seeing" trip I have ever taken!

The next few days would be filled with drills, drills and more drills, - making sure our Combat Packs had everything we would need for at least three days, - extra socks, underwear, tooth-brushes, toothpaste, C-Rations, shaving gear, etc. We would practice how fast we could get from our quarters to our disembarkation station, that was previously assigned to us. We did it during the day and at night so we would get familiar where everything was. One night we tried it again and everything was going OK until I hit topside and I was moving across the deck at full speed when I hit a cable that almost tore my head off. I did a complete flip, - but I got to my station on time, - a bit dazed. You can bet your boots that I knew where that cable was on the drills to come! We would write letters, visit the

Chaplain, check our gear over and over again to make sure we had everything needed for our first assault.

It was Aug. 7th and we were awakened about 3:AM., cleaned up, put on our combat clothing, went to breakfast, - don't remember what it was, but we ate what we could. After eating & getting back to our quarters the word came, - "proceed to your disembarkation stations" and the assault troops moved out. Some of us had other assignments, - Mike and myself were assigned to the 5 inch gun on the fantail, - I to the magazine and because of Mike's former experience on the Battleship, U.S.S. Tennesee, he became the "Gun Captain". We did not have to fire and a couple of hours latter we were relived and ordered to report to our unit, - we were going in. We got our gear and reported to our station, went over the rail, down the cargo net and into a Higgins boat. We headed in to the beach which would be on the harbor side of Tulagi. As we were going in, it was late in the afternoon and a couple miles ride in the Higgins boats, I was thinking to myself, - "How am I going to react, will I do my job, Mom, pray for me, and would I be scared!!" Well, that last thought was already answered, - I was scared!! The closer we got the more we would hear the sound of gunfire, the rat-a-tat-tat of machine guns and an occasional blast from our Navy warships. We landed unapposed and were immedially took up defensive positions. My position was about half way up the hill facing the beach &

we were expecting a counter attack, from the Japs, that night, - but it did not happen. During the night there was sporadic gunfire, including one of our machine guns, manned by Leonard Rawlings, who machine gunned a Jap who was trying to swim to Tulagi. One night while I was in my foxhole it started to rain, - I put on my Pancho and stayed in my foxhole, - it started to rain harder and harder, - my foxhole was filling up with water so I got out and laid down next to my hole, - I fell asleep and when I woke up in the morning I found I had sled down to almost the bottom of the hill. I picked myself up, - went back to my position & resumed my duty with a dry rifle I had under my Pancho during the night. A couple of days after we landed my Lieutenant told me and one other to go to the Ammo Depot and pick up a case of .30 Caliber Rifle Ammo. It would be dark in a little while so we hurried to the Depot, got the ammo & headed back to our unit, - but by the time we got back, - it was dark, - not good. We were stopped by a Sentry who asked us for the, "Password", - what password, we werent given one. We asked the Sentry to get our Lieutenant and he would verify who we were, - this took about an hour total, but our Lieutenant arrived, - recognized us and asked the Sentry to pass us through, which he did. Glad that Sentry didn't have an itchy trigger finger.

      After a couple of weeks the island was declared, "secured". We then started taking on other jobs like building a road around the island and I learned to operate a big, "Diamond "D" Truck. I was also the Assistant Demolition person to our Expert, Emory Ashurst, Cpl. and we would blow-up anything we were told to. - including, "duds", unexploded bombs. One time an inter-island, "Yipee Boat", used to run supplies from Tulagi to the "Canal", ran aground at the entrance to the harbor and it was blocking the field of fire for one of our coastal artillery guns, it had to be moved. Emory and I were ordered to move it. We made several dives down to the boat to check on where the best places were to place the explosives. When we checked out what the cargo was we found it was loaded with canned food, another problem. When we set the charges we had to be sure the cans would not be flying all over the place and maybe hurt someone, - we thought we did that!! We were all set to, "blow" it, - we took a safe position away from the, "danger area" and I yelled as loud as I could, "Fire In The Hole", to warn every- one that an explosion was to take place in the area. Emory pushed the handle down on the plunger and there was a big, "boom", and the, "Yipee Boat", slowly sunk into the deeper water, - but the cans were flying all over the place, - operation successful!! The, "Pioneers", also built the first, "Marine & Navy" Cemetery on the Island of Cavutu.

The night of the second day the Jap Navy came down the, "Slot", to engage the U.S. Navy in a ferocious sea battle. We could see the flashess and hear the explosions, - the night at times would light up like daylight. We thought our Navy was kicking the hell out of the Japs, - but come the morn- ing it was just the opposite we would find out.

The morning of 9th we looked out to sea and all our ships had left, - there was none to be seen!! They left without completing their unloading which meant we were going to be hard pressed for needed supplies. That same day our ships would come limping into the harbor badly damaged with a lot of casualties on board. Our job was to remove the dead from the ships and bury them in the cemetary on Tulagi. I'll never forget the bodies that were torn apart, burned so badly that one could not recognize them as a human being. We also removed some of badly injured sailors and Marines so they could be treated and then sent to the nearest hospital available. For days, after the sea battle, bodies would wash up on the beach; we would bury them. The sight of these bodies, burned to a crisp, socked with fuel oil, body parts of all kinds; it was horrible!! These are the pictures that people back home would never see. There would be more sea battles to come but this time around our Navy would be ready for them. The Jap Navy, in the nights to come, would come down the slot and blast away at Henderson Field on the "Canal" and us on Tulagi. We could hear the shells coming in and we had nowhere to hide, except a "fox hole" and I know I dived into the first one I could find and prayed they would miss me; they did!! The nights were as black as the ace of spades until they would send up flares that would light up the area like it was daylight. There wasn't much we could do but take

the pounding and pray. As hot as it was I would be
as cold as an ice cube, shivering til my teeth rattled.
This would happen every time the Japs would come
in to shell us and I was not the only one!! It was a
nerve racking experience and would happen many
times in future engagements.

    We not only had to put up with the Japs but
with sickness, - malaria, dinghy fever, jungle rot,
dysentary, (the Tulagi Trots), and elephantitus. At
one time over half of the troops were down with,
"malaria", including me. The only treatment available that the Corpman, (medic), had was quinine, -
in powder form and the way they gave it to us was
by putting a dose in a piece of toilet paper, rolled
it up and said, "open your mouth", and when we did
they would throw the ball of quinine in our mouths,
and most times the toilet paper would break, - what
a terrible taste that was!! When we first landed
on Tulagi we only had the water we carried with
us, - a cantee full and that wasn't to last very
long. Our Doctor was consulted about the water
problem and all he said was, "send the men down
to the beach and tell them to bring their canteens,"-
we did. The Doctor dug a hole in the beach until
the water came up and then he would take a
canteen, fill it up, drop three drops of Iodine
in it, shake it up and told us to drink it. We all
hesitated, and he said, "drink it, - it's O.k., - it
won't hurt you", - so we did. The water was as
black as the night and all you could taste and
smell was the, "iodine". Not the best appetizer!
Later on we would get a salt water purifier, -

of which I was put in charge of. The machine did a wonderful job,- the water didn't
taste to bad and there was plenty to keep
the lister bags full. Our religious beliefs
were taken care of by a cracker jack of a
Catholic Chaplain. One day when he was saying mass, for the troops, on a makeshift alter
at the bottom of the hill his finishing words
were, "Amen, lets go kill some Japs",- while he
was twerling a couple of pistols. Another time
the only preacher available was a Jewish Rabbi
who said to us,-" you are all invited to join with
us in prayer regardless of your religion. During the service, close your eyes, and say your
own prayers",- it was a wonderful day of worship. This is a great example of serving our one &
only, "God",- we can do it together now just as
we did during the war.

There will be more episodes about our Tulagi.
stay further on in the book.

We left Tulagi, Feb. 9th, 1943,- we of all the
troops that landed on "D" day were there the
longest, and we were very happy to leave these,
"God", forsaken islands.

Japanese Air Force!

The first to Die from the Second Division in defense of their country and to defeat the enemy were the Marines buried in this joint Marine-Navy cemetery on Tulagi, cared for by native workmen.

" Embarrassing Moment "

It must have been late Sept. 1942 and the heroic fight for the "Canal" was still going on, - the fighting for Tulagi, and the other islands was over, - but we were still on the alert for any infiltraiters. We were now defense troops and Tulagi became a supply depot from where supplies were sent over to the "Canal". Now our Navy and Merchant Marine ships started coming in.

The weather back home was beginning to cool down for the coming of winter, - but the weather on Tulagi continued to be hot and humid. We now had a little more time on our hands to do other things, - like go for a swim. There was a guy in our outfit that I got to be good friends with, - his last name was Withey, - don't remember his first name, - but I found out he was a very good swimmer. He was so good that he was given a try-out for the U.S. Olympic Swimming Team, so I asked him if he would teach me to be a better swimmer, - he agreed. One day we walked along the beach, the harbor side of Tulagi, to pick out an area where we could practice away from the prying eyes of the troops and the Command Center on top of the hill. For the first couple of days everything went O.K., - I was learning a lot from Withey, - he could really swim and we were having a lot of fun. On the third day things would change drastically, - a day I'll never forget!! We went down to the beach, as usual, took all of our clothes off, as usual and

44

placed them, out of sight, along the pathway that went around the island,- and later it would become a road. As usual we, waded into the water, started swimming, and I was practicing some of the things Withey had taught me. He was swimming along side of me and coaching me as we moved through the water. All of a sudden we heard a voice, coming over a bull-horn, loud and clear, telling us to stay where we were and that a boat was coming to pick us up,- and they did. They took us aboard and the Officer in charge gave us a tongue-lashing like we had never heard before!! He told us how dangerous it was,- that we weren't supposed to be out there, and not to do it again! We thought we were going to get the, "book", thrown at us,- but what they did was to take us down the beach a ways,- a long way from where our clothes were. By this time most of the island was alerted to the situation unfolding on the beach. What we were ordered to do was,- walk, no running, back to where our clothing was,- bare-assed naked!!! As we walked back along the beach we were greeted with,- cheers, whistles, and many other greetings you can imagine for yourself. We lived through this,- "embarrassing moment",- but for quite a while the guys didn't let us forget about our, "nude stroll" down the beach of beautiful Tulagi.

Shortly after this incident, my friend, Withey, came down with, "elephantitus",- the swelling of parts of the body,- like the testicles. He was sent back to the, "States", for treatment and since then I have never heard from him or about him,- but

but I do think of him and our, "embarrassing" moment". He was a great guy and I hope he is Okker

It took all of us to do the job!!!
The Army, Navy, Air Force, Marine Corps, Coast Guard and Merchant Marine.

"The Merchant Marine"

This story is about the first Merchant Marine ship to sail into Tulagi Harbor with much needed supplies,- ammo, food and medical supplies,- which were running very low on the, "Canal", and elsewhere. It was great to see that ship come in,- it meant that the shipping lanes were once again open and the much needed supplies would be coming in,- including real food,- no more Japanese rice!

I don't remember the date the ship arrived but my guess would be late in September. Days, months, holidays, were hardly ever remembered. Pretty soon one day ran into another, time didn't count, but we knew when it was daytime or nightime.

The ship dropped anchor about mid-afternoon and the crew prepared the ship for unloading,- the covers were removed, the hatches opened, the booms and cargo nets were ready, and the boats were lined-up along-side the ship. The boats were to transport the supplies to the beaches of Tulagi and we would unload them. All was ready to go,- it was going on 5° P.M. and suddenly all activity aboard the ship stopped. We wondered what the hold-up was,- what the hell was going on,---- the ship had been shut down!! Word was sent to the C.P., (Command Post), on Tulagi, that the crew on the ship had stopped unloading,- that was the wrong thing to do! Very soon the ship's Captain got a message,- "either you proceed with the unloading or we will take over,"- they didn't respond,- we took over. All through the night we worked our butts off unloading the

ship, we were pooped! I rember at one point
during the night I and others got so tired we
didn't think we'd be able to take another step or
pick up another carton. I decided I was going
to take a break for a couple of minutes, a
couple others joined me. We sat down on a concrete slab and before you knew it, we had all
fallen asleep. How long we slept, I don't know,
I do know that I was awakened, very abruptly,
with a kick in my ribs and an Officer yelling,
"Get your butts up and get to work", and we did.
This is proof that no matter how tired and exhausted one may get you'll always find you have a
little extra energy left and this would happen again
and again in battles yet to come. They, the Captain and the crew, must have finally awoke to
realize that they were in a, "War Zone", and Union
work schedules didn't work here, they went back,
real quick. It took the rest of the second day to unload ship and that night we would get some much
needed rest. The next morning, seeing that I would
have some time, I thought it would be a good time
to check and clean my B.A.R., (Browning Automatic
Rifle). I picked a nice spot, on the side of the hill
where I could place the parts as I cleaned them.
I had a good view of the harbor and the ships at
anchor. As I was cleaning my B.A.R. I would look up
every little while and scan the harbor, the sky and the
ships. This one time I looked up I saw two specs in
the distance, they looked like birds, over Florida
Island, but they kept on coming toward Tulagi. The
closer they came the more I could make out they

were, — Airplanes, but were they ours or the Japs! In seconds they opened up with machine guns and dropped two bombs in the area of the ship we just unloaded, — they didn't hit a thing, but they came in so low we could see the pilots. They sure gave us a scare, especialy the crew of that Merchant Marine Ship. It didn't take them long to up-anchor and get under-way, — I think they were in a hurry to get out.

All this time I'm siting there with a field-stripped B.A.R. and I often wondered would I have had a crack at them if my B.A.R. had been assembled! I guess not, because there was no Air Raid Warning & the Jap planes came and went in less than a minute. We never did find out where they came from!

The Merchant Marine, like all of us, — when the war started, were as green as could be in the eper-ience of war. None of us knew what the future had in store for us, — but we would find out in the first offense against the Japanese, — Aug. 7th, 1942. We would find out in the Guadalcanal Cam-paign that the Jap Military were terrific fight-ers, merciless and willing to die for their Emper-or and take as many of us as possible with them.

The U.S. Merchant Marine did a terrific job, around the world, getting the supplies they carr-ied to all the Allies. Their job was not an easy one, as History will tell. They had to face all the dangers of the sea and our enemies. They had to hope that their convoys would get through to their destin-ations with the help of the Allied Navy's and Air-forces. Many ships and crews would be lost as a

result of enemy action. Regardless of the bad
weather or the enemy,- they did their job!!!
May, "God", bless you all,--
   The U.S. Merchant Marine.

To the Victors goes the Spoils of War!

Subject: One Nation Under God

A college professor, an avowed Athiest, was teaching his class.
He shocked several of his students when he flatly stated he was
going to prove there was no God. Addressing the ceiling he shouted:
"God if you are real, then I want you to knock me off this
platform.
I'll give you 15 minutes!" The lecture room fell silent.
You could have heard a pin fall. Ten minutes went by.
Again he taunted God, saying, "Here I am God. I am still wating."
His count down to the last couple of minutes when a marine just
released from active duty and newly registered in the class. He
walked up to the professor, hit him full force in the face, and sent
him tumbling from his lofty platform. The professor was out cold!
At first, the students were shocked and babbled in confusion.
The young Marine took a seat in the front row and sat silent. The
class fell silent.....waiting."

Eventually, the professor came to, shaken. He looked at the young
marine in the front row. When the professor regained his senses and
could speak he asked; "What's the matter with you? Why did you do
that?

"God was busy. He sent me.

"The Doughnut Makers"

When we landed on Tulagi we didn't expect our ships to leave,- which they did, taking with them unloaded supplies of ammo, water, food and medical supplies. We felt like we had been deserted,- it was a scarey time! With food becoming a primary concern our Company Commander decided to appoint a team to see what could be done to scrounge up some food. Rudy Singer and myself were appointed to do the job. First we sent a few guys out to search the island for anything we could use. The pickings were a little slim but they did come up with some flour, sugar, rice and dried fruits. Our regular cooks and their equipment did not land with us,- they would arrive much later. Next we had to find a place to do our cooking and we did. It was a little shack about half way up the side of a hill on the harborside of the island,- it looked like it had been used for that purpose before. With what we had to work with and the ample tropical fruits, including bananas, we were able to provide some decent food,- even if there were a few wiggly creatures in the rice,- they were free and no charge.

One day while we were in our little cook shack cooking up some doughnuts we saw General Vandergrift,- 1st Marine Division Commander, walking along the pathway at the bottom of the hill. He was on Tulagi for a meeting with the overall Command. As he was walking along it seemed as if he was smelling something and he stopped a couple of times,- looked around and finally he spotted our little shack and started walking up the hill toward us. As he entered we snapped to attention, he said, - "at ease, relax, and get on with what you were doing," - he then asked what we were making, - doughnuts we replied. We offered the General a sample, - he accepted and not only had one - but a couple of samples. He remarked; - "Not bad, not bad, at all"; - he "Thanked" us and then asked if we had a cigarette. I told him that there had not been a cigarette around for some time, - he just nodded his head and left. After the word got around that the General had stopped at our cook shack and sampled our doughnuts we became known as the, "Famous Doughnut Makers"

The "C" rations we brougt with us when we landed were not the tastiest food around, especially if you had to eat the contents straight from the can, - heated they tasted much better, - but who had time to heat them!

While on the island we suffered through many of the tropical diseases including dysentary, - which I hope they didn't blame on Rudy and my cooking.

We endured one, "Hell of a place", - a place that will take its place in History as one of the greatest, hardest, and nerve racking battles of World War Two. It was the beginning of the end for the Japanese Empire!!

"WOW - Real Food"

From almost the first day of our landing on Tulagi we had been surviving on captured Japanese food and our own C-Rations, - some real food would be great. One day one of our guys caught a pig, - we were going to have a great treat, - fresh meat. A spit was built, the pig was prepared for roasting and got a good fire going, - we were ready for a feast! I and the rest of the Platoon sat there and watched as the pig was being turned and slowly roasted. We did take turns turning the pig and it was looking real good, - the aroma was getting to us. Like all good things, this meal we were all looking forward to would come to an abrupt end. A Marine Doctor happened to come by and asked what we were doing, - he could very well see what we were doing, - his next words were, - "Don't eat it, bury it, it is deceased." The "Doc" explained to us that we were not immued to the tropical deceases as the natives were. We had tears in our eyes as we buried the pig & some chickens we had caught, - but we soon have another chance at some real food.

There was a guy in our outfit, - I think his name was, "Criss", but I'm not sure. That name keeps poppin-up in my mind, - so we'll go with it. "Criss" was kind of a quiet guy and I didn't get to know him very well. I do know that he was working on some kind of system to catch fish. What he did was get a couple empty gallon jugs, - where he got them nobody knew. He then attached a stiff wire to the handles of the jugs, and anchoed them to the sea bottom with weights. Next he fashioned and sharpened a good sized hook with a line attached to the stiff wire between the jugs. Then one day when his gadget was all assembled he bated it with some leftover food and just before sunset he swam out to where the water was about 15 feet deep and put his invention in place, - the trap was set, what would the morning reveal? Early the next morning, "Criss", swam out to check on his trap, - we heard him holler, with excitment, - "I got one, I got one", - we all came running down to the beach to see what he had caught. He pulled in a 6ft sandsharck, it was a beauty. That evening we had our first taste of fresh food in a couple of months, - it tasted like steak, - "Thanks", to, "Criss", and his invention. This time the Doctor gave us the "O.K.", to eat the shark-steak and, "Criss", did not catch another creature of the sea again! We did have the memories of "Real Food".

One we heard a shot, - like a rifle being fired. At first we didn't know where it came from until we saw people running toward this one tent and calling for a Corpman. In a little bit we found out that it was, "Criss", who had been shot. It was reported that he had shot himself in the foot, - accidently and it was his ticket home. Never did hear what happened to him, - hope he made it O.K..

In the days and weeks to come we would have to endure the night shelling by the Jap

Navy, which I think was the only time during my tour of duty, in the Pacific, that we had this happen to us. It was a scary, nerve-racking time in my life,— I don't know how anyone could take that continuous pounding and pressure! Then there was, "Midnight Charlie", who would fly over our positions every night and drop a bomb. You could set your clock for midnight & every time he came over you'd be right on the dot. I don't think he ever hit anything,— he just wanted to keep us from getting any rest,— he did!

From the Barbary Coast to the Belleau Wood, from the Chosin Reservoir to Khe Sanh, from Guadalcanal to the bloody sands of Iwo Jima, leathernecks have proven themselves to be a fighting force without peer.

"What Stills"

It was October of 1942 and we were still on Tulagi and the U.S. Army had arrived to take over from the Marines. My outfit, Co. "D", 2nd Pioneer Battalion were ordered to help move their supplies off the beach, – we were glad to help. Never saw so much food and equipment in a long, long time; they even moved in the, "Kitchen Sink". It had been a long time, since we had anything decent to eat especially fruit and fruit juice. We did get to try some of the islands tropical fruits and coconuts, but if you ate to much of the stuff you most likely come down with a bad case of the, "Tulagi Trots". Up to this time we were surviving mostly on captured Japanese food, – mostly rice. So, when the Army arrived and the cases of food were coming ashore we diverted a few cases of food, – especially fruits and juices, to our area and the Army never missed them!

It wasn't to much later when it became very noticeable that some of the troops were getting a bit tipsey, – we tried to blame it on the "P.T. Boat Squadron", located down the beach a ways. I had visited with them a couple of times and I knew that they were concocting a pretty potent brew, – made up with torpedo juice and cut with pineapple juices. The same – thing was done with canned heat. Yup, – I had a taste!!

The Commander of the P.T. Boat Squadron was the very famous Hollywood actor, –

Robert Montgomery, and he was hidden behind a very black beard, — very handsome.

    The higher-ups on the island didn't believe the booze was coming from just the crews of the P.T. Boats. They were sure there were other possibilities, — like "stills", because of the frequent, "tipsey" incidents

    One night, after we had tapped our still for a few drinks, Sgt. Mike, climbed up the hill to his tent located above a gravel pit, and went to sleep. During the night he woke up for a piss call and took a step in the wrong direction, — down the side of the gravel-pit he tumbled. He got up, brushed himself off, climbed back up the hill and again went to bed, — he never knew or remembered his tumble. We still talk about that tumble to this day!

    A few days later and unanounced the Army M.P.'s converged on the island and made a clean sweep from stem to stern looking for stills and the makings. By the end of the day they had found and destroyed quite a few stills, — but they never found ours, — we did a very good camouflage job.

    Know where all those cases of fruit & juices went, — the ones the Army donated to us! If you said into the stills, — your right!!

"When The Lights Come On Again"

Once again we were onboard our ships sailing away from the islands of, "Hell", to a place we hoped would be much better. Were we happy to leave,—"You Bet We Were!!" A short time after we sailed we found out we were headed for a place called,—Wellington, New Zealand,—we never heard of it,—but we were to fall in love with this beautiful Country in a very short time. As our ships approched the shores we couldn't believe our eyes,—what a beautiful country side,—the fijords, the green hills and the big snow-capped mountains. We were already in love with this Country and hadn't even landed yet!

We docked, disembarked, boarded the waiting trucks, and we were off to our Camp up in the mountains; above the town of Lower Hutt. After we settled in we finally got some, "LIBERTY", and a chance to go to Wellington. To get there we had to take our military trucks down the mountain, (what a ride), to the town of Lower Hutt where we would get the Tram to Wellington.

On one of these trips,—by pure accident, (on purpose), I bumped into this very pretty young lady,—I introduced myself, said I was sorry for bumping into her and could I walk with her,—she said it was allright. From that moment on we became very good friends,—and I thought I was falling in love!! After we walked for awhile she said she had to get home and before she left I made a date with her for the next day. I was to meet her at the place where we first met and her work place, in that building, at about 5: P.M., — I said I'd be there. I was all excited, — I never felt like this before! After all this was my first, "date", with a, "female" and I was as green about women as anyone could be. (I'm sorry, but I don't remember her name). I met her the next day, as planed, and took her to a restaurant, her choice, because I was not familiar with what eateries were in the area. She picked a very nice restaurant in down-town Wellington, — not far from where she worked. We had a very nice dinner, a couple of drinks and we talked a lot about our lives and the future. I talked about how much I'd like to come back someday, but that all depended on what would happen now and until the war ended, — she agreed. It was getting late and for her was another work day to morrow. We left the restraunt, — I offered to get a cab, (which there were very few), — she suggested we walk and that her home was not far from where we were, — I said O.k., let's go. I didn't think we would ever reach our destination, — we walked and walked right to the top of this hill over-looking the city of Wellington. We didn't see to much because there still was a, "black out", through out the Country. We were, "pooped", — at least I was, from the hike up the hill, — so we sat down on the side of the hill to rest for awhile. All of a sudden, while we sitting there, we could hear sirens whaling in the distance, — thought there was an, "air raid", — but then we heard church bells and just a lot of noise echoing through the hills. Then slowly the lights of New Zealand were coming on again, - what a beautiful sight that was and I'll always remember it, including the young lady I was with. This meant that the threat of a Japanese invasion had been, "stopped". We hugged, cheered, laughed and cried at the same time and my friend was so, "thankful", to us for what we did. I was happy for all the people of New Zealand, - this was a great time for them. I'll never forget these wondeful people and the night the, "Lights Came On Again". I never got to see my friend again or get her address, - but I did have the memories of a wonderful young lady that I met in Wellington, New Zealand. My dreams of returning to New Zealand never happened. When I got home my mother asked me not to go, she said that I was needed here at home, for many reasons, - she was right, so I stayed home. Quite often I think about, - "what if I returned", - I'll never know but I will always cherish my visit forever.

Our Camp in New Zealand, - Camp Judgeford - 1943. We renamed it, - "Camp Moonshine".

This was the first and only time I had the chance to see or hear any group visiting the troops. Sure enjoyed the Navy's Chief Bandmaster Artie Shaw's music.

No uniform needed,—"It's, Mail Call",—in New Zealand.

Philip S. Trier-Cook

Our New Zealand
"Messhall"

P.F.C. Leonard Rawlings

On "messhall duty".

When we landed on,
"Tulagi", Leonard was on
duty with his, "Machine Gun"
and was credited with killing
the first Jap, that night, in
our Platoon. Aug. 7th, 1942.

"Gus" at Camp Moonshine."

"Gus" Gustafson

"Gus", was a great
guy and the Company
"Handyman". There was
nothing he couldn't do.

"Shaving Lotion and Cologne"

This incident takes place in Wellington, NZ, where our Camp was located up in the mountains. Our time of rest and relaxation had come to an end and the Second Marine Division was getting down to some serious training for our next campaign. Sometimes we'd leave Camp in the early morning hours and be gone all day, returning after dark, pooped out! The training and endurance exercises would help prepare us for our next assault. Whenever we left on these maneuvers there were always a few troops left in Camp because of being sick, guard duty or work details. On this one particular day it was, "Bugger Reds", turn to stay in Camp, - he was a real character, with bright red hair, loaded with freckles and not much over 5 ft. tall. When we returned from the days training exercise we looked forward to a shower and shave, which we did and it felt good. As we returned to our tents to use our after shave lotion and cologne you could hear, one after another, down the row of tents guys hollering, - "my after shave lotion is gone or my cologne is gone." Shortly we realized that all the tents had been raided and anything with alcohol in it was gone. Who could do a thing like that, - was it, "Bugger Red", - he wouldn't do anything like that, - but he was the only one here and he's not around! Between us we decided we had better check him out so we split up in twos and threes and headed in all directions in search of, "Bugger Red". After an extended search, some-

one called out,- "here he is,- we found him",- they sure did!! He was in a supply tent, "crapped out", and laying on a mattress,- he was bombed and with a most peculiar complexion,- green! He was one very sick Marine! I don't know if, "Bugger", ever swore off of, "shaving lotion, cologne and anything with alcohol in it",- but our —
"Mystery Was Solved".

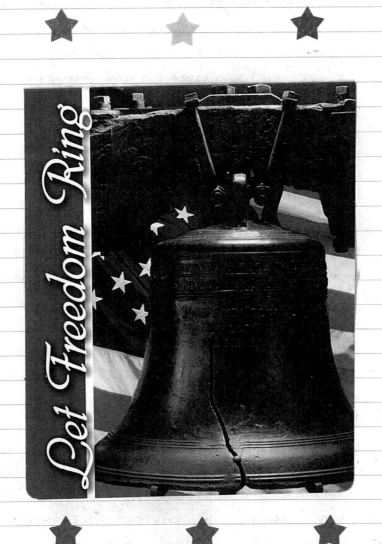

Let Freedom Ring

" My Buddies "

While in New Zealand we were very busy, - had
a lot of good times, met a lot of wonderful New Zelan-
ders, trained and trained some more. Practiced
putting up a portable bridge over a river, - again and
again day after day. Our replacements arrived &
fell into our regular daily routine and most important
we received the new M-1 Garand Rifle to replace the
World War One Springfield Rifle we had on Tulagi.

We were given a 10 day pass to go anywhere
we wanted, - in New Zealand. A family that I got
to know invited me to go with them on a train ride
to Palmerston North to visit there son who worked
in a hospital there. I accepted their offer and
looked forward to a sightseeing trip through the
countryside by train. There would be three of us, -
Mom, her Daughter and me. It was a beautiful trip
but one peculiar thing happened, - the young
ladies Mother left without us, - well I guarantee
you nothing happened and we took the next train
back to Wellington

After the 10 day pass we always had the
weekends to go to Wellington. This brings me to a
true story that happened on one of those weekends.
In town there was always good food available,
plenty of suds, (beer), to drink, - and plenty of
beautiful females to keep one happy.

On this particuler weekend I left Camp Moonshine with two of my "Buddies", - the Rawlings brothers. Once we got down to the town of Lower Hutt,
we caught the Tram to Wellington and when we

got there we set a time, 5:P.M., to meet here at the Tram station, - Sunday, and don't be late getting here. We went our seperate ways, I went to visit with a family I had gotten to know. By family it usually meant a Mother and her Children, - their husbands where in the New Zealand Armed Forces and overseas somewhere. It was rough on them but they did what they could for us and welcomed us into their homes. After a very nice visit with my friend and her daughters it was time to leave to meet my, "Buddies", and get back to Camp. I arrived at the Tram Station in plenty of time but they weren't around as yet. I waited for a bit, when I saw them, they were in bad shape, loaded to the gills. "You better get them under control", I said to myself as I moved out to meet them. First I grabbed them under their arms and told them to, "straighten out and fly right", as we headed for the Tram Station. As we. approched the entrance I spotted some M.P.'s, - I stopped and told them, "the M.P.'s were ahead of us so don't do anything foolish, walk erect and once we are inside make a bee-line for the Tram." Well every- thing went O.K. until they took off down the plat- form for the Tram, - one of them dropped a package of laundry each one was carrying. There was laun- dry scattered all over the place, - we tried to pick up all we could but we had to catch the Tram, - it was getting ready to pull out. We caught the last coach, that had an observation platform on the back of the coach. I herded them out to the plat- form hoping the air would sober them up but they wanted to have some fun as they started to climb up the ladders that were on each side of the platform. I put a stop to that real quick, - practily sat on them until we got to the town of Lower Hutt where our trucks would be waiting for us. When we arrived there I got them on one of the trucks, - no room for me, so I told the guys, in the truck, to see that they got back to Camp O.k.; Marines always take care of their fellow Marines!! Before I could find a place for myself the trucks pulled out and left me standing there, - what do I do now!! What any good Marine does, - start walking! All that I could hope for was that a civilean car came along, - which was very douptfull because of the fuel shortage and rationing, or maybe a Marine vehicle would come along. I had walked a couple of miles when a Marine truck did come along and picked me up, - lucky me! If I didn't make the morning roll-call I would be reported, "A.W.O.L."; - but I did get back in time. When I got back to, "Camp Moonshine", I checked on my, "Buddies", the Rawlings brothers, - they were asleep like two little babies. In the morning, after roll-call, I asked them how they were and did they remember any of last nights events, - they didn't remember a thing but they did have dandy hangovers. "My Buddies".

P.S.- As a rule you are not supposed to get to attached to other members of your unit, - but that is an impossible thing to do. You can't help having some, "Buddies", and getting pretty close to one another. We all trained together, went on liberty together,

67

shipped out together, went into combat, together, - some of us survived the horrors of war,
some gave their all, - "Our Buddies".

After coming home, "we the survivors", had
Company Reunions and we remembered those
we left behind, - the real, "Heroes", of W.W. II !!
When we remembered those who didn't make it, -
tears came to our eyes and we said a prayer
for them. We all knew that some day we would
meet again doing our duty, "Guarding the Streets
of Heaven". To this day and for the rest of my
life I will always remember my, "Buddies", -
what we went through and what we accomplished. I'll love them all, "My Buddies".

"It is the duty of all nations to acknowledge
THE Providence of Almighty God, to obey His will,
to be grateful for His benefits, and to humbly
implore His protection and favor."

George Washington
October 3, 1789
Proclaiming a National
Day of Prayer and
Thanksgiving.

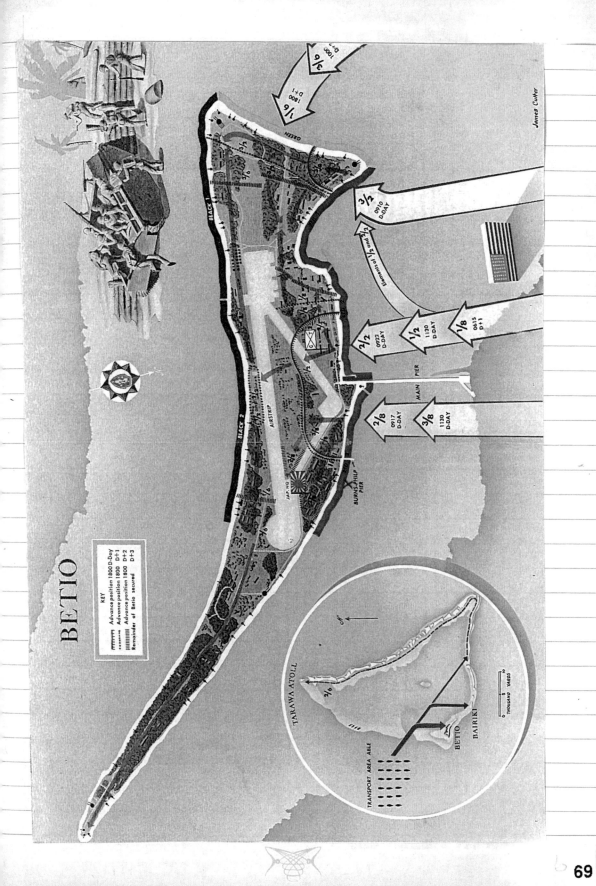

BETIO

KEY

- Advance position 1800 D-Day
- Advance position 1800 D+1
- Advance position 1800 D+2
- Remainder of Betio secured D+3

BLACK 1

BLACK 2

GREEN

AIRSTRIP

JAP. HQ

MAIN PIER

BURNS-PHILP PIER

3/6 1000 D+2

1/6 1800 D+1

3/2 0910 D-DAY

Elements of 1/2 and 3/2

2/2 0922 D-DAY

1/2 1130 D-DAY

1/8 0615 D+1

2/8 0917 D-DAY

3/8 1130 D-DAY

3/6

2/6

TARAWA ATOLL

BETIO

BAIRIKI

TRANSPORT AREA ABLE

THOUSAND YARDS

James Cutter

TARAWA

↑ ↑ P.F.C. Floyd Schouviller
P.F.C. Charles Wysock, Jr. - Tarawa Nov. 20th, 1943.
We went in in an "Amtrack", in the 3rd wave.

HEADQUARTERS, SHORE PARTY GROUP A
SECOND MARINE DIVISION, FMF
IN THE FIELD

TEAM No. 1

FORWARD ECHELON

COMMAND SECTION (1 OFF - 1 ENL)
SLOAN, Frank B., 2ndLt
MORAN, Robert F., Pfc

RECONAISSANCE SECTION (2 ENL)
(Range Marker)
SLOWINSKI, Alexander B., Corp
WOODWORTH, Frank A., Pfc

LAISON SECTION (1 OFF - 2 ENL)
FAQUIN, Arthur C., Jr., 2ndLt
BURKS, Billy G., Pfc
LOPEZ, Paul, Pfc

REAR ECHELON

COMMAND SECTION (1 OFF - 8 ENL)
BROES, Robert W.L., Capt
LANDENBERGER, Arthur E., TSgt
FARMER, William A., StfSgt
SEWELL, Philip S., Corp
MORAN, Robert F., Pfc
CAPRA, Angelo V., Pvt
HAAK, Robert G., ACk
MAGEE, Burt K., ACk
SANDOW, Roy F., ACk

DUMP MARKER SECTION (12 ENL)
MC CUINE, Charles E., Sgt
HUPP, Roscoe W., Corp
PERALES, Joe L., Corp
SOLEY, Lawrence C., Corp
BROCK, Harold E., Pfc
CLEVELAND, Herman H., Pfc
DE MARTINI, Paul, Pfc
ELLIOTT, James H., Pfc
FRANK, Arthur E., Pfc
GREER, Leonard A., Pfc
LANO, Royce C., Pfc
PERRY, Donald E., Pfc

PIONEER SECTION (1 OFF - 16 ENL)
FAQUIN, Arthur C., Jr., 2ndLt
YONKE, Carmen K., Sgt
MAY, Jimmie N., Corp
WHITLEY, Denver D., Corp
TURNER, Harry T., Corp
BITLE, Arthur A., Pfc
BRADY, James C., Pfc
CHRONABERRY, Richard E., Pfc
COULTER, Regenal D., Pfc
DALE, Herbert J., Pfc
FOWLES, Leonard J., Pfc
JONES, John C., Pfc
RINGGOLD, James W., Pfc
STEWART, Thomas M., Pfc
SOLBERG, Robert Y., Pfc
WALTER, William E., Pfc
YOUNG, Gene E., Pfc

SECURITY SECTION (18 ENL)
WOODWORTH, Frank A., Pfc-in Char
ANTONELLI, Nick J., Pfc
BURHENN, George D., Pfc
ACHENBACH, Paul L., Pfc
SCOTT, Foch, Pfc
SHIELDS, Philip F., Pvt
BRAUCHLER, Charles, Pfc
BROWN, Robert E., Pfc
BAUMGARDNER, Richard P., Pfc
HARRELL, Louis J., Pfc
BUTTERFIELD, Milford E., Pfc
GALAWAY, William V., Pfc
ZUCHELLI, Daniel M., Pfc
HOARD, Clarence, Pfc
ASBURY, Walter V., Pfc
BYRAN, Cyril, Pvt
JEFFCOAT, Jesse R., Pfc
DELP, Richard F., Pfc

HEADQUARTERS, SHORE PARTY GROUP A
SECOND MARINE DIVISION, FMF
IN THE FIELD

D COMPANY, 2ND BATALLION, 18 REG.
TEAM No. 2

FORWARD ECHELON

COMMAND SECTION (1 OFF - 1 ENL)
SIMONSON, Arthur K., 2ndLt.
MASTERS, Mike A., Sgt.

RECONAISSANCE SECTION (2 ENL
(Range Marker)
CALDWELL, Joe F., Pfc
CRELIA, Lloyd T., Pfc

LAISON SECTION (1 OFF # 2 ENL)
SAYLOR, Wilford B., 1stLt
PAUL, Christian F., Pfc
SNYDER, Mark G., Pfc

REAR ECHELON

COMMAND SECTION (1 OFF - 8 ENL)
JONES, Robert C., Jr., Capt
GABEL, George P., StfSgt
STUBBLEFIELD, Robert E., Corp
KARPICKY, Frank D., Pfc
FERTADO, Richard M., Pfc
PRICE, Richard, Pfc
MORROW, Harvey I., Jr., Pfc
FEUTREN, George G., Pfc
VAUGHN, Buck J., Sgt

DUMP MARKER SECTION (12 ENL)
DUNN, Oather J., Sgt
BURKE, Theodore J., Jr., Corp
DAILEY, Virgil E., Corp
WESTOVER, Elmer G., Corp
GRAHAM, Gerald P., Pfc
CHIER, George D., Pfc
WEBB, Jack K., Pfc
COTHRAN, George M., Pfc
REED, Jimmie R., Pfc
OPALINSKI, Eugene E., ACk.
WOLF, Erwin J., FldCk
CATES, "O" "A", CCk

SECURITY SECTION (18 ENL)
REED, Richard O., Pfc
BATES, Myron C., Pfc
SINGER, Rudolph A., Pfc
DUCHARME, Alphee, H., Pfc
PRATT, Louis A., Pfc
MC ENTEE, Norman J., Pfc
HOAR, Jerauld E., Pfc
SMITH, James Pl, Pfc
SUSANS, Edward W., Pfc
STELZER, Paul C., Pfc
LOBE, Frank J., Pfc
ALBANESE, Joseph V., Pfc
STRONG, Robert A., Pfc
BRUNNER, Ernest H., Pfc
ROTRAMEL, Donald A., Pfc
POLSON, George W., Pfc
LEWIS, Joseph H., Pvt
DICKENS, Theodore D., Pvt

PIONEER SECTION (15 ENL)
LA POINT, Charles L., StfSgt
BENNETT, William W., Corp
COATE, Gerald E., Corp
ELLIS, Fred R., Corp
CLODFELTER, James B., Pfc
BONAWITZ, Harold G., Pfc
WALZER, William C., Pfc
HERMAN, Samuel, Pfc
FORTENBERRY, Carl E., Pfc
TABER, William E., Pfc
POTEROLA, William J., Pfc
HELLMAN, Lester A., Pfc
URIOSTE, Benni, Pvt
DE GENARO, Anthony, D., ACk
TRIER, Philip S., ACk.

HEADQUARTERS, SHORE PARTY GROUP A
SECOND MARINE DIVISION, FMF
IN THE FIELD

TEAM No. 3

FORWARD ECHELON

LIAISON GROUP (1 OFF - 2 ENL)
JORDAN, Lawrence P., 2ndLt
THARP, Robert E., Pfc
ROBINSON, Doyle H., Pfc

RECONAISSANCE GROUP (1 OFF 3 ENL)
COEN, James N., 1stLt
DORTCH, Richard F., Sgt
GLASER, William, Pfc
CURCIO, Louis P., Pfc

REAR ECHELON

COMMAND SECTION (1 OFF - 8 ENL)
LA TROBE, Osmun B., Capt
HAABY, Emery W., GySgt
KEOGH, Howard F., Pfc
BRIN, Harold P., Pfc
DE AGUERO, John J., Pvt
FRYE, Clarence E., Pfc
HOUSE, Gordon, Pfc
DRAKE, Arlie B., FM1c
DARLINGTON, Aubrey E., FldCk
MALONEY, Joseph M, Pfc

DUMP MARKER SECTION (12 ENL)
SOBOLEWSKI, Joseph F., Corp
BARAN, Paul, Pfc
MAKLARY, Alexander, ACk
RAWLINGS, Leonard C., Pfc
WOODS, James J., Corp
WHARTON, "J" "R", Pfc
BAKER, Everett E., Pfc
KINDER, Charles H., Corp
WYSOCKI, Charles, Pfc
SCHOUVILLER, Floyd H., Pfc
HARRIS, Willie P., Pfc
DUBUQUE, Jack T., Pfc

SANITATION SECTION (3 ENL)
ADAMS, William S., Pfc
BURGESS, Richard C., Pvt
HERMAN, Samuel, Pfc

PIONEER SECTION (11 ENL)
BASS, John C., Sgt
PAKULA, Leo S., Sgt
SCHOLL, Jacob A., Corp
RALPH, William A., Pfc
TOMASZEWSKI, Felix P., Pfc
SMITH, Frank A., Corp
JACKMAN, Robert E, Pfc
MC GARY, David, Pfc
CULLUM, Edgar, Pfc
DUFFY, Howard E., Pfc
FRITZCHE, Eldred N., ACk.

SECURITY SECTION, (18 ENL)
STOFFER, Donald E., Corp
BRODY, Dan, Pfc
HARRISON, Henry L, Pfc
REED, Wilson J., Pfc
WILBUR, Willard E., Pfd
BROWN, Gregory J., Pfc
WALLACE, Robert H., Pfc
BEAULIEU, Robert J., Pvt
HULSE, Roy H., Corp
STREEVER, Roy R., Pvt
KLEBER, John M., Pfc
COSTA, Laurence V., Pfc
CABLER, Harrell C., Pfc
THOMAS, William O., Pfc
ANSLEY, James B., Pfc
METZ, Gerald L, ACk
GUY, James E., Pfc
BROWN, James F., Pfc

These are the three Teams that made the Assault on the Island of Betio-Tarawa Atoll, Gilbert Islands. Red Beach #1, Red Beach #2, and Red Beach #3. Nov 20th, 1943.

"TARAWA"

Why was there a, "Tarawa", on Nov. 20th, 1943!!
Why was there a, "Gettysburg", in the Civil War!!
Why was there a, "Belleau Woods", in World War One,
and many others. Most of these battles were the
Bloodiest, Fiercest and Nerve Racking engagements in the History of the United States. They
were also the turning point in each of their Wars,
which led to, Victory, over our enemies.

Ten years after the battle for Tarawa
25 Officers were asked thier views on the "Battle
for Tarawa." Among the Officers, who were at the
battle were, — Fleet Admiral C.W. Nimitz, Admiral
R.A. Spruance, Lt. General Julian C. Smith, Vice
Admiral Harry W. Hill, Lt. General W.D. Hermle, Maj.
General Merritt A. Edson, Rear Admiral H.B. Knowles,
Brig. Gen. David M. Shoup, Colonel P.M. Rixey, Col.
R.W. Murray, Col. W.K. Jones, Col. R. McC. Tompkins,
Col. L.C. Hays, Col. H.P. Crowe, Col. T.J. Colley, Col.
T.A. Culhane, Jr, Lt. Col. Howard J. Rice, Lt. Col. C.
W. McCoy, Lt. Col. J.E. Herbold, Jr., Lt. Col. Maxie R.
Williams, Lt. Col. John T. Bradshaw, Lt. Col. W.C. Cham-
berlin, Lt. Col. William T. Bray, Lt. Col. Henry G. Lawrence,
Jr. and Lt. Col. Ben K. Weatherwax. They all agreed that
the Island of Betio, Tarawa Atoll, had to be taken, — it
was the stepping stone for the eventual Victory over
the Japanese Empire. I agreed with them, — but there
are no comments from the Sargents, Corporals, Privates,
and etc.

I was a P.F.C., (poor fighting civilian), in
Co. "D", 2nd Batt, 18th Marines, 2nd Marine Division.

One of those was Major Mike Ryan who kept an effective fighting force of Marines together and cleared the Western beach area so that reinforcements could come in on Green Beach to help secure the Island of Betio and the airfield.

Going back to the preinvasion of Betio the scuddlebutt going around was that once we landed we would be able to walk across the island to the other side with little resistance if any at all. That sounded real good, – and then the preinvasion bombardment, by sea and air began. The noise was so terrific you couldn't hear yourself think. My "God" what a pounding they were taking on that island, – nobody could live through that pounding! It was unbelivable and maybe they were right, – there would be little opposition. But, – there was to be a big surprise for us, – the Japs were waiting!!

The first major assault from the sea on a strongly fortified position was beset by a whole series of blunders, – hard and costly, – paid by the Marines at Tarawa. Later, amphibious assaults would profit from the sacrifices made by the Marines in this assault. We should never have been told that there would be little opposition, – if any. Then there was a shortage of Amtracks to do the job, – those who did the planning for this operation should have made sure and secured enough Amtracks to take the Troops in over the coral reef, – but I guess they thought that the 3 waves of Amtracks were enough; – and that the Higgins Boats could do the rest. They were so wrong!! Then the Navy used none armor-piercing

I guess I was a lucky one because I made the landing in an Amtrack that reached the beach just like we practiced. My partner, Floyd, and I were in the 3rd wave,- the last of the Amtracks! All the waves after the 3rd came in in Higgins Boats,- they couldn't clear the coral reef,- so they dropped off the troops they were carrying about 500 yards or more from the beach,- they were sitting ducks for the Jap guns as they waded in,- never faltering and never turning back. To this day, in the year 2007, I wonder what kept these Marines going until they died or made the beach. They were some of the, "Heroes", of the battle for Tarawa!!

My partner and I were supposed to put a Beach-Marker when we landed,- but an Officer, on the beach, told us not to because there was no way a boat with supplies could come over that coral reef. There were many dead and wounded on Red-Beach 3 so we did what we could for the wounded. We used the Medical kits they carried and ours to sprinkle the Sulfa on the wounds and to bandage them as well as we could. It wasn't until late the next day when we got some help in moving the wounded to a medical aid station down the beach about 50 yards or so,- I hope they made it!! While we were moving the wounded, useing anything we could for stretchers, including our panchos, we moved as fast as we could across the beach under continuous enemy fire. We could see the sand kicking up as bullets were hitting all around us,- but we made it to the Aid Station and nobody got hit.

There were many individuals in the course of this bloody "76" hour battle who did what they had to do.

shells which did little damage to the Jap emplacements or to the Japs themselves. The Naval bombardment ended 20 minutes before it was supposed
to, - giving the Japs enough time to man their weapons
while the Marines were still a long way from their
assigned beaches, - Red Beach #1 to the far right,
Red Beach #2 in the center and Red Beach #3 to the far
left which was the beach that my partner, Floyd &
I landed on. The Air Force Bombers was supposed to
drop 2000 pound bombs on Betio just before the
assault, - but it never happened! The elaborate defenses
on Betio were impressive, - concrete and steel bunkers,
mine fields, long strings of barbed wire protected
the beaches. Tank traps protected heavily fortified
Command Bunkers and firing positions throughout
the island. There must have been a couple hundred
of these pill-boxes covered by steel plates, logs &
sand, - which were very difficult to get at and destroy.
Admiral Shibaski, the Jap Commander on Betio said, -
"a million Americans could not take Tarawa in a
hundred years". It turned out he was wrong, - it
took "76" hours. Tarawa Atoll was garrisoned
by about 5000 of Japans best troops, - often
compared to the U.S. Marines, - not any more!!
    When the Tarawa Atoll was secured and we
were getting ready to leave that, "Hell-Hole", called
Tarawa you could see in the faces of the Marines the
horror we had just gone through. We were filthy
dirty, our eyes sunken back into their sockets and
our eyes were staring into nowhere like a bunch
of "Zombies". When we walked off that, "God Forsaken",
island we walked of with pride, - and sadness for the

ones we were leaving behind. We of Co. "D" would remember for the rest of our lives the ones we lost and the ones we buried on Betio.

Our "foxhole buddies" we buried on "Tarawa"

"Thanks", to the efforts of Emory Ashurst and Joe Sobol who searched the beach to find the following— right to left —
R.C. Mckinney, G.G. Seng, R.C. Kountzman, R.L. Jarrett, Max J. Wynnton, C. Montague, S.R. Parsons, M.W. Waltz, H.H. Watkins, H.B. Wanning, J.S. Castle, A.B. Roads, A.R. Mitlick, W.A. Larson, and First Lieutenant R.W. Vincent.

At the gravesite, Emory, led us in prayer and there were tears in our eyes as we said, "Good Bye", to our, "Buddies". We think the ones that were not found were carried out to sea by a fast channel of water within the sea waters.

TAPS

Some Gave All

The first cross on the left marks the grave of First Lieutenant R. W. Vincent

All the crosses were made by Gus Gustafson, - some how he found enough material to make the crosses with the names of the deceased on them.

"IN GOD WE TRUST"

Second Battalion, Eighteenth Regiment, Second Division
Composition: Companies D, E, F, and Headquarters Company

Deaths resulting from the battle at TARAWA, November, 1943

Name	Rank	Company	Burial Location	Date of Death
Anderson, Truitt A.	Pfc	D	Unknown	11-20-43
Bonnyman, Alexander J.	1stLt	F	D-2-18, #17	11-22-43
Carlson, Glen E.	Pvt	D	At Sea	11-20-43
Castle, James S., Jr.	Pvt	D	D-2-18, #5	11-20-43
Coble, Edward D.	Pvt	D	D-2-18, #16	11-20-43
Coloske, Robert E.	Pvt	D	Missing->KIA	11-20-43
Entwisle, Ennis M.	Pfc	F	Missing->KIA	11-20-43
Hudson, Ralph L.	Pfc	D	Missing->KIA	11-20-43
Jarrett, Russell L.	Pfc	D	D-2-18, #11	11-20-43
Kountzman, Ralph C.	Pfc	D	D-2-18, #14	11-20-43
Lanning, Hazen B., Jr.	Corp	D	D-2-18, #6	11-20-43
Larson, Wayne A.	Pfc	D	D-2-18, #2	11-20-43
Lazzari, Donald C.	Pvt	D	* Cem. #1, B	11-20-43
Lind, George	Pfc	D	Unknown	Unknown
Lyntton, Max J.	Pvt	D	D-2-18, #12	11-20-43
Mahoney, John W.	Sgt	F	Unknown	11-20-43
McCoy, Cecil R.	Pfc	D	Missing->KIA	11-20-43
McKinney, Robert C.	Pvt	D	D-2-18, #15	11-20-43
Millick, Arnold R.	Pfc	D	D-2-18, #3	11-20-43
Montague, Charles	Pfc	D	D-2-18, #10	11-20-43
Naffe, Joseph J., Jr.	Pvt	D	Missing->KIA	11-20-43
Nalazek, Edward A.	Pfc	D	Unknown	11-21-43
Overman, Norman C.	Pfc	D	* Cem. #29, C	11-20-43
Parsons, Samuel R.	Pfc	D	D-2-18, #9	11-20-43
Phillips, John E.	Corp	D	Unknown	11-20-43
Roads, Addison B.	Pvt	D	D-2-18, #4	11-20-43
Seng, Gene G., Jr.	Pfc	D	D-2-18, #13	11-24-43
Snyder, Robert A.	Corp	F	Unknown	11-20-43
Swigert, Robert	Corp	D	Missing->KIA	11-27-43
Thomas, Edwin E.	Pvt	F	At Sea	11-20-43
Thompson, Leonard A.	Pfc	D	Missing->KIA	11-20-43
Vincent, Richard W.	1stLt	D	D-2-18, #1	11-20-43
Vollmer, Danial L.	Corp	D	Missing->KIA	11-20-43
Waltz, Merlin W.	Pvt	D	D-2-18, #8	11-20-43
Watkins, Henry F.	Corpsman	USN	D-2-18, #7	11-20-43
Wetternach, Laurence K.	Pvt	D	Missing->KIA	11-20-43
Zalut, Stanley	Pfc	D	* Cem. #20, C	11-20-43

```
FROM:         NUMBER
Company "D" =   31        November 1 - 30, 1943
Company "F" =    5        Muster Roster Total   = 799
Corpsman    =    1        Number dead           =  37
              -----
TOTAL       =   37        Percentage            = 4.6%

 *  East Division Cemetery
```

I hope you are comforted to know that

*When we lose someone who is close
to our heart it is difficult because of
the special bond we share.*

This is what all the invasion beaches looked like after and during the, "Battle For Tarawa". Many were wounded and many gave their all.

"Lord, hold our troops in your loving hands. Protect them as they protect us. Bless them and their families for the selfless acts they perform for us in our time in need. I ask this in the name of Jesus, our Lord and Savior.
Amen"

A direct hit by a Navy 16-inch shell took care of this Jap emplacement.

A moment of Triumph comes when the Stars
and Stripes are hoisted on a topless coconut tree, –
after the bloodiest battles in Marine Corps history.

HONOR THEIR COMMITMENT TO HOME AND COUNTRY

"The Battle Is Over," and we
are walking back across the hard-won Island of
Betio, Tarawa Atoll, Gilbert Islands, to a well
deserved rest.

★ ★ ★ ★ ★ ★ ★ ★ ★ ★ ★ ★

"It is fit and becoming in all people, at all
times, to acknowledge and revere the Supreme
Government of God; to bow in humble submission
to His chastisement; to confess and deplore their
their sins and transgressions in the full conviction
that the fear of the Lord is the beginning of wisdom;
and to pray, with all fervency and contrition, for
the pardon of their past offenses, and for a blessing
upon their present and prospective action."

Abraham Lincoln, declaring a National
Day of Prayer and Fasting following the Battle of Bull Run.

The President of the United States takes pleasure in presenting the PRESIDENTIAL UNIT CITATION to the

SECOND MARINE DIVISION (REINFORCED)

consisting of Division Headquarters, Special Troops (including Company C, 1st Corps Medium Tank Battalion), Service Troops, 2nd, 6th, 8th, 10th and 18th Marine Regiments in the Battle of Tarawa, as set forth in the following

CITATION:

"For outstanding performance in combat during the seizure and occupation of the Japanese-held Atoll of Tarawa, Gilbert Islands, November 20 to 24, 1943. Forced by treacherous coral reefs to disembark from their landing craft hundreds of yards off the beach, the Second Marine Division (Reinforced) became a highly vulnerable target for devastating Japanese fire. Dauntlessly advancing in spite of rapidly mounting losses, the Marines fought a gallant battle against crushing odds, clearing the limited beachheads of snipers and machine guns, reducing powerfully fortified enemy positions and completely annihilating the fanatically determined and strongly entrenched Japanese forces. By the successful occupation of Tarawa, the Second Marine Division (Reinforced) has provided our forces with highly strategic and important air and land bases from which to continue future operations against the enemy; by the valiant fighting spirit of these men, their heroic fortitude under punishing fire and their relentless perseverance in waging this epic battle in the Central Pacific, they have upheld the finest traditions of the United States Naval Service."

For the President,

James Forrestal

Acting
Secretary of the Navy

It wasn't until the, "Battle for Tarawa", was over that I could sit down and think about what we just went through. I know that most of those who participated in this battle would have flash-backs of incidents that happened during the battle,- I know I did. I'd have nightmares and sometimes I'd be hollering,- screaming or crying. I'd wake up in a cold sweat and be shivering even though it was 100 degrees,- my stomach would hurt and I'd think of my, "buddies", who we left behind. I'd wonder,-"why wasn't it me"!! One night I was having a bad night, really bad,- I had a Jap by the throat trying to kill him when all of a sudden I woke up,- it wasn't a Jap,- it was my wife and she was screaming and fighting me off! That was a very scary momet and I, "Thank The Lord", that it never happened again. I would carry these thoughts and memories for ever. Certain smells and noises to this day would trigger my memory bank and would react by hitting the deck or look for a safe place. The war has stayed with me and I'll never forget,-"76" hours of "Hell"! I am now 84 years young and the battle for Tarawa seems like it happened yesterday.

 Honor
Through
Remembrance

" Prisoners "

On the second day of the battle, around mid-morning a Marine Officer came down to the beach, where I was, with two Jap Officers and I was ordered to take them out to a Higgins Boat that would be waiting to pick them up. Before I left with the prisoners I told my partner, Floyd, to cover me, just in case they tried to get away. I prodded them with my rifle and motioned them to get going toward the water. We would have to go out and over the coral reef to the waiting boat. All this would happen while we were still under enemy fire. Both of the Japs had been hit by a flame-thrower, — their burnt skin was hanging from their bodies, — it was an awful sight! As they walked in front of me, across the coral reef the water was getting deeper and soon the salt water hit their exposed and burnt bodies. I have never heard such screams of pain in my life, — I almost felt sorry for them, — almost. I got them to the waiting boat and I presume they would be interrogated. I completed my job and now I would have to go back across the coral reef, still under fire, but I made it back to the sea-wall safely.

★ ★ ★ ★ ★ ★ ★ ★ ★ ★ ★

"We hold these truths to be self-evident, that all men are created equal. That they are endowed by their Creator with certain unalienable rights, that among these are life, liberty and the pursuit of happiness."

Declaration of Independence, July 4, 1776

" The Vision "

    The true experience I am about to tell you is known only by a few people including my wife and my mother, who has since passed away.

    In World War Two I was a member of Co."D", 2nd Batt., 18th Marines, (formerly the 2nd Pioneer Battalion), 2nd Marine Division. Our mission was to go in with the assault troops and set up avenues for supplies to come in and to evacuate the wounded.

    On Nov. 20th, 1943 we were at a place called, "Tarawa", and I was a part of the, "Beach Party," going in in the 3rd wave in an Amtrack, (a tracked landing vehicle). I was lucky, we made it to Red Beach 3, O.K.! On the way in Tarawa exploded into an inferno of bullets, fire, smoke and a deafining sound of noise from the Navy ships that were pounding the island. What surprised us the most was the intense fire the Japs were throwing at us as we came in. There was to be no walk across the island, we were going to have to fight our way across!! This was going to be very difficult to do our job because of the coral reef, the intense fire coverage of the Japs and the shortage of Amtracks. The beach-head was measured in yards and there was a sea-wall made up of palm logs and my partner and I got up behind it, the only protection we had. I was leaning against an upright log, my partner, Floyd, was to my right, (as in the picture). I had just moved to a kneeling position when it seemed to get quiet, all of a sudden a vision of my mother appeared before me, for only a couple of seconds, - it was then that I knew that I would be all right. It was seconds, after I saw my "mom", that there was a very loud, "crack", exploded right above my head. We were being fired at from a half sunk Jap ship out in the harbor and one had me in his sights, - "Thank God", that he missed!! Shortly after the ship was bombed and put out of action.

The "Vision" was of a picture of my mother that I had looked at many times in my youth. "Thanks Mom", for being there with me, - I wasn't scared any more during the, "Bloody Battle For Tarawa".

When I got home from the war I looked for the picture but it was gone, disappeared, - maybe it still is on, "Tarawa".

The sturdy, "Grumman F4F Wildcat", was the primary Navy and Marine Corps fighter at the beginning of World War II. "Thanks", to the guys who flew them!!

"Liberty In Hilo"

Once again we were on board troop transports and it was a great relief to get off that island of, "DEATH", called, "Betio", in the Tarawa Atoll. We were on our way, - to where we didn't know, - but we would be told somewhere along the way. I and others were on the biggest troop transport that I had ever seen, - it was strictly a troop transport, not like the ones we came on, which were combat loaded with Marines and their equipment. We didn't care what ship we were on, - as long as we got our three meals per day, had a nice clean bunk to sleep in and showers to take, - it was like, "Heaven". The word was finaly passed down, - we were on our way to, - Hawaii, - that sounded real good. We didn't do much of anything the rest of the trip until we reached the, "Hawaiian Islands", and the Port of Hilo on the big island. We disembarked from the ships, boarded the waiting trucks which would take us up to our camp which was located between two mountains and it was cold. The camp was called, "Camp Tarawa", - they had to remind us! The trucks would take a special road, built special to our Camp, over the Lava Beds. It was about 70 miles to camp and when we arrived we looked like the Ace of Spades from lava dust, - it was fun trying to wash it off. Shortly after we were ordered to, "pack up your gear and get ready to move out", Co. "D", was ready and again we boarded our trucks and headed down over the Lava Beds to Hilo. We would take over the former P.O.W. Camp, (Prisoner of War). We would operate from this, "Base Camp", to do guard duty and work parties.

One day during our stay at the stockade we got a day of liberty and about a half dozen of us took off for town, did a little shopping and ended up in a local gin-mill. The liquor in Hawaii was made from the sugar cane grown in these islands and it had a kick. The good state-side stuff was hard to find, but that was O.K. we could get our kicks from whatever they had. After getting acquainted with the other patrons who welcomed us and, "Thanked", us for what we had accomplished in the Pacific. They invited us to have a drink and we did; several times. We were having a great time when, Gus, fell off the bar stool he was sitting on and we razed him and hollered at him, "Hey Gus get up, - get off the floor,"- and he did! Soon it was time to leave, - we said our, "Good-bys", and, "Thanked", them for a good time;- after all it didn't cost us a cent; - we couldn't buy a drink! As we stepped outside the Tavern there was a little dog, - a Terrier I think, it was, trying to get across to the other side of the street, which was very busy. So, yours truly, feeling pretty good, decided he was going to help the dog get across the street. I walked out to the center of the intersection, - stopped all the traffic and my, "buddies", helped the dog to the other side of the street. We did our, "Good Deed", for the day.

On another day when a group of us were on a, "work-detail", we came across some Navy Pilots who were preparing to have a, "lu-au", - a Hawaiian Feast,

and they were apologizing to us and they were
sorry for dropping their bomb load on the Marines
at Tarawa. We were sorry to, but those things do
happen, it can't be helped. They had set up an outside bar and we were invited to have a drink, -
several of them, - and all the time we talked &
talked they kept on saying they were, "Sorry".
We under-stood how they felt and we told them,
"this is wartime and anything can happen, - keep
up the good work", - and we left, - feeling pretty
good.
      While we were still in Hilo a Navy Squadron
put out a call for volunteers to man the guns on
their planes. I had never been in an airplane or
flown in one, - so I thought this would be a good
time to find out about flying, - so I volunteered for
the chance, along with a couple of other guys.
We were taken to the airbase, - fitted with what we
needed for the flight, including a parachute. I was
to fly with the Squadron Commander and before
I set foot in the plane he said, "If you make a
mess you'll clean it up with a toothbrush", -
"Yes Sir", I replied and took my place in the turret
of the gun bubble and I took off the parachute,
because it didn't fit with me in the turret. In the
meantime we had taken off and climbed way
up in the blue and while I was still familarizing
myself with the machine gun the Commander put
the plane into a dive, which I was not ready for,
and I hit my head on the machine gun, - not to hard,
but over the planes intercom I said to the Commander -
"let me know the next time your going to dive, - let

90

me know". The rest of the flight was great and at one time they were flying inches over the ocean. Those Navy guys sure could fly those planes and what a thrill it was for me.

Our stay in Hawaii was coming to an end, — & we made a lot of friends while we were there, — but now it was time to, "move out". We again boarded our ships and headed out to sea, — but this time it was for a practice landing before we moved on to our next campaign, — Saipan!!

This is the Island of Maui where we made practice landings for our next assault.
L. to R. - Lt. Walter McNamara, Don Stoffer, Floyd Schouviller, Charles Wysocki, Jr. and Lou Curcio
D-2-18

SAIPAN

Tapotchau

MT. TOPOTCHAU

OBSERVATORY HILL

Garapan

RADIO STATION

AIRSTRIP

LAKE SUSUPE

Charan Kanoa

GREEN 1
GREEN 2
GREEN 3

D+3
D+1
D+7
D+9
D+12
D+14
D+17
D+18
D+16

NAFUTAN PT.

ASLITO AIRFIELD

AGINGAN PT.

Charan Kanoa

MAGICIENNE BAY

CT-8
0843
D-DAY

CT-6
0843
D-DAY

1/29
1450
D-DAY

CT-2
1800
D-DAY

2nd DIVISION

TANAPAG HARBOR

MUTCHO PT.

Garapan

Mukunsha

CT-4
CT-8

CT-3

ARPI

James Cutter

Saipan

Sgt. Mike Masters
wounded — note
medical patch
on buttocks

Mike was my Platoon Sgt. and this wound
put him out of action for good. This is the beach
we landed on under heavy enemy fire.

"In all of the far-flung operations of our own
Armed Forces the toughest job has been performed
by the average, easy-going, hard-fighting young
American who carries the weight of battle on his
own young shoulders.

It is to him that we and all future generations
of Americans must pay grateful tribute."

President Franklin D. Roosevelt.

Another view of the beach we landed on
and secured, then moved inland. "D-2-18."

L.S.T.'s -
unloading Marines
and supplies. I
came in in a
"Higgins Boat"
June 15th, 1944.

The first troops ashore on Saipan wait for reinforcements. During WW II, amtracs landed Marines on beaches which would have been impossible to reach by boat.

Second Marine Division

P.F.C. Charles Wysocki, Jr. is in this landing, June 15th to Aug 9th, 1944.

X - Sgt. Wesley C. Worthington

"MIKE" →

SOBOL →

STUFFER ? →

PAMEMBER ET ?
(PUBLISHED IN LIFE MAG)
0-2-1B MARINES

Here we go again, and as you've seen in the previous couple of pages the next target would be another place we never heard of, - "Saipan", in the Marianas Islands. The assault date would be - June 15th, 1944. The trip to "Saipan" was uneventful but the day we arrived off the Island all hell broke loose; the Navy opened up with its big guns what a thunderous, ear-splitting sound that was - a very welcomed one. While the Navy was blasting away the Air Force was doing its part, - dropping bombs all over the place. Every time I have seen one of these pre-invasion bombardments I am amazed that there is anyone still alive, - but there always is! While the island was being blasted we were going over the side and down the cargo nets into the "Higgins Boats", that were much improved over the original ones. We reached the "line of departure", waited for the signal to head for the beach, - which came very quickly and we moved out. Frome our boats we could see heavy black clouds of smoke hanging over the beaches, raging pockets of fire, flashes of exploding shells and bombs along with the tremendous noise. As we approched the beach we were ordered to back off and wait for further orders. We found out later that the beach we were supposed to hit was under terrific enemy rifle, mortar and artillery fire. Shortly we were ordered to go in on another beach where we successfully landed, - still under heavy enemy fire. After the beach was secured an Army unit took over, we became, "Infantry Support". We moved to an area that was flat from the beach to the base of the mountains and ideal for a Jap counter attack. Orders came down to take up defensive positions and dig in. My, "foxhole", buddy and I started digging in a hurry so we would have a nice deep hole for protection during the night. Our position was on the right edge of this flat area and about 70 yards inland from the beach. We set up a schedule so that one of us would be on watch at all times through the night. Very early in the morning the Japs executed a, "tank-attack". They came out of the foothills, roared down this area headed for the beach, - they were trying to drive a wedge in our lines, but our own, Sherman Tanks, anti-tank guns, called, "bazookas", took care of the Jap attack! I have to confess, - I didn't see any of this battle and through all of the turmoil and the noise, - I slept through it !! I was so exhausted that I didn't hear a sound, - my, "foxhole", buddy couldn't wake me up, even though he said he tried! When I did get up and had a look at all the destroyed Jap tanks, - the closest being about 25 yards away from our foxhole, - I gave a sigh of relief and thanked the, "Lord", for watching over us. Again we moved out and headed for the town of, "Garapan", which had been flattened by our Naval guns earlier in the assault. Our job was to secure the town and make sure there no Japs around, - only dead ones! We did have a scare one night while on patrol through town, - an odor of gas was detected and we were ordered to put on our, "gas masks", - which we did, - those who had one. In the course of the assault some of the troops threw their, "gas masks", away but they kept the pouch it came in to carry extra grenades, clothing or to carry souvenirs in it. Lucky for those who did not have a, "gas mask", - it was a false alarm. The odor came from some very large batteries that were leaking. After that episode no one threw their "gas masks", away, - they learned their lesson. Then we got a break, - we were relieved and sent back to a rest area to await further orders, - which came sooner than expected. During the night the Japs pulled a, "Banzai", and had driven all the way up to where our artillery was firing point blank at them, - the attack was repulsed with many casualties. During the attack we were ordered to take up defensive positions to repel any further attacks. It was a forced march up to our positions and while we double-timing it to the area in the hills my right leg went out on me and I couldn't walk, - so a couple of my, "buddies", grabed me and tossed me on top of a truck until we got to where we took up our positions in, "foxholes", on the side of a hill, - we were ready, but nothing more happened through the night. All night long star-shells were being fired to keep the area all lit-up, - it was a nerve-racking night. From our position we could see the aftermath of a battle, - there were bodies everywhere, - theirs and ours!! What a horrible waste of life!! Early that morning we were ordered to a rear area to help load L.S.T.'s for our next engagement.

   At this point I want to go back to the original assault when I was wounded in both my elbow areas. It happened a couple of days after we landed. A group of us were advancing through a wooded area that was being used as a fuel dump when all of a sudden the Japs opened up with artillery fire from the mountain area directly in front of us. I for one dove for cover behind a tree and as I was flying through the air a shell exploded and pieces of shrapnel were flying all over the place. My arms were extended in front of me when a piece of shrapnel tore into my arms around the elbow and it felt like a hot poker was sticking me. A Navy Corpman was called and still being under fire he got to me, stopped the bleeding, cleaned the wound, and bandaged it up. I was taken off the line to a rear area for a few days of rest and then I was returned to duty. There just are not enough words of, "Praise", for the, "Corpman", who with no hesitation tend to the wounded under some of the worst conditions one could imagine. They are the, "Unsung Heroes", of the war!!

When we were relieved of our positions in the foothills of Mt. Topotchau we continued on to the North end of the island,- Marpi Point, where many of the Islanders were jumping off the cliffs, to their deaths on the rocks and ocean below. The natives were, "brain washed", by the Japs who told them they wold,- be tortured, raped, and then killed,- but the survivors found out that was not true!! They were given the best care possible! I remember one incident when the Island's residents were coming out of their hiding places in the hills, -

very scared and not sure of what was going to happen to them! I was standing high up on the side of this hill directing traffic to an area at the bottom of the hill where they would be taken care of, - fed, clothed and given medical help. As I was standing there searching the natives for anyone who might be trying to infilterate and blend in with the natives, this little old looking woman, carrying a baby came along and she looked exhausted, wobbly and sick. I thought she needed help, - so I stopped her and motioned to her to give me the baby, - she backed off and shook her head indicating a "NO." I again motioned to her that I wanted to help her and the baby get down the hill. This time, being not sure still, she gave me the baby, - I smiled and I cuddled it in my left arm, slung my rifle over my right shoulder and put my right arm under hers and led her down the hill to safety. I then gave the baby back to her, and this time she smiled as I waved to her and returned to my position on the hill, - feeling good about what I had just done. When our help to the survivors of Saipan was finished we rested for a few days and then got ready for our next assault on another island not to far from Saipan.

⭐ ⭐ ⭐

"The quality of our American fighting men is not all a matter of training, equipment or organization. It is essentially a matter of spirit, that spirit is expressive in their faith in America"

President Franklin D. Roosevelt.

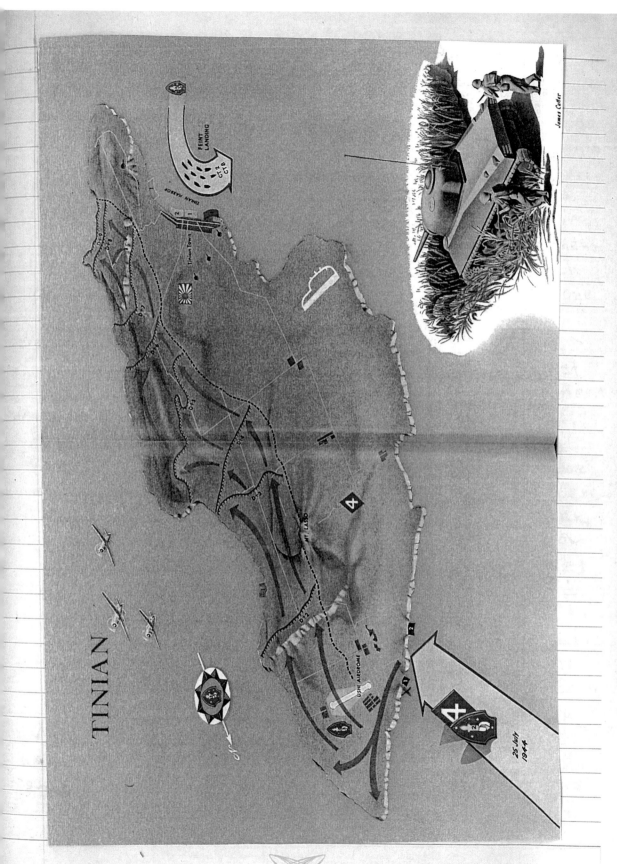

TINIAN

FEINT LANDING

CT 2
CT 8

TINIAN HARBOR

TINIAN TOWN

USHI AIRDROME

MT. LASSO

25 July
1944

James Cutter

TINIAN

Our next assault would be just down the road, about 3 miles from Saipan on an Island called, "Tinian", which was much flatter than the mountainous Saipan. These Islands would later be used by our B-29's for the air assault on Japan.

The assault on, "Tinian", would one of great surprise for the Japs who thought we would be making an assault near, "Tinian Town", which was on the East side of the Island near the South end of the Island. A fake landing was made at, "Tinian Town", but the real one would take place on the, "North-east end of the Island which was not an ideal place to land, - but we did !! There were two beachheads, - each one just wide enough for an, "Amtrack", to land. It was a very rocky area with jagged coral edges. We worked our way through the crevices and rocky coral terrain, - past burned up bodies of Japs who had been hit with, "Napalm", dropped by our planes. In most cases you could tell it was a Jap only by the remains of a belt buckle or a partialy burned rifle. As we passed through, - very carefully, the area the stench was almost unbearable and some of the bodies were still smoldering. As we came out from this rugged area of violent death we could see the Airport which had been worked over by our long range artillery firing from the coast of Saipan. The Airport had already been taken and secured by the troops in front of us.

It didn't take to long to overun, "Tinian", and secure it. We started at the North end on July 26th and ended up on the South end on Aug. 9th 1944 where there was a deep ravine with the Japs on one side and our troops on the other side. We could see the Japs going in and out of the caves and firing their Artillery pieces and other weapons at us,- we would return the fire with our own weapons. How long it took to clean them out,- I don't know because we were ordered back to Saipan. Our job on "Tinian", was much like the one we had on Saipan,- "support troops".

A few days after we returned to Saipan a miracle happened one morning at roll-call. A list of names was read followed by this announcement,- "If your name was called,- you are going "Home",- pack your gear and be ready to move out". My name was called,- I couldn't believe what I heard, but from the reaction of those whose names were called it must be true. We congradulated each other, hugged one another, shock hands and it was a moment of happiness, undescribable joy. Late that afternoon we got the word, "to move out", and as we did we said, "good-bye and good luck", to our, "buddies", who wouldn't be leaving with us. We boarded the biggest Army Transport I have ever seen,- our, "Unholy Four", ships were midgets compared to this Army Transport. I didn't care how big it was as long as it was headed for the good ol' U.S.A. and home.

The war would be over for some of us but we still had, "Buddies", over there and they would be going to Okinawa,- we prayed for their safety.

This is the beach-head we established on Tinian. The coast-line in this area was very rugged, — not an ideal place for a landing, but we did on two beaches, — each one wide enough for an Amtrack to get on the beach. I waded in from an L.S.T. and with others moved in to the left and headed for the airstrip, — top of picture. This maneuver was a big surprise to the Japs!!

I, with others landed here x, then moved across the airstrip to the East side of the Island. The 2nd Division went up the East side of the Island and the 4th Division went up the West side to it's conclusion

L.V.T.'s going in with their load of assault troops. This time I waded in from an L.S.T.

The Corpsman's Creed

1898 cadeusis

Hospital Corpsmen (HMs) are members of the United States Navy Hospital Corps. The Hospital Corps is the only all enlisted corps in the United States Navy. Corpsmen serve in a wide variety of capacities and locations, including shore establishments such as naval hospitals and clinics, aboard ships as the primary medical care givers for sailors while underway, and with Marine Corps units as battlefield corpsmen.

The Hospital Corps has been part of the United States Naval service since 1799, when congress instituted a service-wide provision to include a surgeon's assistant on all ships of the fleet. The title of this specialty training, also known as 'rating' in naval terminology, has changed over the years from loblolly boy, surgeon's steward, apothecary and bayman. The latter three required the rate holder to be a recipient of private medical instruction.

On 17 June 1898, by act of congress, the Hospital Corps was established, though the actual name of servicemen under that rating would change several times (known as "Pharmacist's Mates" throughout World Wars I & II) before ultimately becoming "Hospital Corpsman."

During World War I, 684 personal awards were issued to Hospital Corpsmen, who distinguished themselves while serving with United States Marines in numerous battles, among them Belleau Wood. In World War II, Pharmacist's Mates hit beaches alongside Marines in every battle of the Pacific. They also served on ships and submarines.

The rating of Hospital Corpsman is the most decorated in the United States Navy, with 23 Medals of Honor, the most of any single group in the U.S. Navy; 174 Navy Crosses; 31 Distinguished Service Medals; 943 Silver Stars and 1553 Bronze Stars.

The Hospital Corps has the distinction of being the only corps in the U.S. Navy to be singled out by Secretary of the Navy James Forrestal after the conclusion of World War II.

Fourteen ships have been named after Hospital Corpsmen. Due to the vast array of foreign, domestic and shipboard duty stations in which hospital corpsmen are called to serve, as well as the fact that the United States Marine Corps has no medical personnel of its own, the Hospital Corps is the largest single rating in the United States Navy.

The Field Medical Service School has locations at Camp Pendleton and Camp Lejeune, where sailors bound for service with the Marine Corps attend classes to earn the rating of Field Medical Service Technician. This is specialized training emphasizing physical conditioning, small arms familiarity, and fundamentals of Marine Corps life–to make up for the lack of traditional field training corpsmen receive during Navy boot camp.

This course is seven weeks long.

A common description of the Vietnam era corpsman was "A long-haired, bearded sailor who would go through the very gates of Hell to tend to a wounded Marine."

Tom McLeod, Historian

Plasma for the wounded is administered under fire, on the beach by suspending bottle on rifle. Some casualties were evacuated on the first day.

At beach aid station a wounded Marine is attended by a Navy Corpsmen.

The white dot on the helmets indicate that person as a member of the "Shore Party", as I was.

The Navy Corpsman who were assigned to a Marine unit were,—in my opinion, the unsung "Heroes" of the war. I know because one took care of me when I was wounded. There is not enough praise for these guys who put their lives on the line to help others.

"God Bless Them All Always."

It's a weird feeling when you have to leave your "Buddies", to go home knowing that some of them would not be going when you do. After being with these guys for almost four years and going through what we did,—battle after battle, you feel like your losing a brother. Memories are great because you can remember the good times we had.

C.H.

The psychological aspect of trying to go through the war meant you had to keep your sense,—your own self,—you had to really look at yourself every day and say,—"I hope I make it to the next day." You had to have that thing:—"Well, if it's my time, it's my time,—right! you see all your buddies go or get wounded and that's why it is so tragic! said by a W.W.II Veteran. . .

" War Is Hell "

If, "Hell", is anything like the "Horrors of War",-
I pity those who will have to go to war! Yes,- "War
Is Hell", and it must be stopped forever,- but how do
we do it! The Combat Veterans of past wars will
soon be gone and their wartime experiences with
them. So, for the record I'll try to tell my story
of World War Two! Before I start let me mention
that what I say, what stories you have heard,
from other Veterans, how many books you have
read about war or how many movies and documen-
tries you have seen you will never know what "War",
is. You have to be there, to see it, to feel it, to hear it,
and smell it,- these cannot be reproduced. Neither
can the thoughts that go threw the head of one
facing the possibility of being killed,- the sweat
that pours out of your body, your nerves are
tingling, you think about what you have to do
when you hit the beach,- but when you do you
automatically do what you have been trained to do. Many times I've been asked if I was
scared,- you bet I was and anyone that says
they weren't,- are liars!! Each engagement,
the feeling would get worse and you began
to wonder,- "How much can the human body
endure",- I would find out!
       I was nineteen when I enlisted in the
Corps and eager to get at the Japs and pay
them back for their, "sneak", attack on Pearl
Harbor. I went through, "boot camp", at the
Marine Corps Base in San Diego, California.

109

I was a true, "raw recruit,"— I knew nothing about the military. I was never away from home and I had never held or fired a rifle, — this was to change in a hurry! After the rigors of, "boot camp", and our, "combat training," I was assigned, (I volunteered), to the 2nd Pioneer Battalion of the 2nd Marine Division.

One day, early in July 1942, after days of practice landings, we again boarded our ships, — the, "Unholy Four." I was on the U.S.S. President Hayes, — the others were, Pres. Adams, Pres. Jackson and the Cresent City. These ships would take units of the 2nd Marine Division to Guadalcanal, — our first assault against the Japanese Empire.

The main assault was to be by the 1st Marine Division reinforced by units of the 2nd Marine Div., — which included us, — the 2nd Pioneer Battalion. The Guadalcanal Campaign included Tulagi, Cavutu, Tanambogo, and Florida Islands. In my opinion the battle for the, "Canal", was one of the toughest battles of the war for the following reasons, —

 1. - The heat and humidity

 2. - The Jungle

 3. - The sickness, — malaria, dingy-fever, Tulagi Trots and elephanttitus.

 4. - Jungle Rot

 5. - World War One equipment we had

 6. - Our ships leaving with much needed supplies and troops.

 7. - The duration, — Aug. 7th, 1942 to Feb. 9th, 1943

 8. - The Naval Battles and the shelling of our positions.

9. - Our inexperience for Combat
But we learned about our enemy, many things about their operations and their willingness to die for their Emperor, - we would obliege them.

For 6 months we endured the shelling and bombing by the Japs, the attempt to infilterate our lines, living off captured Jap food, (mostly rice), and wandering if we would survive.

We watched and heard the Naval battles that were taking place around Savo Island and in the Slot. We could see the flashes of the guns when they were fired and the explosion when they hit, - but what we didn't know was who was doing what to who? In the morning we found out we, the good guys, didn't do to good. We watched the crippled U.S. ships come into Tulagi Harbor, - we helped the survivors, some wounded, some burned, some whose insides were badly injured from swallowing fuel oil end salt water. The dead that were taken from the ships or washed up on the beach were buried as soon as possible, - some were so badly burned they were not recognizable. There were tears in our eyes, - but this was a horrible lesson in warfare.

It's hard to describe the feelings I had during the Jap bombings and shellings or to hear the crack of a rifle shot. I do know I was scared!! My body would shake and tremble all over, - I thought my head was going to explode, - I'd break out in a cold sweat, - I didn't know where to run, - all I thought was to take cover and I'd dive into the closest foxhole, - even if someone was already in it. This all happened at the same time.

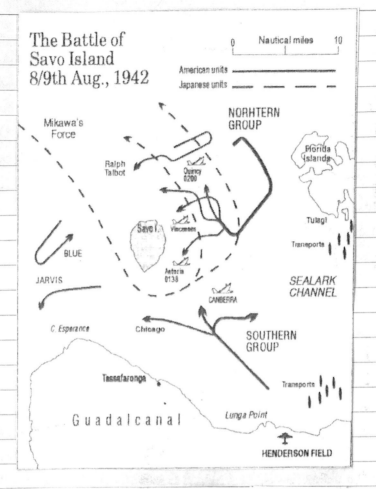

The Battle of
Savo Island
8/9th Aug., 1942

0   Nautical miles   10

American units ————————
Japanese units —— — — —— —

Mikawa's Force

NORHTERN GROUP

Ralph Talbot

Quincy 0200

Savo I.

Vincennes

Astoria 0138

BLUE

JARVIS

Florida Islands

Tulagi

Transports

SEALARK CHANNEL

CANBERRA

C. Esperance   Chicago

SOUTHERN GROUP

Transports

Tassafaronga

Lunga Point

G u a d a l c a n a l

HENDERSON FIELD

SAVO ISLAND

In a serene setting Savo Island stands as a permanent monument in memory of
those brave men who fought and died in her adjacent waters of Iron Bottom Sound

The heavy crusier Portland before the battle and

after it took a torpedo in the fantail area.

"Let us have faith that right makes might; and in that faith let us to the end, dare to do our duty as we understand it."

Abraham Lincoln.

The transport President Jackson, one of the "Unholy Four", take on Jap "Betty" torpedo bombers. The smoke cloud is a "Betty" that has crashed.

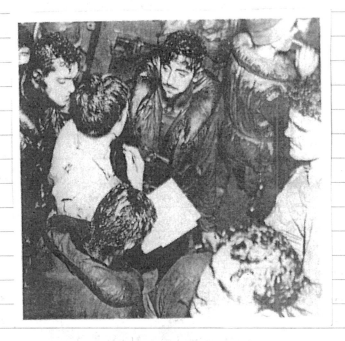

Fuel soaked survivors of the battle. They were the ones, who were lucky!!

The Army arrived in October, during an air raid, to relieve the Marines and mop-up the remnents of the Jap Army. We didn't leave until the 9th of February, 1943, – we were the last to leave from the original landing force. We were tired, worn out, we needed a lot of rest and relaxation. We would get it at our next stop, – New Zealand.

We would fall in love with this Country and its people. A great time was had by all and I for one will always remember my visit to this beautiful Country and the people I met. While there we got our replacements and the M-1 Rifle. It was time now to get down to serious training for our next campaign. On November 1st, 1943, before dawn, our ships left Wellington Harbor and set sail for our next objective which we would find out in a couple of days.

The day came and the word was, another Island we never heard of, – "Tarawa", in the Gilbert Islands, the Island was named, "Betio". Early in the morning of November 20th, 1943 we prepared to, "hit the beach", – my second campaign and landing! The beaches, the airstrip and the whole island were being bombarded by our Navy ships and the Marine and Navy bombers. It was an earth shaking bombardment and an unbelievable thunder of noise that made one tremble. How could anyone live through it, – the Japs did! This was to be an easy landing, – it would take about an hour to go from one side to the other, – but the Japs had other plans for us. It turned out to be one of the great and bloodiest battles of W.W. II and in the History of the Marine Corps. Much was to be learned from this battle that would be used in future assaults. It was a good thing that I heard the, "crack", of the bullet that hit above my head other wise I wouldn't be writing about it today. After, "76", hours the bloody battle for, "Betio", and the, "Tarawa Atoll", was over and time to say, "Good-bye", to our "Buddies". We were the only ones, that I know of, who buried their, "Buddies". They were all marked with a Cross with their names on it and a seperate Cross in front of them indicating their unit, - "D-2-18". Thanks", to Emory, Joe and Gus, who made it possible for us to wish our, "Buddies", a safe trip to the, "Gates of Heaven", to do "Guard Duty".

The battle was over but the troops were dazed and exhausted, - our clothing was filthy, our exposed skin and faces were black from the smoke, gunpowder and dirt that floated over the Island. The bodies of the dead were blotting and you could see the magots taking over, - it was terrible and words cannot describe what I saw those days but the horror of, "Tarawa", will be with me for the rest of my life!!

We left, "Tarawa", on November 24th, 1943 and our ships headed for the Hawaiian Islands and, "Camp Tarawa", located on the slopes of Mauna Loa on the Parker Cattle Ranch. Again we rested, received our replacements and trained for our next assault. While on the Island of Hawaii,

Mr. Parker, threw a, "Rodeo", for the 2nd Marine Div., complet with a barbecue, beer and bucking broncos. A great time was had by all!! Once again we said, "Good-bye", to the beautiful Islands of Hawaii and the friend we had made.

Late in May, 1944, we again boarded our ships, which were docked at Hilo Harbor and once again we headed out to sea, destination unknown!! Before we left the Hawaiian Islands we made some practice landings on some of the other island in preparation for our next assault, "Saipan", in the Mariana Islands. This would be my 3rd assault.

We arrived at our destination on the morning of June 15th, 1944, and again the bombardment of the Island of Saipan was well underway. The noise again was blowing our brains out, you never get used to that pounding, unbearable noise. We made the landing and my Sergeant, Mike, got a million dollor wound that sent him State-side for good. A few days later I would catch a piece of shrapnel in both my arms, but not bad enough to be sent State-side. I felt sorry for the Natives of Saipan who were committing suicide, they were brain-washed by the Japs who told them the Marines would torture, rape and kill them, but for some it would be to late to know that was not true. Because a Country, Japan wanted to expand their boundries through war and conquest innocent people, like those on Saipan, had to die and suffer at the hands of the Jap invaders.

Saipan was now secured and we were to get

117

some much needed rest, – but not for long, – there was another island to take, – called, "Tinian", – next door to Saipan.

    While still on Saipan we were preparing for the assauld on, "Tinian", – loading the L.S.T.'s with what ever would be needed for the asseult. On July 26th, 1944 we assaulted, "Tinian", on two beaches, – each one wide enough for an Amtrack to get on the beach. I was on an L.S.T. with others and we were dropped off about a hundred yards off the beachead. We had to wade in and lucky for us there was no enemy fire. The differance between the two islands was that, "Saipan", was mountainous and, "Tinian", was pretty flat. This was my 4th assault on an enemy held island and by August 9th, 1944, the battle for, "Tinian", was over. The 2nd and 4th Marine Divisions did what they had to do to secure these two islands.

    We were ordered back to Saipan and a couple of days later, at a morning roll-call, a bunch of us were told we were going back to the States! What a wonderful feeling that was!!

    The trip home was uneventful except for the day we sailed under the, "Golden Gate" bridge. You could hear us cheering all over the Sanfrancisco Bay area, – what a wonderful day that was. We were, "home", in the good-ol U.S.A..

    Shortly after arriving in the U.S. we docked at the Treasuer Iisland base and then onto the Marine Base in San Diego, – where we started from over 3 years earlier.

While at the Marine Base in San Diego I ran into a couple of guys that were with us at Tulagi and sent back to the States for one reason or another. They were so glad to see us they invited us to have a drink with them, – it was O.K. with us. Off we went in their car out to the "boon-docks", where they broke out a bottle of Gin and passed it around until it was gone and we were a little, "tipsey". I told my friends, – sorry I don't remember their names, – I had to get back because we were leaving that evening for Camp bejune, – the Marine Base in North Carolina. They dropped me off on the far side of the Parade Grounds and I would have to cross it to get to the assembly area where the trucks would take us to the train depot. I was about half way across the Parade Grounds when the Gin, the Sun and the Heat hit me! My, "buddies", who were watching for me saw that I was in trouble so they ran out to get me, – they hustled me the rest of the way, put me in a truck with my gear and when I woke up I was on the train, – my "buddies", had taken good care of me. They "needled" me all the way to Camp bejune! The train we were on was a regular passenger one and very friendly passengers, – so, we had a very enjoyable trip. When we arrived in Washington, D.C. our train was going to have a lay-over for a couple of hours, So, "Sarge", – one of the Marines I met on the train, decided we were going to go into town and take two of the young ladies, we had met on the train, with us. We found a niece restaurant, – had a very nice dinner, a few drinks and returned to the train, – we were never missed, but we had a great time, and we did get to Camp LeJune the next day and a new era would start for, P.F.C. Charles Wysocki, Jr..

Now, the question is, – how do we put an end to "WAR"!! Do it by educating the people, and the leaders around the world that the way to, "Peace", is not "War". War only destroys human beings, cities, towns and Countries. If there is ever another World War it will be the end for all of us, – no one will survive!! We must prevent, "WAR", through education and peaceful negotiations.

"Peace, Not War."

"It is the Soldier, not the reporter, who has given us
    freedom of the press – – – –
It is the Soldier, not the poet, who has given us
    freedom of speech – "
            Author Unknown.

Long may it Wave

"My Career As A Public Speaker"

It was early in September, 1944 that I returned to the States from Saipan where I had been wounded, on the third day of the assault. My wounds were taken care of and I completed the taking of Saipen and Tinian. I then returned to Saipan where I was becoming a casualty of, "Combat Fatigue", - I think that is why I was returned to the States. Eventually I ended up in the Philadelphia Navy Hospital where I was treated for a number of ailments including, "Combat Fatigue".

Around March of 1945 I was picked, by the Hospital Staff, to go on a Salvation Army Fund Raising Campaign with a Soldier from the Valley Forge Army Hospital, - Frank was his name. I had never made a speech before any group in my life, - so this was going to be a great experience and part of my, "Rehab", before being returned to a, "Civilian". Frank and I toured the State of Pennsylvania making speeches to many clubs and organizations, - always chaparoned by, Col. Bayless of the Salvation Army.

One day, while in my hotel room, in Philly. I got a speaking assignment at a, "Women's Club", from Col. Bayless and he told me to be there by 3: P.M.. That afternoon I left for my assignment with plenty of time to get there. As I was walking through a busy downtown intersection there was a loud explosion, - I hit the deck, - right in the middle of the intersection!! What an embaressing moment with everyone staring at me. Out of the crowd came a Marine to help me get up. He knew what was happening and he said to me, "I think you could use a drink." At first I said, "No", because of the assignment I had. He insisted we have a drink, there was plenty of time, so we did. After a couple of drinks it was time to go, we said our, "good-bys", and I headed for the, "Women's Club", where Col. Bayless was waiting for me, he was getting worried about my showing up! I cleaned myself up, combed my hair, had a drink, of water and I was ready to meet the ladies. By the time I was to make my speech I was feeling the drinks and I really didn't know what I had said to the ladies. Col. Bayless met me backstage and congradulated me on the, "Best Speech I Had Made", I wish I knew what I said, but from the applause it must have been good!! End of career!!

The explosion was a back-fire from a truck. Today at the age of 84 I still jump at loud noises.

My being in the War gave me the opportunity to meet many people and because of that I am a better person and a better human being today.

C. H.

"Assaulting The Beaches"

Many years have gone by, 65, since the battles and my experience in some of those battles in the Pacific Theatre of War during World War Two. It might have been a long time ago but some of the memories and incidents seem like they happened just yesterday,- I don't think they'll ever go away. Even today there are things that bring back memories,- different odors, noises, voices, pictures and movies. I am going to try to tell you of my thoughts, feelings, and experiences in assauting the beaches of,- Tulagi, (Guadalcanal Campaign) in the Solomon Islands, Tarawa Atoll, Island of Betio, in the Gilbert Islands, Saipan and Tinian in the Marianas Islands. I would be wounded on the Island of Saipn.

It all started on February 5th, 1942 - the day I enlisted in the United States Marine Corps, in Milwaukee, Wisc.. Then off to, "boot camp", at the Marine Corps Recruit Depot, San Diego, Calif.. It was a pretty rugged, "boot camp",- there were many days and nights when every bone and muscle in my body ached. The DI's were trying to make Marines out of a bunch of, "grunts", and most times they succeeded. I made it through, "boot camp", and then volunteered for a new unit called the, "Pioneers". We would be used as, "Combat Engineers", "Shore Party", or "Infantry" of the 2nd Pioeer Battalion, 2nd Marine Division.

Early in July, 1942, we left the States on

board the U.S.S. President Hayes, my ship; the other ships were the, Pres. Jackson, Pres. Adams and the Crescent City, - they would be known as, "The Unholy Four". Wherever we were going was unknown but we did know that it was going to be first offense against the Japanese Empire and our first combat experience. We finally got the word that our target was going to be a place we never heard of, - "Guadalcanal", in the Solomon Islands. There would be other, "unknown islands". Besides the, "Canal", the other islands that would be involved in this operation were, - Tulagi, Cavutu, Tanambogo and Florida. I, with my unit would land on Tulagi.

We were aboard our ships for almost a month, with a stop at the Tonga, Islands for a one day break to stretch our legs; then back aboard ship and on our way again. As we sailed to our destination life aboard ship was pretty routine, - eating, sleeping, exercising, guard duty, letter writing, meetings and taking in the beauty of the ocean during our liesure time.

As we neared our target you could feel the tension growing and on day before the assault we checked our gear, packed and repacked our back-packs with 3 days of C-Rations, underwear, extra socks, toilet articles, including toilet paper, wrote a letter, visited the chaplain, checked our rifles, our ammo and then tried to get some sleep before the 3:AM. revellie. After revellie we would do our morning chores, get in line for breakfast and then get

The Six Marine Div's. In World War Two
Pacific Theater

1st Marine Div. - Guadalcanal, Cape Gloucester,
    Peleliu and Okinawa

2nd Marine Div. - Guadalcanal, Tulagi, Tarawa,
    Saipan and Tinian, & Okinawa.

3rd Marine Div. - Bougainville and Iwo Jima.

4th Marine Div. - Marshalls, Saipan, Tinian & Two Jima.

5th Marine Div - Iwo Jima

6th Marine Div. - Okinawa

Duty Honor Courage Semper Fi

ready to leave the ship as soon as we got the word, "Marines proceed to your debarkation stations". When the word came we would move as fast as we could to our stations, — wait for the order to disembark, — and over the side and down the cargo nets we'd go into our "Higgins Boats", assemble and head for the line of departure. We'd wait for the signal to move out and head for the beach. This would be the procedure for most of the assaults on the Islands in the Pacific. The one exception would be my Platoon landing on the Island of Tulagi. Although some of our, "Pioneers", did land with the assault waves, my Platoon did not go in until late afternoon. Prior to going in I was thinking, — this is going to be my first combat experience, what's it going to be like, how am I going to react, will I do my job, what's going to happen to me, and always in the back of my mind were the thoughts of home and family. I did not see any combat on Tulagi, but did experience several Jap Navy bombardments and air raids of the island which were very sca- rey and nerve racking. I'd be sweating, freezing and shaking all at the same time and the fox- holes were never deep enough! Today, April 2007, I often wonder, — "How the Hell" did I ever live through those days of, "horror".

   I and my fellow Marines were on these Islands the longest of any of the D-Day troops, Aug. 7th, 1942 to Feb. 9th, 1943. While there we enjoyed all the comforts; mud, rain, heat, mosquitos, malaria, dinghyfever, dysentery, elephantitus and fatigue! I was lucky I got to try them all, except elephantitus. At one time 50% or more of the troops were on the, "sick list", - good thing the Japs didn't know. Tokyo Rose didn't know either!

I have never seen a bunch of guys so happy to leave this, Island Paradise, as we were. We earned a well deserved rest in a beautiful place called, - "New Zealand"!!

After getting our rest, training, and replacements we again boarded our ships, said "Goodbye", to our New Zealand friends and headed for our next objective. Early in the morning of Nov. 20th, 1943 we arrived off the "Tarawa Atoll", and the Island of, "Betio". We again went through our morning routine and then prepared to leave the ship. This time we would load up in, "Higgins Boats", and at the, "line of departure", we would transfer to the, "Amtracks". We would be in the third wave, the last of the, "Amtracks", - the other waves would come in in the, "Higgins Boats".

Before we left the ship we had to have a good breakfast, - one that would fill our bellies for a long time, - like steak and eggs. Some guys didn't have any trouble eating, others did, like me. My stomach was doing flip-flops, - but I knew we had to eat, so we did our best to get some food "down", - for only, "God", knew when we would get our next decent meal!

From the time we left the ship until the campaign was over there was very little said, - except what was necessary. Everyone had their own thoughts and said their own prayers.

As we left the, "line of departure", there was no time to think of anything else but the job ahead of us. We could hear and see the guns of the, "U.S. Navy", bombarding, "Betio", and the, "Air-force", above us droping bombs. Smoke, unbearing noise, bullets flying over us and hitting our, "Amtrack". We were thinking, nobody could live through that bombardment, - would we be surprised!!

It's hard to describe what's going on around you as you prepare to land on an enemy beach, - you have to experience it, you have to be there!!

Our, "Amtrack", churned its way through the surf, over the coral reef and onto the beach. We rolled over the side as fast as we could and headed up the beach to the, "seawall", for protection. I was one of the last to leave our tracked vehicle and when I landed I was reaching for the, "beach-marker", - my right leg was under the track of the vehicle and it started to back up, - boy, did I move in a hurry, - to pull my leg out from under the track. I did lose my shoe but I was able to retrieve it after the, "Amtrack", pulled out. When I moved up to the, "seawall", there were bodies and debris all over the place, - what a grizzly sight it was!! At the time we didn't who was alive or dead. It wasn't till later in the day that my partner, Floyd, and myself were able to help some of the wounded. On the second day, afternoon, we were able to get help and moved the wounded to an "Aid Station", - all this time being under fire from the Nips. What was happening was something we didn't expect and we weren't going to be on the other side of the island in a couple of hours. We were in for the fight of our lives!! If hell is anything like the, "76", hour battle for, "Tarawa",- I've spent my time in, "HELL"!!

I made it through the battle without a scratch,- but I did lose, 30 pounds and it took over 8 days before I could get any food or water down,- to stay down! As a result I would be treated for a nervous stomach.

It usually is after a battle that you start to think about all the things that happened and could have happened. Sometimes I'd shiver, just thinking about the posabilities! I have, "Thanked God", many time for sparring me and giving me another chance at life.

We left, "Tarawa",- tired, dirty, and very much in need of some rest and sleep. We were a bunch of miserable looking Marines as we walked off that island of death.

Our trip to Hawaii was uneventful, peaceful,- and gave us a chance to, "Crap out" (get some rest),- which we did most of the way. We docked at Hilo on the big island and were transported by truck over the lava beds to our camp up in the mountains,- "Camp Tarawa". I don't know why they had to name the Camp after that hell-hole,- we didn't need to be reminded!

A great time on the, "Big Island", was enjoyed by everyone while we were there. We had liberty in Hilo, the Parker Ranch people had a Rodeo for the 2nd Division Marines and we had a close-up look at the, "lava fields", on our private road over them.

The road stretched for 70 miles from Camp to Hilo over the "lava fields", and by the time we reached our destination we were covered with lava dust, - what a mess, - what a ride!

Our outfit was transferred to the old P.O.W. stockade just outside of Hilo. (Prisoner of War), to do guard duty and work parties.

Norman J. McEntee

Shields, Strinden, Harrell

At a lake near Camp Tarawa.

Turner, Harrell, Strinden

Shields, Harrell, Turner

Before we left the area we made some practice landings on some of the Hawaiian Islands like Maui,- the one we landed on. We were practising for our next assault,- Saipan, in the Marianas Islands. On the 15th of June, 1944, we arrived off the coast of "Saipan". We went through our regular routine of getting ready to go in once again. I said my prayers, as I presumed everyone did in their own way. While waiting to go over the side my thoughts drifted to home and would I ever see it again! I also said to myself, "this is my third assault, - would I make it, - how much more can a body take", and then it was time to go. There was no time to think about anything else. We made the landing, - again under heavy enemy fire, and about the third day I would take a piece of shrapnel in the elbow area of both arms. I was patched up by a "Corpman", and in a couple of days I would be sent back to duty. The battle for Saipan was being well on its way to be secured.

We were prepairing for our next assault, - the Island of Tinian, - right next door. On July 25th, 1944 we moved out from the beaches of Saipan and headed for, "Tinian", in L.S.T.'s loaded with Amtracks and Marines. This assault would be a text-book maneuver, - one that would baffle the Japs completely. A fake assault woud be made on Tinian Town, - located on the Southwest end of the Island. In the meantime we were landing on two beaches on the Northwest end of the Island, - the fake worked perfectly. We left our L.S.T. and waded in through the surf to the beach unharmed. We worked our way through a very rocky area filled with a lot of dead Japs who were killed by, "naphlam", (liquid fire), dropped by our planes. It was a ghastly sight of bodies burned to a crisp. The stench was so bad your nose would burn and your eyes water. It was so bad that you had a hard time breathing, but we had to keep going. Once we emerged from this area the land became pretty flat. The 2nd Division would go up the East side of the island and the 4th Division would go up the West side, to the conclusion of the battle for "Tinian."

This concludes my part of the assaults on four different islands, World War Two!!

P.S. - These islands, Saipan and Tinian, would be used by the U.S. Air Force to bomb Japan and drop the "Atomic Bomb", from, "B-29's", - "To End The War"

B-29 Enola Gay
Replicating the Enola Gay, the famed B-29 Superfortress that dropped the atomic bomb on Hiroshima,

Thanks!

Atomic Warfare is Here ▶
A lone B-29 Superfortress drops a single bomb and changes the world forever.

WWII

LIMITED EDITION

Enola Gay Commander Colonel Paul W. Tibbets, Navigator Captain Theodore J. VanKirk and Bombardier Major Thomas W. Ferebee.

VJ Day Newspaper
This reproduction of Washington D.C.'s *The Evening Star* from August 14, 1945, presents the heavily-anticipated news of Japan's surrender. You'll see a retrospective of the Pacific war, a photograph of Henry Fonda receiving his Bronze Star... even political cartoons and sports news.

EXTRA The Evening Star 5 Cents

WHITE HOUSE ANNOUNCES THE WAR IS OVER

MacArthur to Receive Surrender of Japanese

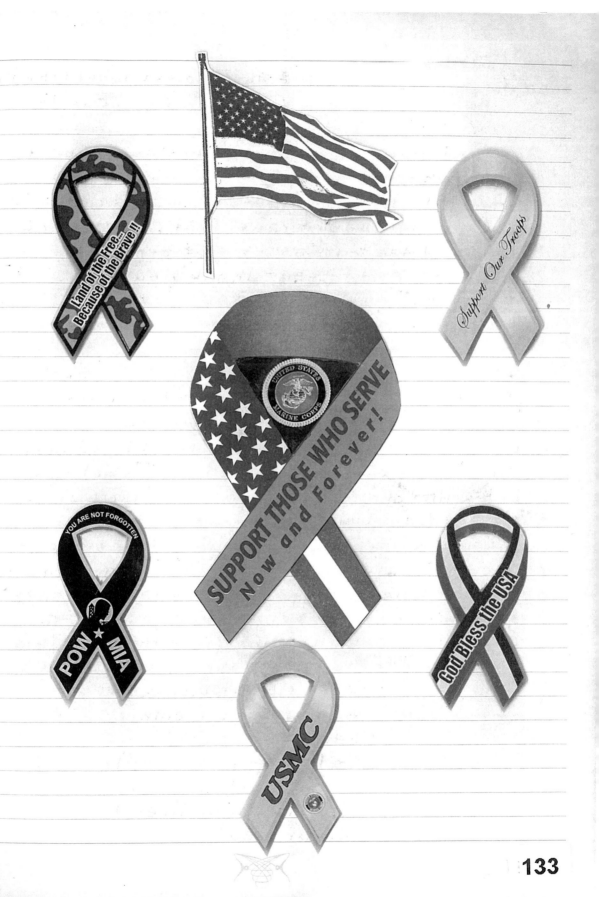

"Prayers"

Father Denis Edward O'Brien
U.S. Marine Corps Chaplain,

Father O'Brien said it best, "our basic freedoms, - freedoms that so many Americas tragically take for granted, - were fought for and won by the Veterans. That's why every day is a good day to remember the dept we owe our Veterans, - and to say, Thank you."

As D-Day neared brief church services were held daily on the hatches. On one transport the priest, a husky barrel-chested, red-haired man, stood on the deck just above the men gathered below him on a hatch. The men, for the most part, stripped to the waist, their dog tags and reigious medals glinted in the hot sunlight as they kneeled on the canvas tarp. The sermon was in man's language. The Padre began, "It takes guts for a man to meet his obligations to God." While he was reading from the Bible his voice would be drowned from time to time by a voice coming over the ship's loudspeaker with important messages. In the evenings the troops would line up in the passageways for a few minutes with the Padre, - in any available ship's office.

Yes, - "God" was in our lives then and as, "He" is now in our lives!

Mass aboard one of our troopships and yes we prayed for, "God's" protection,— I know I did!!

Lee Powell

1908 - 1944

Lee Berrien Powell was born on May 15, 1908 in Long Beach, California. Powell was a pretty good action hero, and had demonstrated same as the star of two classic Republic serials of 1938, THE LONE RANGER and THE FIGHTING DEVIL DOGS. There's a bit of eerieness about Powell's starring role as a Marine in THE FIGHTING DEVIL DOGS, as he would be wearing a real Marine Corps uniform during World War II and fighting his way through various Pacific island junglesHe enlisted in the Marines on August 17, 1942 in Los Angeles, and reported to the Marine base at San Diego, California as a recruit. Powell saw action at Tarawa (in 1943) and Saipan (in 1944). On July 30, 1944, Sgt. Lee Powell, serial number 442926, 18th Regiment, 2nd Marine Division, died on Tinian (Marianas Islands). World War II era reports indicated he was killed in action, and that information has been carried forward to current times.

Television/movie actor and retired Marine Corps Officer Brent Davis has done some investigation into Powell's death on Tinian, and info follows:

1. Brent referred me to a recent book about Hollywood personalities in the Marine Corps. That book is *STARS IN THE CORPS - Movie Actors in the United States Marines* by James E. Wise, Jr., and Anne Collier Rehill (ISBN 1557509492, Naval Institute Press, 1999).

"Sgt. Lee Powell lived through some of the bloodiest battles of the Pacific War. But then, on the same day that the Tinian battle ended, he died of acute poisoning. Newspapers at the time assumed he had been killed in action, but Sergeant Powell's USMC files report not only the alcohol poisoning, but some sort of "misconduct", the nature of which was "undetermined". Hypothetically, it must have had something to do with cutting loose a bit too much after having survived the hellish battles in which he was involved, perhaps by celebrating with vast quantites of methyl alcohol. Even

small amounts of this highly toxic substance can kill; it can only be hoped that the courageous and successful warrior at least got to have one last good party with his buddies.

But the United States's erstwhile masked man carried the mystery to his grave. He was buried in the Marine Cemetery on Tinian and later, at the request of his father, moved to the National Cemetery of the Pacific in Honolulu.

Sergeant Powell, age thirty-five when he died, was posthumously awarded the Purple Heart, the Asiatic-Pacific Area Campaign Medal with two stars, and the Victory Medal World War II. The latter two awards were sent to his widow in September, 1948."

2. About a dozen years prior to the publication of the above mentioned book, Brent was thinking about authoring a screenplay called "The Death of the Lone Ranger", and conducted his own research into the death of Lee Powell. In 1988-89, he was able to contact a dozen or so Marines who knew or served with Powell. Some were on Tinian. Some had recollections about Powell's death. Others simply reported what they heard via the grapevine. Their comments and recollections coincide with the info in the Wise book — Lee Powell (and one or more other Marines) found or concocted some kind of beverage to celebrate the Tinian victory. Powell was taken ill and passed away (and one of the Marines celebrating with him had to be hospitalized and was temporarily blinded for several weeks).

The former Marines had some additional remembrances of Powell. Some were in their late teens and Powell was in his mid thirties and one referred to him as a "father figure". Others noted "... would remember Lee with affection" and "... we all liked him" and "I remember Lee fondly" and "he had a singing voice that was beautiful" and "Lee was really a great guy, a good story teller, and such a generous person ..." and Powell was "a good Marine". Several recalled that they found out about Powell portraying the Lone Ranger and and got in some good-natured ribbing with taunts of "Hi Yo Silver!". Another mentioned that "Lee never did try to impress any of us, if anything, he played down his notoriety."

For those who may not be familiar with WWII history, Tinian was a key island in the Pacific and an airbase would be constructed there. On August 6, 1945, a B-29 Superfortress bomber named the Enola Gay would take off from Tinian on its atomic bomb run to the Japanese mainland and a city named Hiroshima.

Today, few people recall Lee Powell and his brief Hollywood career. But for those who do, he will always be remembered as the first cinema Lone Ranger.

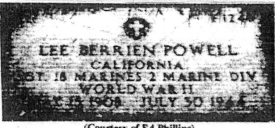

(Courtesy of Ed Phillips)

Above - the grave marker for Lee Powell at the National Memorial Cemetery of the Pacific, Honolulu, Hawaii (AKA The Punchbowl), Section F, Gravesite Number 1246.

"I have a tender reliance on the mercy of the Almighty; through the merits of the Lord Jesus Christ. I am a sinner. I look to Him for mercy; pray for me."

Alexander Hamilton's
last dying words,
July 12, 1804

JUST A COMMON SOLDIER
(A Soldier Died Today)
by A. Lawrence Vaincourt © 1985
http://www.vaincourt.homestead.com/

He was getting old and paunchy and his hair was falling fast,
And he sat around the Legion, telling stories of the past.
Of a war that he had fought in and the deeds that he had done,
In his exploits with his buddies; they were heroes, every one.

And tho' sometimes, to his neighbors, his tales became a joke,
All his Legion buddies listened, for they knew whereof he spoke.
But we'll hear his tales no longer for old Bill has passed away,
And the world's a little poorer, for a soldier died today.

He will not be mourned by many, just his children and his wife,
For he lived an ordinary and quite uneventful life.
Held a job and raised a family, quietly going his own way,
And the world won't note his passing, though a soldier died today.

When politicians leave this earth, their bodies lie in state,
While thousands note their passing and proclaim that they were great.
Papers tell their whole life stories, from the time that they were young,
But the passing of a soldier goes unnoticed and unsung.

Is the greatest contribution to the welfare of our land
A guy who breaks his promises and cons his fellow man?
Or the ordinary fellow who, in times of war and strife,
Goes off to serve his Country and offers up his life?

138

A politician's stipend and the style in which he lives
Are sometimes disproportionate to the service that he gives.
While the ordinary soldier, who offered up his all,
Is paid off with a medal and perhaps, a pension small.

It's so easy to forget them for it was so long ago,
That the old Bills of our Country went to battle, but we know
It was not the politicians, with their compromise and ploys,
Who won for us the freedom that our Country now enjoys.

Should you find yourself in danger, with your enemies at hand,
Would you want a politician with his ever-shifting stand?
Or would you prefer a soldier, who has sworn to defend
His home, his kin and Country and would fight until the end?

He was just a common soldier and his ranks are growing thin,
But his presence should remind us we may need his like again.
For when countries are in conflict, then we find the soldier's part
Is to clean up all the troubles that the politicians start.

If we cannot do him honor while he's here to hear the praise,
Then at least let's give him homage at the ending of his days.
Perhaps just a simple headline in a paper that would say,
Our Country is in mourning, for a soldier died today.

——————— ✧ ———————

The truth has been spoken here !!

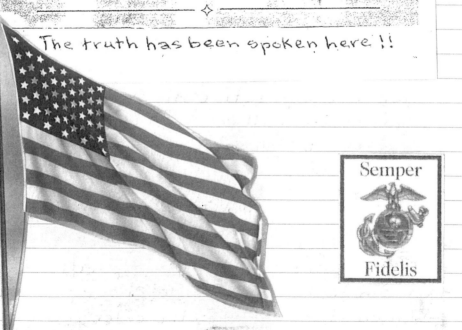

Semper

Fidelis

"DECK, Courtmartial"

This happened before I left the States in 1942 while we were on ship to shore maneuvers off San Diego.

My group of recruits had just finished our, "Boot Camp", training at the Marine Corps Recruit Depot, San Diego, California when we were told about a new outfit that was being organized called the, "Pioneers", and were looking for volunteers. One usually does not volunteer for anything in the Corps,—but in this case a bunch of us did. At this time we were not told what our job would be but we would be told in the near future. What was more important was the training we needed for combat and the ship to shore operations. We boarded our ships,— which were to become known as the, "Unholy Four",—they were the U.S.S. President Hayes, Adams, Jackson and the Crecent City. The four ships would go out to sea and day after day we would practice disembarkation from the ships with full packs and all other need- ed equipment. Every day we would hear over the ships intercom,—"Marines, proceed to your disembarkation stations", and then there would be a big rush to get our packs on, grab our rifles, helmets and what-ever else we needed. We would dash through the gangways, up the ladders to the main deck and assemble at our previously assigned stations. When the order was given to to, "disembark",—over the side we would go, down the Cargo nets we'd go into a, "Higgins Boat". This procedure, at times, could be very scary and dangerous. If you let go of the Cargo Net to soon you could drop 15 to 20 feet into the Higgins Boat and hurt yourself pretty badly or you might miss the boat completly and your chances of surviving would be zero. These tragedies did happen!

After training for weeks and being aboard ship without any liberty we were getting pretty restless. One day we found out that some of the Sailors and Marines were being given, "shore leave", for the weekend. The question was, - how could we get in on this? I and about a half dozen of my, "buddies", decided we were going to go in with those who had permission to leave the ship. We got all dressed up in our, "Forest Green", uniforms and proceeded to the, "gangway", and fell in with the others who were leaving the, - "U.S.S. President Hayes. So far so good, - no questions asked! We boarded the "Liberty Launch", and headed for San Diego, - we were free for the weekend.

I wanted to go up to Laguna Beach, - at that time a very small town, on the California coast, - to see a very nice young lady whom I had met in San Diego on a recent liberty. She was the only person, at that time, that I knew in the short time I was there. I don't remember much about her except that she was a wonderful lady and I was a 19 year old kid and lonely. I hitch-hiked up to Laguna Beach and lucky for me she was home. We spent the day together and at one

141

time we were sitting on a bench just talking about each other and taking in the awsome beauty of the surrounding area including the beautiful blue of the Pacific Ocean. It was a wonderful day that I will never forget and for a 19 year old kid who was away from home for the first time and had no experience with women,- this wonderful young lady,- I don't even remember her name,- made me feel real good about myself and the future. Now it was time to leave and get back to my ship. We said our "good-bys", and I, "thanked" her for being with me that week end. I hitch-hiked back to Diego and the pick-up dock to wait for the "Liberty Launch", to come in. Everyone was there, including my "buddies", and some sailors. We didn't have to wait to long when the launch arrived and loaded up to capacity including all of the Marines. I was told to wait for the next launch, and that was O.K. with me,- I thought I had plenty of time to get to my ship. I waved to my "buddies" as they pulled away and said, "I'll see you aboard ship." Well, I finale made it back to the ship,- and what I didn't know was that at the morning roll-call, that I missed,- I was put on report as absent,- unaccounted for! That Sunday night,- late in the month of June, I went to bed and had a good nights sleep. The next morning when I and the others went top-side,- there was no land to be seen anywhere. During the night our ships up-anchored and where on the way to our first engagement with the troops of the Japanese Empire. At the time we didn't know where we were going, - but when we were told, - we never heard of the place, - "Guadalcanal", in the Solomon Islands. Shortly we would get to know the, "Canal", and the surrounding islands very, very well!

That same morning I was invited, (commanded), to be present at the Officer's Command Center to explain why I was missing at the Company roll-call the day before, - I thought I had better tell them the truth that I, "jumped ship", to visit a lady friend of mine. I did that, but I did not tell them about the others and they didn't ask me. After I told what I did and why I answered their questions the best I could and admitted, - "I made a mistake"! I was told to sit down, - I made an about face, (pretty snappy), and sat down to await their verdict. The Officers hearing the, "Courtmartial", left the room to an ajoining one to decide what they were going to do with me. If you think I wasn't scared as to what my punishment was going to be, - I was, - very much! All kind of thoughts were going through my mind, - this is wartime and I could receive the most severe penalty for my, "jumping ship", - would it be prison! While I was sitting there, - it seemed like an eternity that they had been gone, - and the longer they were gone the more I thought my punishment would be. When they returned, the Officer in charge called everyone to, "Attention", - I snapped to, "Attention", and held it until I was given the command, "At Ease", which I executed. He then ordered me to come forward, - I did, and he proceeded

to read me the, "riot act," and I was thinking, —
they are going to throw the, "book," at me! When
he finished, "dressing me down," he asked me if
I understood that what I did was a very serious
action in the time of, "WAR". I said, — "I do, Sir! He
then asked me if I had anything to say and I
said, "no Sir". There was nothing I could say, — I
made a mistake and I was going to pay for it. He
then rapped the gavel on the table and again
called everyone to, "Attention", which I again
executed. He then proceeded to read the official court records, — "You, Private Charles Wysocki, Jr, have been found guilty of leaving the
U.S.S. President Hayes without permission, —
but in your favor you did return to the ship
and your unit. The panel of Officers have
sentenced you to a, "Deck Court Martial",
and you will be confined to the ship with
no special previliges for a period of 30
days. I was told to report to the Comman-
ding Officer of our outfit, — "The Pioneers",
for further instructions. I was dismissed
and with a sigh of relief I made an, "About
Face", and left the room. As I left I thought
to myself, "You are one lucky Marine", — it
could have been a lot worse!

    A, "Deck Court Martial", is not a perman-
ent blemish on ones, "Military Record", — it would be
removed from my records after I had completed the requirements of my sentence. I would
also have to meet the specific standars of the,
United States Marine Corps, — which I did. I

did meet with our Company, Captain _ _ _ _ _, who wasn't to happy with me. As a punishment for my, "stupidity" I was given all the, "crappiest", jobs that could be found on a troop ship. For the next 30 days I would do what I had to do to get the, "Deck", removed from my records. It would take over 30 days to go from San Diego to the, "Canal", and I had no plans to do anything or go anywhere!!

I had learned, - the hard way, - the rules and regulations while in the Military are to be obeyed, - if not, your in trouble! My experience in the, "Corps", has carried over to my civilian life, - "Obey the rules and the laws of the, U.S.A. and you'll stay out of trouble, - you'll have a good life!

I am proud to have served my Country in the, "United States Marine Corps", - with my, "Buddies", in, "D-2-18", - from Feb, 5th, 1942 to July 17th, 1945, - World War Two!

U.S. Marine Corps . . . The Marines of World War II never faltered in their relentless drive to clear the Pacific of Imperial Japanese invasion forces. Island after island, wave after wave, the Marines exhibited great valor and selfless service. They smashed Japanese stronghold after Japanese stronghold, - returning home victorious in 1945.

"Military Issue"

THE FINAL INSPECTION

The Gunny stood and faced God
    Which must always come to pass.
He hoped his shoes were shining,
    Just as brightly as his brass.

"Step forward now, Marine,
    How shall I deal with you?
Have you always turned the other cheek?
    To my Church have you been true?"

The Marine squared his shoulders and said,
    "No, Lord, I guess I ain't.
Because those of us who carry guns,
    Can't always be a saint.

I had to work most Sundays,
    And at times my talk was tough.
And sometimes I've been violent,
    Because the world is awfully rough.

But I never took a penny,
    That wasn't mine to keep.
Though I worked a lot of overtime.
    When the bills got just too steep.

And I never passed a cry for help,
    Though at times I shook with fear.
And sometimes, God, forgive me,
    I've wept unmanly tears.

I know I don't deserve a place,
    Among the people here.
They never wanted me around.
    Except to calm their fears.

If you've a place for me here, Lord,
    It needn't be so grand.
I never expected or had too much,
    But if you don't, I'll understand."

There was a silence all around the throne,
    Where the Saints had often trod.
As the Marine waited quietly,
    For the judgment of his God.

"Step forward now, my Son,
    You've borne your burdens well.
Walk peacefully on Heaven's streets.
    You've done your time in Hell."

Author unknown:
Presented by Padre Womak, a former proud
Navy Corpsman and brother Marine.

Dedicated to the Great Task

We honor our fallen best with unwavering devotion to democracy

THE ACCOUNTS APPEARED the same day in a Midwestern newspaper reporting on the return home of the remains of two young American soldiers, ages 21 and 24. The 24-year-old Marine sergeant died just a week earlier from injuries sustained while defusing a bomb in Iraq. Some 3,000 mourners lined the route of a procession bearing his flag-draped coffin to a service attended by hundreds of friends and loved ones. The day before at a nearby airport, the remains of the 21-year-old Army private arrived from the U.S. Army's Joint POW/MIA Accounting Command at Hickam Air Force Base in Hawaii. This young man was reported missing in action November 28, 1950, at the Battle of Chosin Reservoir deep in North Korea. He likely died the day after Chinese troops poured across the border to drive the American and United Nations forces back south. No one knew this young man's fate until Army scientists and anthropologists recovered his remains and those of three others on the eastern shore of Chosin. Fifty-six years later, the soldier's younger brother—the last living member of his immediate family—welcomed him home.

These two young men who were returned to their hometown on the same day may have left that place more than a half-century apart, fought and died in different wars under vastly divergent circumstances, but they are forever united in their unspent youth and their families' grief. They are united as well by the rituals, respects and tributes our nation bestows upon those who give their last full measure of devotion to their country. In reality, though, words are inadequate gestures that can only begin to honor those who answer the call to do our democracy's bidding on the battlefield. The true measure of our gratitude is our devotion to the ideals for which they died.

In our nation's most celebrated dedication ritual at Gettysburg on November 19, 1863, the keynote speaker was leading intellect and orator of the day Edward Everett. He described how the ancient Greeks typically honored their lost warriors with rituals written into law. At Marathon, where Greece's existence was in the balance, an even greater tribute went to the fallen as they were entombed on the battlefield itself, forever hallowing that ground. As Everett said of the dead at Gettysburg, so should we say of the two who died in Korea and Iraq and the legions of young who have perished in our service: "No lapse of time, no distance of space shall cause you to be forgotten."

The second speaker that day at Gettysburg, Abraham Lincoln had a mission not simply to honor the dead and dedicate a graveyard but to somehow convince citizens that the awful bloodletting that had occurred there was not only essential, but needed to go on. As our cover story reminds us, in some 200 meticulously crafted—and long remembered—words, Lincoln somehow did that and, at the same time, redefined the meaning and ideals of America for generations to come.

"My Life" continued

"My Life" continues in the summer of 1940, on a Sunday afternoon at my house. Two of my friends were visiting with me and we were in the living room, on the floor, looking at maps of the U.S.A., talking about where we'd like to go on a trip. My Dad, who was sitting behind us, in his favorite chair reading the Sunday paper and listening to us, with one ear, when he looked around the edge of the paper and said to us, "If you want to travel,—join the Navy"!! We looked at each other, as if to say, "why not," The next day we went to the Navy Recruiting Office in the Federal Bldg, Milwaukee, Wisc.,— to enlist. My friends passed their physicals,—I didn't,—the Navy Doctor found that I had a, "Hernia," and it would have to be fixed before I could enlist. I said, "good-bye to my friends and wished them the best. They left for the Great Lakes Naval Training Station and that was the last I heard of them or what happened to them! I went home,— told my Mother about the Hernia, arrainged to have the operation, had the operation, recuperated and on Feb, 5th, 1942, I again went to enlist in the Navy. When I arrived, that morning, Feb. 5th, 1942, at the Federal Building, where all the Military Recruiting Offices were located, there were lines a mile long for all the branches,— except the Marine Corps. I didn't want to stand in line,—so, I went to the Marine Recruiting Office and enlisted,— no problems and left that evening,— 6 P.M., for the Marine Corps Recruit Depot, San Diego, California. The war with Japan had been going on since Dec. 7th, 1941, - so, I knew I was going to be involved, - what, when and where would not be to far off!! I would become a member of the 2nd Pioneer Battalion and participate in the Solomon Islands Campaign, the Gilbert Islands Campaign and the Marianas Islands Campaign, - where I was wounded. In the days, months and years that were to come, a 19 year old kid, like myself, would, with thousands more, would experience all the horrors of war. We would be witness to the most unbelievable destruction at the hands of our Navy and Air Force, - against the Japanese held islands. Today I don't think I could bare the sight of the bodies torn apart by bombs, shells, bullets, mortars, flame throwers, napalm and much more! On top of that there was the unbearable noise and stench of decaying bodies, - so bad you could hardly breath! Only those who were involved in combat know what the catastrophe of war is and they cannot describe it, - no one can!!

When we left the, "Canal", we went to a place we would fall in love with, - beautiful, New Zealand. I was now 20 years old and I would have my first involment with a female, - it was a great experience!! I'll always remember the wonderful people of New Zealand and the good times we had there. The people of New Zealand were having there own problems with the possibility of a Jap invasion but that wouldn't happen since we stopped them at the, "Canal", - they were very grateful to use. Most of their young men were in the New Zealand Military and deployed somewhere helping to fight the enemy wherever they might be. Their families, children, wives and sweethearts, were doing whatever they could for the war effort. Even with the rationing they invited us into their homes and fed us,- they did what they could to make us feel at home,- the young ladies did to !! Memories,- yes, I'll have memories for the rest of my life.

It was hard to leave New Zealand, but we knew it was time to move on,- we still had a job to do. Our next assault would be a place called, "Tarawa", in the Gilbert Islands. It would be the, "Bloodiest", battle in Marine Corps History and it would last for, "76 Bloody Hours". Then we would go to, "Hilo, Hawaii", where we would rest, train and prepare for our next assaults. First it would be Saipan and then Tinian in the Marianas Islands. I would be wounded during the Saipan Campaign,- by a piece of shrapnel in both arms,- which would heal nicely.

After these battles a bunch of us would be informed that we, going back to the, "States". "WOW",- what a surprise !! I felt like the weight of the world was lifted off my shoulders and I'm sure the others felt the same. While we were waiting for the order to, "move out", we were saying, "so long", to our, "buddies", we were leaving behind,- they had one more battle coming up,- "Okinawa". We wished them the best and, "God Willing", they would be home soon. The order came to,- "move out", and

150

we proceeded to the dock area where landing boats were waiting to take us out to a troop transport. While waiting our turn I spotted a bunch of "seabags", (canvas bags in which we put our belongings),- and one had my name on it,- so I knew they were our out- fits, "seabags". I asked the Officer in charge if we could pick-up our bags as long as we were there,- his answer was a very stern, "NO",- "they'll be shipped to your next station." The year was 1944, August, when we left Saipan,- with no, "seabags",- and now it's the summer of 1946,- I was home in Milwaukee, Wisc., when a Railway Express Co. truck dropped off a package for me,--- it was my, "seabag",--- it was empty,- except for a couple of, "field scarfs", (ties), and a web best,- that wasn't even mine,- had some- one else's name on it. To bad we couldn't have picked-up our, "seabags", when we had a chance to when we were leaving Saipan,- at least we could have had some clean clothing. I was really ticked off at the Corps for not properly taking care of the contents that were in my, "seabag", and then have the guts to send me an empty one! So, we had to wear what we had on and what we had in our packs. Every time we took a shower we would take it with our clothes on,- and wear them till they dried.

  The ship that was going to take us back to the States was a big Army Transport,- never saw a transport as big as this one. I counted six decks down,- all for troops to bunk,- so, I know there were more decks,- it was a big one!

When we went aboard the ship, up the gangway, no cargo net this time, we looked like a
bunch of, "ragtail" Marines. We were still wearing
our combat clothing, carrying our gear and all
the souvenirs we could carry. I had a Jap Rifle,
and other items in my pack.

I don't remember the trip to the States, - I
guess I was catching up on my sleep and rest, -
but I do remember the day we passed under
the, "Golden Gate Bridge", - there was so much
noise, - cheering, hollering, screaming and waving of arms, - in happiness, and joy!

After fighting the Japs for almost three
years, - at times under unbearable conditions,
physical and mental, - not knowing what the next
moment would bring. Many of us would suffer
for many years, some for the rest of their
lives from, "Combat Fatigue", and their wounds.

Our ship docked at, "Treasure Island",
California, and while we were waiting for our
transportation to take us to the Marine Base
in San Diego a man approached us and introduced
himself, ---- it was Tony bazzerie's father! We
talked for a bit, - he welcomed us home, - and then
asked about his son, Tony, and how did he die!
This was a very difficult and soul searching
time, - but he had the right to know. A couple of
us took him off to the side a bit and told him that
Tony died charging up the beach through some
barbed-wire and all the time cussing the Japs
until he was cut down by a Jap machine gun.
The last I saw of him, he was draped over the, -

"barbed-wire", on the beach of, "Tarawa"!! I could
see tears in his eyes and I felt bad that I and the
others had to tell him about, "Tony", his son! It was
time to go,- Mr. Lazzerie, "thanked us", and we
said our, "good-bys",- boarded our trucks and as we
left the area we could see him waving to us.

When we arrived in San Diego, the Marine
Base, we were fed and believe it or not we were to
be billited in the same eight man tents we were
in prior to leaving the States for combat duty.
After a good nights rest we were issued a complete new, "Forest Green", uniforms, cap, shirts,
shoes, belt, and underwear,- we felt like new,
"boots". We stayed at the, "Base", for about two
weeks,- with no, "liberty",- but we pretty much
could do what we wanted to do. One day, thinking
that every thing was the same as it was when
I was there in 1942,- I was going to go to the, "PX",
and the, "slop-chute", the way I always did before.
As I proceeded down the walk, behind the barracks,-
I was stopped by the M.P.'s and taken to the O.D.'s
office,- and asked what I was doing in that
area. I was kinda confused,- why shouldn't I
be there,- I always went this way before,- then
they told me,- I was in a restricted area. Restric-
for what I asked! To the, "Female Marines"; I
was told,- which I didn't even know there were!
The, "O.D.", (Officer on Duty), let me go with a warning,- "stay out of this restricted area and tell your,
"buddies", the same." "Yes Sir", I said, saluted, and
did a snappy, about face and left. I did tell
my, "buddies", and we had a special name for them -

"B.A.M.'s", which means,-"Broad Assed Marines",-cute!
The second incident, which I told earlier in the book was about my meeting a couple of guys who were on Tulagi,- but were sent back to the States for health reasons. We did some celebrating with a few drinks and my, "buddies", who were waiting to move out came to my rescue and got me on the train for Camp Lejune, N.C.. Also our Washington, D.C. escapade is told earlier in the book. We finally arrived at Camp Lejune,- and guess where they stuck us, - - - - in the, "boon-docks", in eight man tents! In my tour of duty, in the, "Corps", I was never billeted in a barracks! My bed was in a tent, a bunk on a ship or good o'l mother earth. The only time I was in anything but a tent was when I was in a hospital.
After arriving at Camp Lejune we were issued our ribbons, stripes and the Second Div. patch. One day, when a few of us were on our way to the base tailor, a group of, "B.A.M.'s", stopped us, - one was a big o'l Sergeant, and she wanted to know what we were doing,- it really was no, "damn", business of her and her friends. We didn't say a word, we just reached into our pockets, pulled out our ribbons, stripes and the Second Marine Div. patch,- we flashed them in their faces, - - - - they made an, "about face", and high-tailed it as fast as they could out of the area. We were never bothered again. I was a little upset at this female Sergeant,- I spent almost 3 years overseas and made 4 D-Day assaults

and I got to be a P.F.C., (Private First Class), - how the hell did she become a sergeant!! I guess that's the way it had to be!

Another time, when we finally got a, "liberty", pass for the weekend to go to Jacksonville which was new to us, - none of us had ever been there. There were a half dozen of us who were going to go in together. We got all dolled up, - made sure our ribbons were all on properly and we headed for the main gate. The O.D. on duty that day was a well known movie star by the name of, - - Tyrone Power, - he stopped us, checked us out and said our shoes were dirty, - what did he expect when we had to walk up from the, "boon-docks, - he wanted a, "spit-polish", pair of shoes on each one of us, - before we could leave the Base. We said, "Yes sir", saluted the Lieutenant, moved out and stepped behind the, "guard house", rubbed our shoes on the back of our pants until they were nice and shiney. We waited a bit and then went back to the gate and Lt. Power passed us with flying colors!

When we got to Jacksonville we tried to get a hotel room, but they were all taken. The, "B.A.M.s, Navy, "WAVE,'s and the local girls got there first. The only way to get a place to stay for the weekend was to be invited to share a room by one of the ladies. I got a beautiful, redheaded, "WAVE", - - what a weekend I had. This would happen every weekend, - the gals would grab a towel, soap and a toothbrush and get to the hotels before the guys did. Glad I didn't get

155

"liberty", every weekend!!

I was at the Base for only a couple of weeks when I was taken to the Base Hospital, - for observation! From there I was sent to the Navy Hospital, Philadelphia, PA, where I would be treated for the next 4½ months for "Combat Fatigue", - a nervous stomach, real bad headaches, jungle rot, and psychiatry sessions. I was told my problems started when I was on Saipan. I would do crazy things, - like head for the front lines without my rifle, getting up and not knowing where I was, having horrible nightmares, hot and cold sweats and more. I didn't know I was doing some of these things until they told me I was!

After a couple of months of treatment I was improving and one day my Doctor came to tell me they had received a telegram from my Mother asking if I could come home for a few days because my brother, "Bob", was coming home. He was in the, 121st Field Artillery, 32nd "Red Arrow", Army Division and he served his time in the Pacific in the New Guinea and the Philippine Islands Campaigns. We hadn't seen each other in over 5 years she wrote, - permission was given and my Mother was notified. I didn't have any money so I was told to talk to the Red Cross who had an office on the ground floor of the Hospital. I was given permission to see them. When I got to talk to them I told them what I needed and why, - they agreed to give me enough money to get home and then I had to sign a paper stating that as soon as I got back I would have to give the money back. The cost of a ticket in those days wasn't very much, - maybe $20 or $30 dollars one way. I didn't like the agreement of having to pay it back, - but I did.

It was great to get home to see my brother again after all these years, - but even greater to see my "Mom", again. For the first time since we went away to war the whole family was together and we celebrated our good fortune. There was even a picture and story of us in the Milwaukee Newspaper. But as always the good times must and did come to an end.

I had to go back to the Navy Hospital, - a bit tired and worn out, but with grand memories of our reunion. After I returned to the Hospital my condition steadly improved and I began to help-out around the Hospital, - like taking the blind to their sessions and appointments. I'd line them up, - like a "Congo line", - have them put one hand on the shoulder of the person in front of them, - then we'd go dancing down the hallways to wherever they had to go and then take them back to their wards. Sometimes I'd visit the amputee's ward to talk to the guys and try to cheer them up. On my visits I got to know this one Marine amputee who was upset and angry because he couldn't accept losing his leg. He wouldn't let the medics fit him for an artificial leg, so I got to talking to him about it, - telling him how much more a new leg would help him. I think he was coming around to understand

TOGETHER AGAIN — Milwaukee's snow, even though soot-ridden looks great, Sgt. Robert Wysocki, 2363 N. 59th St., left, and his brother, Pfc. Charles Wysocki Jr., 4215 N. 21st St., agreed yesterday. They've just returned from overseas and haven't seen a snowflake or each other for more than three years. *Sentinel photo.*

PFC. CHARLES WYSOCKI, JR.
SGT. ROBERT WYSOCKI

September, 1944
First time together in over 4 yrs.

PFC. CHARLES - U.S.M.C.
Co. "D", 2nd Batt., 18th Marines
Second Marine Division

Tulagi, (Guadalcanal Campaign)
     Solomon Islands.
Tarawa, Gilbert Islands
Saipan, Marianas Islands (Wounded)
Tinian,   "

SGT. ROBERT - U.S. ARMY
Battery "C", 121st Field Artillery
32nd Army Division

New Guinea, & Phillipine Islands

ARMY

MARINE

what was best for him. I was pleased with his attitude,- but when I went to see him again he was standing,
with his crutches, and again complaining about his
artificial leg. I thought,- something has to be done with
this guy,- and I proceeded to kick his crutches out
from under him,- he hit the floor like a ton of bricks,-
and looking at me he said, "why did you do that!" I
replied, "do you want to sit on your butt for the rest
of your life or are you going to do something about it!"
The next time I saw him I was pleased,- he was walking around on his new leg,- I waved to him with a
thumbs up gesture and he returned it!

While still in the Navy Hospital I was picked
to go on a fund raising campaign for the, "Salvation
Army," in the state of Pennsylvania. My partner was
a fella named, "Spence", who was picked from the
Valley Forge Army Hospital. We were to talk to
different organizations about our association
with the Salvation Army and the contributions
made by them to the Military around the world
At the close of a successful campaign and at
the Victory banquet I got to meet the founder of
the Salvation Army,- a wonderful lady,- Mrs. Booth.
I also had the honor to be the first speaker of the
evening,- I made it very short. Also had the
privilege to make a radio appearance on the, "Salute
To America", program in Philly. I talked about my
experiences in the fight against the Japanese in the
Pacific.

In the later days of my Hospital stay I was
allowed to leave the Hospital,- but I had to have a
Hospital person with me. As chaperons I had a,-

Navy WAVE, a Navy Nurse and a Navy Corpsman take me out a few times. One time, the WAVE, took me to a Piano Bar where a Black Man was playing, and he was real good. After a couple of visits we got to know him pretty well and one night after his show he invited us to come to his apartment, - my escort said it was O.K.. When we got there, - what a great surprise we got, - the suite was full of entertainers from around Philly. What a great show we had into the wee morning hours. We also got to meet our friends young son who was a child prodigy, - around 7 or 8 years old, - and what a talent he was! He played the piano for us and you wouldn't believe how this young man at, that age, could make that keyboard sing. This night was a most entertaining one and one I'll always remember.

As part of my rehabilitation I was sent, from the Hospital, to a battery factory whose employees were mostly female. They would ask me for a date, - what a choice I had! This was a situation where you'd say to yourself, - "What a way to go."! I didn't last to long in that place!

I was selected, by the Hospital, to attend a ceremony at, "Independence Hall", - where the, "Liberty Bell", was on display. It was a very "Patriotic and Inspiring", program, - I got to touch the awsome, "Liberty Bell", that rung on July 4th, 1776 to proclaim the, "Independence", of the U.S.. It was a wonderful day for me and for all who could attend, - even though it was raining that day!

One day, I'm not sure of the date, but I think

it was in late June, that I should report to the Hospital Auditorium, "on the double", and when I got there I saw a bunch of Marines and Sailors lineing up in front of the stage, what for I didn't know. A Navy person took me to the line-up and put me in it. Shortly we were called to, "attention", as a group of Officers came in. One of the Officers read the, "Order Of The Day", which stated that those assembled here were to receive the, "Purple Heart", medal for wounds received in, "Combat", – or words to that effect. Now I knew why I was there and a feeling of, "Pride", when the, "Purple Heart", was pinned on me. We were, "congradulated", and, "thanked", for our service for, "God and Country". Again we were called to, "attention", we, "saluted", and then, "dismissed". What a wonderful day for this, "Marine"!!

Shortly after the Medal Ceremony my Doctor came to see me, – to tell me I was going home, – I told him I wanted to stay in the, "Corps", to make a career of it, – his answer was, "Great, – but your career just ended, – your going home!!! I was sent to the Phil. Navy Yard to await my, "Honorable Discharge", which came on July 17th, 1945. Yes, my military career was over, – six months short of four years, – but I will always be a, – "Marine"!! Once a, "Marine", always a, "Marine"!!

When I got home, July of 1945, I didn't do much but take it easy for awhile, and go shopping for a new wardrobe, – because the clothing I left behind, when I enlisted, were all gone, – plus other of my belongings. I asked the family, "what happened to all my stuff, – but nobody knew –

anything, - although I did notice my Dad wearing some of my clothes. What a home-coming, - I felt like they didn't expect me to come back!!

On V.J. Day I was shopping, in downtown Milwaukee, still in my Marine blues, when the announcement came that the Japanese had, - "SURRENDERED"!! The place went crazy, - people poured out onto the streets, - horns, whistles, bells, sirens, people hollering, screaming and crying all at the same time. I was attacked by a group of young ladies and a couple of sailors, - hugging, kissing, shaking my hand and litterly jumping on me. Then they took me over to one of those public photo machines, located in the lobby of Plankington Arcade Bldg, and took a bunch of pictures, - for souvenirs. What a wild day I had, - but, "Thank God", - the war was over!! After awhile it all settled down a bit and I was able to get a streetcar to get home. My uniform was still in one piece, - I still had all my ribbons and my hat, - which several times someone tried to grab for a souvenir. But I survived the, "Battle of V.J. Day".

Now it was time to go to work, - so I went back to Blatz Brewing Co. to get my pre-enlistment job back, I worked on a Carton Machine and that's the job I wanted, - but the employment office had other plans for me, - a job in the, "box shop", where cases of returned bottles were dumped and cleaned for future use. It was a dirty, filthy and dangerous job, - many who worked in that dirty hole ended up with cut

This was the "Home" I left in Feb. 1942 to join the "Marines" and the one I returned to on April 1945.

This is me just before I joined the "Corps" and I'm wearing the sweater that I didn't want to part with, - I never saw it again

163

fingers, hands and arms from the flying broken glass. When the men left for Military Service. women took their places and when we came back they didn't want to give those jobs up. I wasn't going to argue with them, - I told them to, - "take your job and shove it", and I left with no job! I should have reported them to the Government for not giving me my job back as the, "Law", said they were supposed to do, - but I was tired of fighting! I had a couple of jobs after that but couldn't hold them, - I was having problems coping with the, "civilian way of life. The last job I had was a, "Window Clerk", for the U.S. Postal Service and again I was having problems, - sleeping, drinking, nightmares, sweats and people. All this time I was going to the V.A. Hospital at Wood, Wisc., - just west of Milwaukee, - for help and treatment. It was around 1964 that I had to take many medical tests, as did my wife and children. One day the Doctors called me and my family in for a conference, we were told that I, - while overseas, had picked up a rare blood disease, - one of 7 others around the world, - I couldn't pronounce the name. The Doctors said they didn't know to much about this disease but that they would do whatever they could to help me. They also said that my time on earth would be about a year or two, - I fooled them, - I'm still here, in the year 2007!! Age 84! Shortly after this diognosis I was declared a 100% service connected disabled Veteran. and the U.S. Postal also retired me, - age 39!

Going back to 1946, when I was working at the, "Square "D" Company," Milwaukee, a fellow worker and friend decided to get married and he had to deliver the bridesmaids dresses but didn't have a car,- could I help him out. I talked to my Dad and told him the situation,- could I borrow the car to help my friend, Art,- he said O.K., I called Art and told him we had a car and a couple of days later we were delivering the dresses,- all but one! When we got to the last home, Art said I should come with him which I did. I was standing at the bottom of the stairway, that went up to the second floor, when the lady of the house called out, "Art is here",- a couple of seconds went by and at the top of the stairs appeared a beautiful young lady who was to become my wife! Art said to me,- "this is your date for to-night", and then he introduced us,- her name was,- "Bernice", and she was dressed very beautiful,- as she always would be. In comparison I was still in my work clothes,- but we went out any-way,- and I was in love!! We were married on, Feb. 15th, 1947, at St. Hyacinth's Catholic Church.

During the courtship of my future wife there was a terrific snowstorm that paralyzed the City of Milwaukee and surrounding area. The city was at a standstill,- nothing was moving! A group of us set-up an, "Aid Station," in a local tavern called, "The Stables", and all the neighbors pitched in to help make firelanes for the Fire & Police Departments,- it took a lot of schoveling! We also took food and milk to those in need in the area,- by 'sleds! We did what we could to help.

165

There was no way to get around and I wanted to see my girl, "Bernice", - so I decided I'd walk to her house. I lived on the North-side of town and she lived on the South-side of town, - a distance of at least 30 miles. I don't recall the date, but I took off early one morning, about 6 AM, and started plowing through the snow, - resting whenever and where-ever I could, - very late that afternoon I arrived at my futures home, - knocked on the door and Bernice answered the door, - "surprise", I said, "it's me!! She was speechless! No one believed I had walked all that way, - just to see my girl, - but I did!! I had dinner with the family, stayed over-night, slept on the davenport and left the next morning, - for the hike back to my house and, "Happy", I got to see my girl." Those who heard about my escapade thought I was either crazy or in love, - or both! I made it both ways!

Our wedding day was something to write about: First, - the day was bitter cold, but there was a very good crowd in attendance, which was pleasing to us. Next the photographer, we hired to take pictures at the Church and the hall, - didn't get a thing, - something was wrong with his camera. The pictures we did get were snapshots from our friends and relatives they took.

The next episode took place when we went to the hall, for our reception, to find out we were not getting the hall we thought we had rented. We found the upper hall occupied and when we complained we were told we

My "Bride"- Bernice P. Gaszak.
On Feb. 15th, 1947 she became Mrs. Bernice P. Wysocki.

★ ★ ★

had rented the lower hall; not the nice big upper
hall. I had no proof for what we thought we had
rented; only a receipt saying we rented a hall.
Lesson,- get everything in writing, with all the
specifics!! Then all through the evening the lights
would go out, in the lower hall; and the custodian
would do whatever he could to get them on again.

And then we caught people sneaking in from the bar, adjoining our hall, trying to swipe pieces of our wedding cake, - we put a stop to that in a hurry! That's not all, - a light rain was falling and the roads became very icey and my best-man, who was to take the gifts to my house and also pick up the tuxedos to take them back to the rental place was nowhere in sight, - he got bombed and his wife took him home. Everything was left up to us, - we took all the gifts to my house, - driving very carefully over the slick and icey roads, - then driving back to our down-town hotel, - the Ambassador Hotel. We arrived at the hotel later than we were supposed to, - the management didn't think we were coming, - so they gave, the, "Bridal Suite", to someone else. They also cancelled the reception they had planned for us, - but we did get a room, - with a murphy-bed! We had to get up early the next morning, "Sunday", to take the tucs back and go to Church. In those days you had to bring back what you rented the next day or pay a penalty. Everyone had a good time that, Saturday", and our marriage, - even with all the problems we had, - was united by, "God", - has passed the 60 years on, February 15th, 2007, - with my, "Dream Girl".

After our marriage, Bernice and I lived at my folks home and we all got along real well, - especially my Mom with, Bernice. We lived upstairs, in my bedroom, for about 6 months, - until one day my Dad said, "I think it's time you get your own place", - we had been trying but there was not a

Bernice — Charles
Celebrating 60 years of marriage, on 2-15-07,
with our family and friends. I'm 84, lucky me!

thing available. I told my wife what my Dad had
said, — so she composed a verse and put it in the
Milwaukee Journal, —

    "No house no home,
    No tea for two,
    A couple of rooms,
    Sure would do —"
    Call, (our phone number here)

    It worked, — we got a call and a rental. The
caller said the verse is what made him call us.
We now had a place of our own, — but no furniture
or appliances, — there was a shortage of everything,
due to the need of the troops coming home. A
friend of ours told us about a place called,

"Railroad Salvage",- a place where all kinds of items,- that were in train wrecks, were for sale,- as is. We furnished most of our home with items from this place and after we cleaned, doctered everything,- it looked just as good as new,- almost. My Dad had some connections with business places where he worked and was able to get us a range and a re-frigerator,- lucky us! A bed was still needed and my Mom & Dad had an extra one which they gave to us to use,- until we could get our own. In the years ahead we got all we needed for our home. We moved about 3 times,- always bettering our-selves.

Two years after our marriage we star-ted a family,- dispelling the thoughts of many neighbors and relatives that we mov-ed up our wedding date because Bern was pregnant. Our first born was a healthy baby girl,- Sept. 8th, 1949,- we called her,- Patricia Ann,- our second was a boy,- not so healthy,- he was born with a cleft pallete,- Aug. 18th, 1951,- we called him,- Paul Douglas,- our third was again a healthy baby boy,- March 10th, 1955,- we called him,- David Charles. The family Doctor then told Bern she should have no more babies,- we didn't. Paul,- through the help of a very wonderful, Plastic Surgeon, went through a series of constructive surgery. This was a very trying time for Paul and for us! Even-tualy everything turned out O.K., and he went to the University of Wisconsin, Whitewater, and became a very fine teacher,- he now lives in Flagstaff, Ariz.. Pat went to the University of Wisconsin, Milwaukee, and also became a very fine teacher. She married a wonderful man,- Jeff Jinkins and had three children,-Elizabeth, Ryan and Michael,- they live in Algonquinn, Ill. David was going to the, Wisconsin School of Engineering, Madison, Wisc. We are very proud of our children!

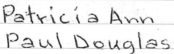

Patricia Ann
Paul Douglas

"Our Children —"

David Charles
(deceased)

David was a very intelligent student and a very talented bowler,- in January of 1975 he was to become a semi-pro bowler,- but that was never to happen. He had come home for a visit,- Thanksgiving, 1974,- and then back to school. The morning he left, with a friend of his, it was drizzling and I told him to drive carefully,- as all fathers do. We said, "Good-bye",- not knowing it would be our last! He was on his way and the weather was getting worse as the day progressed,- the roads were getting slippery and icey! Very late that same day we got a phone call,--- it was from a hospital in Oconomowok, Wisc.,- telling us David was in an accident! My wife and I were, in shock, as we left to drive,- in the snow,- for the hospital. I'll never know how I drove the car, 30 miles, with the wind and the snow blowing, making driving very difficult,- but I did! I remember us running through the snow,- no boots and really not dressed for the winter weather. When we got into the hospital we were taken to a private room where we were told,- David didn't make it!! I asked to see my son and they took me to him,- I stayed with him for awhile, prayed for him and said, "Good-bye", and, "God be with you"! It was time to go back home,- in the snow, and as we were driving back on the interstate a highway patrol officer stopped me for speeding,- I guess my mind wasn't on my driving. When the officer found out what had happened he said he was sorry, and told me to keep my mind on my driving! It was a horrible night and the

172

days and nights to come would not be any easier, -
especially for my wife. We were told the accident
happened on a State highway not on the express-
way as we had thought, - and that David was not
driving, his friend was. David must have taken
the scenic route and the area where he did some
small game hunting to show his friend. According to the Police report David's car skidded on a
curve, crossed over into the oncoming traffic
and was hit broadside by a big pick-up truck, -
they didn't have a chance! David's friend, with
a most serious condition did eventually survive.
A couple of years later he committed suicide -
he never did get over the tragedy! David was
19 and we were thankful, "to the Lord", for
giving him to us for those years. He is buried
at the National Cemetary, Wood, Wisc., where
my wife and I will also be buried. We had to pick
up our sons belongings at the school in Madison
and from the wreck. It was a very sad time, -
especially when we saw the car, - it was twisted
like a horse-shoe, - must have been a terrific
impact. We know he's in, "Heaven", with his maker,
because we can hear him bowling every time
it thunders.
    After the funeral I had to get Bernice
away for awhile until she could get over this
great tragedy, - but where! I was looking through a magazine one day when I came across
an ad for a free 1 week vacation in Green Valley,
Arizona, - hey, this sounds real good! I talked
to our close friends, Ralphh & Doris, who had -

been with us through this whole ordeal, if they would like to go with us, - they said, "yes". I called Fairfield, the construction company, in Green Valley, offering this vacation package. I made a reservation for the four of us and we were on our way! It was February, 1976, when we arrived in Green Valley and the weather was beautiful! We got there in time to celebrate our twentyninth wedding anniversary at the "Country Club of Green Valley. We all had a great time!! We both put down cash on homes, - but we had to cancel our purchase because of complications from the accident, - a lawsuit against us! When we got home we got the problem taken care of and then returned to Green Valley, - summer of 1977, bought our present home, returned to Milwaukee, sold the "Doll House", and returned here on December 1st, 1978. It was snowing when we left Milwaukee and the first day we were in our new home, no furniture, we slept on the floor, - and woke up in the morning to about two inches of snow, - it does that once in awhile here and brings out all the cameras. Our Poodle, "Peppie", a miniature, enjoyed romping around in the snow that disappeared by 10; AM...

Bern loved her new home and a ball shoping to get it all fixed up. We settled down in our new Green Valley home, - a Townhouse, and fell into the Green routine. There were so many things to do here that everyday you could do something different. We joined a Pinoc-hle card club, a bowling league, and took part in many Community programs.

"Peppie"

"Peppie", is gone now, but was a great companion and travler. He could smell a McDonald's a block away, - he loved their, - "French Fries"!!

I transfered my American Legion membership to Post #66 here in Green Valley, and became very active in it. I became the Post Adjutant, - for over 10 years; was the Post Commander for 3 terms and was appointed to the Building Comm. in 1982. I became the Chairman in 1987 and in that capacity I contacted the President of the Park Corporation located in the town of Sahurita, our neighboring community. My wife and I met with Mr. Park and presented our plans for a Post #66, "Post Home", - he was very receptive to the plan. We would meet, with Mr. Park,

"Our House"

This is the house we bought — ★

This is the "Home" we sold
22 years later, 1978. Called —
"The Doll House"

It was 1956 and we decided it was time to get our own home!! We looked and we looked and finally came up with this house with the help of a State of Wisconsin G.I. Loan. This house was going to take a lot of work, — but with my brother, Bob's, skills we would remodel the house, inside and outside, — to what you see on the left.

All of our children would grow up in this their "home".

We would live here until 1978, when my wife and I would move to "Green Valley, Arizona."

We purchased this "Townhouse", in Green Valley, the summer of 1977. We have lived here going on 30 years.

To live in this area one person had to be 55, - I just made it, to qualify in this retirement subdivision called - "Continental Vistas".

The way it looked -

Bern and Chuck - 2005.

several more times and in May 1991 I signed an Agreement between the Park Corp. and the American Legion Post #66, - located in Sahurita, Ariz., - for almost 5 acres of land; - next to the Titan Missle Museum, that would be donated to the Post by Mr. Park. What a day of joy for all at Post #66; - we finally did it, - we got the land!

"American Legion Post #66"

Now we would have a lot of work to do, - we increased our, "Fund Raising Campaign", hired Architect, Dick Rief, and The Chestnut Construction Company. Prior to the start of construction we went over the building plans and eliminated a couple of projects that could be done at a later date. Now we had enough funds to start the construction, - a 5,000 sq. ft. building. Every day we watched the, "Post Home", take shape and soon we would be able to get inside to do the painting, - that was a fun time but a lot of work. On Feb. 3rd, 1996 a, "Grand Opening and Dedication Ceremony," was held. We did the impossible; we had our, "Post Home," - thank you, "Mr. Park," and thank you, "Good Word." In the years to come I would start many programs including, - Bingo, Flea Market, Post Newsletter, Post Military Library, & Memorbelia Room and more.

Charles Wysocki, Jr. Green Valley, Ariz.
— Post Commander - 1991-92, 1992-93, 1994-95
72 years old, 1995.

In the year 1990 I approched our Post Executive Board with a plan; a Green Valley, "Avenue of Flags". It was approved and I was appointed Chairman for the project. I formed a Committee and we proceeded to form a, "Fund Raising Campaign", - Contact the Pima County Officials and the Green Valley Coordinating Council. All went well, - our plans were approved. Now we had to design a flagpole and ground sockets to put the poles in. Also the poles would have to be easy to store, handle and transport. A friend of mine, at that time, the owner of the, "Tucson Map & Flag Co.", was contacted and told what we needed. He said he'd work on it and a few days later he called me to come to the store to see what he came up with, Burt Miller, a Post #66 member, came up with exactly what we needed, - so we contracted with him to have the poles made. Next we had to determine where each flag pole was to be placed and a ground socket embedded. U.S. 3X5 Flags were ordered, - some from David Monthan Air Base and some from Washington, D.C.. A dedication Ceremony . was held and Green Valley had its, "Avenue of Flags", sponsored by, "The American Legion Post #66." There were 95 flagpoles along, - La Canada Blvd., between Esperanza Blvd. & Continental Rd.. It took about 2 years from conception to completion. After the dedication, the, "Avenue of Flags", Committee was turned over to a Civilian Committee made up of people from the Green Valley Community.

The putting up and taking down of the flagpoles is done by volunteers from the, "Lions, VFW, Elks, American Legion," and others. I and the Committee were a very happy and proud group this day.

All these years I have been a patient at the V.A. Hospitals in Milwaukee, Wisc. and Tucson, Ariz.,- since 1945,- for many medical problems. The one condition, to this day, that I have not been able to overcome is the fear of crowds! I'm better today than I was a few years ago,- but wherever I go my wife is always with me, or close by,- and knowing that she is there,- makes me feel more comfortable.

I cannot say enough about the wonderful care I have received from the Doctors, Nurses, Staff Members, Volunteers at the V.A. Hospitals I have been a patient. "God Bless," them all.

Now, I am in the twi-light of my life and sharing it with my wonderful wife of 60 years,- Bernice. She helped me through my, "War years," and drinking problems,- after the War. Because of her I am still here,- and I did quit drinking and smoking about 50 years ago,-this is 2007!

We did a lot of fun things, as a family,- traveling all over the State of Wisconsin, picnics, cookouts, Boy & Girl Scout activities, and more,- all without our own car. We'd travel with friends and relatives who had cars,- by chartered busses, streetcars and taxies sometimes. Then my Dad suffered a stroke. Dad gave me his car with a stipulation that I was to take him and Mom wherever they wanted to go; I did that. The car was a Pontiac, don't remember the year, but it was a very nice car, our first one! We have never owned a brand new car!

My years in Green Valley, 30, with my lovely wife, Bernice, have been very happy and wonderful years. We have made many friends, traveled around this beautiful State of Arizona, surrounding states and Mexico, plus all the Casinos! We have traveled to Germany, Greece, Tahiti, Hawaii, Canada, Islands of the Mediterranean and visited every state in the U.S.A., including Alaska. We used every means of travel, with the kids and by ourselves, by cars, trains, buses, airplanes and cruise ships. I'm glad we were able to travel when we did because today our traveling days are over due to my medical problems. I'm like an old car, I need new parts!! It's been over 10 years that our traveling has ceased, but we have had the fortune of having our children, grandchildren, relatives and friends come to Green Valley for a visit with us, "I love them all".

This has been my life story up to, June, 2007, someone else will have to write the final chapter - - - - -

Charles Wysocki, Jr. - 84.

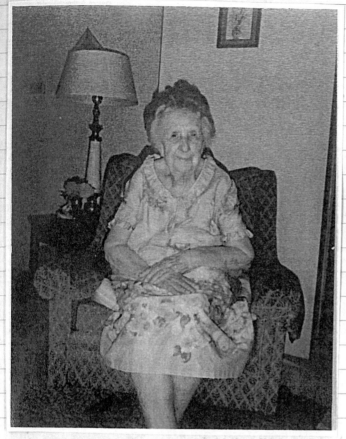

This is a picture of my Mother, Emma, taken when she was in her 90's. She passed away at age 96.

This is not the picture of, Mom, that I saw in my "Vision," on Tarawa. The one I saw she was in her early 30's and in an Indian costume. She was beautiful and I miss her very much!

⭐

This is a picture of my, Mom, and my, Mother-in-law,- Lucille Gaszak. They got along like two peas in a pod. They were wonderful.

Charles & Bernice —
Celebrating their "60th Wedding Anniversary" with
their Children, — Paul Douglas Wysocki, Flagstaff,
Arizona and Patricia Ann Jinkins, Algonquin, Ill..
February 15th 2007

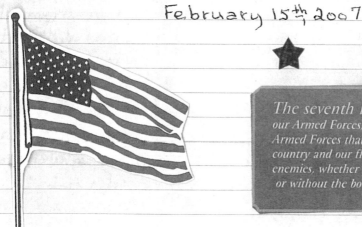

The seventh fold is a tribute to our Armed Forces, for it is through our Armed Forces that we protect our country and our flag against all her enemies, whether they be found within or without the boundaries of our republic.

Celabrating the end of WWII.

Me,- Charles Wysocki, Jr.
    My Dad,- Charles Wysocki, Sr. (Carl)
    My Brother,- Robert Wysocki

    We are in the rec room of my parents
home, shortly after the War ended in 1945,
hoisting a few to victory and our safe return
from the horrors of War.

Charles, Jr. - W.W.II, U.S. Marine Corps.
    2nd Marine Div. - Co. "D", 2nd Batt., 18th Marines.
Charles, Sr. - W.W.I, U.S. Army
Robert, - W.W.II, U.S. Army, 32nd "Red Arrow Div."
    121st Field Artillery.

Patricia,
Daughter

Jeff Jinkins,
Son-in-law

Elizabeth

Grandchildren

Ryan
"Eagle Scout"

"Jinkins Family"

Michael
"Eagle Scout"

"Rotation Point System of World War Two"

    The Marine Corps set up this system around 1944, - that's when I heard about it, - as follows -

Time in Service, - 1pt. for each month.
Overseas Service, - 1 pt for each month.
Campaign Landings, - 5 pts each Campaign.
Purple Heart Award, - 5 pts each award.
Commendation Awards, - 5 pts. each award.
    Presidential Award

Total requirement for W.W. II rotation plan from overseas was, - 45 points.

Some Marines of the 2nd Marine Division had averaged enough points under this plan for 2 or 3 rotations. I had enough pts. for 2+ rotations. P.F.C. Charles Wysocki, Jr.

Time in Service	28 pts.
Overseas Service	37 "
Campaign Landings	20 "
Purple Heart Award	5 "
Commendation Awards	
Presidential Unit Award	10 "
Total pts.	100 "

" World War Two Statistics "

Draftees:
Comprised 66% of all four services.

Typical Soldier:
1.- Single and 28 years of age, finished sophomore year of high school; 14% had attended college.
2- 73% of GI's served overseas; ratio of support troops to combat was 10-1.
3.- 17,000 women served abroad.
4.- Casualties: The U.S. suffered up to, 293,000 killed in action; 115,000 were non-combat and over 670,000 were wounded in action.
5.- In the Army, 37.5% were dischared for psychiactric reasons, these were referred to by the GI's as, "Nervous in the service", or just, "Fed up with the set-up."

As one Marine put it: "The medics say my wounds will heal, but none of us will be completely cured for years.

In conclusion: "We fought Japan because we were attacked by them. We fought Germany because it declared war on us.
We fought for democracy, for our families, for our loved ones and for our nation.
We fought to rid the world of evil and to preserve "Peace", around the world.

"I Want Them To Know"

Oliver Wendell Holmes, Jr. said, —

"Historic continuity with the past is not a
duty it is a necessity, — but what have we done?
We have taken great delight in ripping apart
historical values and anchors, as well as
leaders from the past."

Sadley, though, many young people today
have not just forgotten the brave deeds of our
men and women in all the wars, — because they
have never been taught about them in the first
place. Nor do they appreciate the dept our
nation owes to our Veterans and the Americans supporting the war efforts. That's because in this, politically correct, time many of
our nation's schools don't teach about the heroism and the sacrifices made for our freedom
in all our nations wars and crisises.

I want our children to know how 55,000
ordinary Americans changed the world forever
by acting against all human instinct to
charge ashore on the beaches of Normandy
in World War Two. I want them to know about
the surprise attack on Pearl Harbor and how,
with our backs to the wall, we went on the
offensive against the Japanese at Guadalcanal.
I want them to know our American forces fought
back with a strength, power and pride we didn't
know we had. For four years our Troops, Navy,
Air Force and the Coast Guard fought the Nazis
and the Japanese back to Berlin and Tokyo. Along

the way there were many casualties among our troops and the civilian population. I want our children to know of the brutal concentration camps where thousands of innocent civilians were murdered. I want them to know how our prisoners of war were killed and how sadisticly they were treated in the Prisoner of War camps. These men and women were all, "Heroes", then and still are now, but many of our young Americans don't know the first thing about our proud Veterans. They don't know what, where or the meaning of names like, - Midway, Guadalcanal, Tarawa, Omaha Beach, Battle of the Bulge, Iwo Jima, Battle of the Coral Sea and many, many others including battles of the Civil War, Revolutionary War, Vietnam, Korea, Gulf Wars and others. World War One was the war to end all wars, - but it didn't and no war will until governments realize that killing and destruction are not the answers to, "PEACE".

I, and all the Veterans of all the, "Wars", - hate and despise war in all its forms of horror, death and destruction. We want the world to be at, "PEACE", forever and we want the Goverments of the World to find peaceful means to seattle their differances. It has been proven through the years that those who want to rule the world will be destroyed and those who want and love freedom will prevail. Freedom is not free, - we have to fight and die for it!! With God's help we, the people of the world will bring back the meaning of values.

There must be values in the home based

on the "Word of God". Values are clear statements of
policy upon which a home, business, organization,
church or Country are established and built. Authority, is a value that is based on God's ordained
leadership. Obediance, is a value that has its foundation in character. We cannot save ourselves or
sanctify ourselves,- only, "God", can do that. I want,
not only the children, but every person and Government in the world to know that we,- the Veterans
of all the wars were there, we saw, we fought, we
heard and we smelled the battles of war,- as
we still do to this day. I personally know the
horrors, destruction, the human body being torn
apart, men being pushed to the limit of their
endurance and beyond,- yes, I know,- I was
there!!

Then years later you get some, "Clown", out
there who wants to change, "History", by saying
this battle or that battle was an unnecessary
one,- like the, "Bloody Battle For Tarawa",- Nov. 20th,
1943,- one that I took part in! I landed in the 3rd
wave with my partner, Floyd, and other assault
troops in an, "AMTRACK". How do they know if it was
necessary or not,- they weren't there,- but we
were and we know it had to be taken no matter
what it would take to do it! Those who want to
change, "History", most times they weren't around
when the battles took place. How did they think,
we who were engaged in that battle,- the families
and loved ones of those who gave their all for their
Country and Freedom For All would feel,-
I know I didn't feel to good about what was

said, – in fact I was very angry that someone would have the, "gall," to say you suffered and died for nothing! Robert Sherrod, the War Correspondent, said in a statement, after war, how shocked he was by the way his combat stories were altered, – just to sell papers. The truth must always be told, – no matter how much it may hurt someones feelings.

The public must be prepared for whatever the future may bring! Todays children must be educated in our schools, churches, and their homes about, "WAR," so that they can tell their children and so on. The faith of, "God", must be put in the lives of all of us, – as it was in us as we prayed for, "God's", protection during the war, – and has continued through our present and future lives. There are those who do not believe and I say to them, – stand in front of a full length mirror, – look at yourself and say, – who gave me eyes to see with, – who gave me a nose to inhale the life giving air, – who gave me legs to walk and run with, – who gave me a brain to think with, and who gave me the rest of my body that makes me a human being. If you think it was by evolution, – why then isn't it continuing today. If it was by scientific means, – why are they still looking for answers!!

God, Jesus, Allah, the Mesiah or a Super Being you may think is the orgin of life and the universe, – we will all find out the day we die, – only none of us will be able to come back and tell what we find out. Only, "God", has the answers. We were all given a free will to do what we want to do with our lives and when the end comes we will be rewarded or punished for what we did with our lives. Which do you want, - what Kind, - what kind of life do you want to live.

During the war, that I was in, there were no atheist in the fox holes, - that I know of. I believe in, "God", and I pray to, "Him", every day for Peace in the world and to put an end to all Wars. I ask for Peace in the world and Happiness for all the People and all the Nations for ever and ever. Will you pray too!!

I want the children and the world to know and believe!! The glory of life comes from what we revere and hold dear.

Let me close with the following: -
We, the people, cannot thump our noses at our moral duty to others and our Country. We must not fail our children in giving them the character gifts our parents gave to us, - self respect, honesty, independence, thrift, respect for others, moral standards, and much more. Our children, of all ages, must be taught, - obedience, loyalty, patriotism, love of Country, and most of all, - to believe that we will be rewarded, - one way or another, for whatever we have done with our lives!! We must support our Government in its decisions to preserve Democracy and the Freedoms we now enjoy. We must support our Military, - regardless of our personal feelings.

No matter where they are sent and no matter what they have to do to protect the Freedoms of our Country; they are our children, husbands and loved ones; so support and pray for them! Everyone must be made aware to the fact that this Country can be destroyed; as have other countries been down through history! Unless there is a moral rejuvenation in America and the world we will continue to, "decline". The youth of our Country are our hope for the future. The return to basics; those values rooted in our conscience, that reveres the, "Highest", will truly be the guideline for the future. I want everyone to know that the future is their future. Will the future bring, "Peace", or will we face the, "Weapons of Mass Destruction". Will we return to the values and fundamentals of our forefathers, or will we continue to, "deteriorate"!!

"God Help Us"

Charles Wysocki, jr.

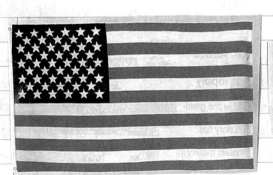

U.S. Flag

The flag of the United States consists of 13 equal horizontal stripes of red alternating with white, with a blue rectangle bearing 50 small, white, five-pointed stars. The 50 stars on the flag represent the 50 U.S. states and the 13 stripes represent the original thirteen colonies that rebelled against the British crown. Nicknames for the U.S. flag include "the Stars and Stripes" and "Old Glory," with the latter nickname coined by Captain William Driver, a 19th-century shipmaster.

"These Were The Bad Of World War Two"

"Japanese Bayonet" "+"
World War II.

Admiral Tanaka

"Japanese Zero" "Jap Mitsubishi"

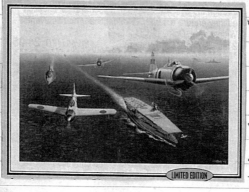

"Awakening
the Giant!"

Japanese
Zeros from
the imperial
Japanese
Navy's flagship carrier Akagi
proceed to the opening strike
at Pearl Harbor, - Dec. 7th, 1941

They are not
cheering anymore!

195

"↑"

"Yamato's Final
Voyage!"
In April, 1945, the Jap
battleship Yamato, surrounded   "↑"
by the rest of her Task Force, heads south toward
Okinawa on the mission from which she will never
return.

The Jap men are no longer around, - but they
left their pictures behind for us!

196

"Japanese Landing Barge" –

Late, the first night on "Betio", Tarawa Atoll, a barge, like the one above, was coming into the beach very slowly. We could see it very clearly by the light of the moon and the star shells that were going off all night long. Word was passed down the line, – "don't move, be quiet and don't shoot." We wondered, – why was that, "barge", coming over the coral reef with no problems! As the, "barge", hit the beach, Marines, in the immediate area, tossed grenades into the, "barge", and nothing more happened. Later, toward the morning, Marines boarded the, "barge", and found only a half dozen dead Japs, killed by the grenades. That was a scary couple of hours!!

197

"Captured Jap 70 mm Field Piece"

A piece of shrapnel from one of these is what hit me and left very fine slivers of metal in my arms. They float around and every once in awhile a sliver will hit a nerve and I'll have pain until it breaks loose and moves on til another time.

These guys didn't want to play the game anymore, on the Island of Tarawa, so they put themselves to sleep permanently!

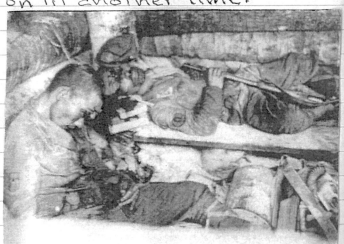

" These Were The Good Guys Who Took Care of the Bad Guys "

December 8, 1941 Newspaper
This reproduction of *The Baltimore News-Post* from December 8, 1941, takes you back to the day after Japan attacked Pearl Harbor and the Philippines – the day when the war that Adolf Hitler started by invading Poland became a worldwide conflict.

"The Doolittle Raiders"

April 10th, 1942 aboard the USS Hornet eight days before their famous "Tokyo Raid."

Lt. Col. James H. Doolittle.

Doolittle's B-25 takes off from carrier *Hornet*

Action in the Slot

Tom Freeman. The Japanese destroyer Makigumo goes down at the hands of PT-124 in 1943.

LIMITED EDITION

Number 20 for Joe

Roy Grinnell. Marine Corps ace and Medal of Honor recipient Joe Foss downs a Betty bomber over Guadacanal, scoring the 20th of the 22 victories he would achieve in 30 days of combat.

God Bless America
LIMITED EDITION

PT-109

PT-109 is immortalized as the boat commanded by John F. Kennedy. It was powered by three twelve-cylinder Packard engines, and equipped with four torpedo tubes, machine guns, and an anti-aircraft gun.

"If we lose our history, we lose our national identity."
—Joe Foss, CMH

Amphibious Assault Vehicle Model

Amphibious Assault Vehicles were instrumental in carrying Marines

"LCM"
Troop & Equipment Carrier.

Willys Jeep

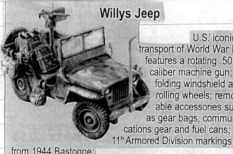

U.S.' iconic transport of World War II features a rotating .50 caliber machine gun; a folding windshield and rolling wheels; removable accessories such as gear bags, communications gear and fuel cans; 11th Armored Division markings from 1944 Bastogne;

Gato Class Submarine

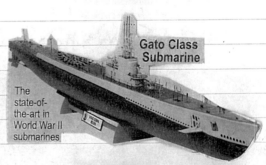

The state-of-the-art in World War II submarines

M4A3 Sherman the world famous M4A3 Sherman tank of World War II.

one of the Allies' most useful and versatile vehicles which was capable of carrying a 2½ ton load over land or water.

DUKW Amphibious Vehicle Set

Semper Fi Skies

John Shaw. On May 13, 1943, Capt. Archie Donahue of VMF-112 becomes an "ace in a day" by shooting down five enemy aircraft in one mission near Guadalcanal – a feat he repeated two years later while flying with VMF-451 over Okinawa.

LIMITED EDITION

LIMITED EDITION

God Bless America

Iwo Jima
A Hard-Won Haven

John Shaw. Iwo Jima, a volcanic speck in the Pacific for which the U.S. Marines paid dearly, became a thing of beauty to B-29 crews that had to make emergency landings after missions against Japan in early 1945.

God Bless America

LIMITED EDITION

Battle for the Islands

Nicolas Trudgian. Dogfighting at tree-top height, VMF-121 Corsairs rip into a formation of Betty bombers as they try to make their escape following their attack on shipping. On fire, the Betty in the foreground is doomed, and will shortly become one of 58 enemy aircraft destroyed this day.

B-25B Mitchell

the bomber flown by Lt. Ted W. Lawson who, along with his crew, crashed in the China Sea after their successful bombing of Tokyo on the famed Doolittle Raid

B-25 Mitchell

THE Bs WWII

B-17 Flying Fortress

B-24 Liberator

Wings of Freedom

— "And Then Came The Marines!!"

"Assault."

"Counterattack"

Against the Japs assaulting Henderson Field, – Guadalcanal, October 26th, 1942

"Tarawa"

"Bloody Tarawa", – 76 Hours.

Nov. 20th, 1943.

"Trophies: Victory at Tarawa"

"Hitting the Beach"

"Hand Grenade"

"1.5 Ton Truck"

".50 Caliber Machine Gun"

God
Bless
America

LIMITED EDITION

Imperial Sacrifice
Robert Bailey. In April, 1945, Lt. Hal Jackson and a fellow pilot, both flying Corsairs with VBF-10, evade deadly anti-aircraft fire from the sinking Imperial Japanese battleship Yamato after successfully delivering their bombs on target.

"75mm recoiless rifle"

Sherman Tank.

For freedom and all who defend it!

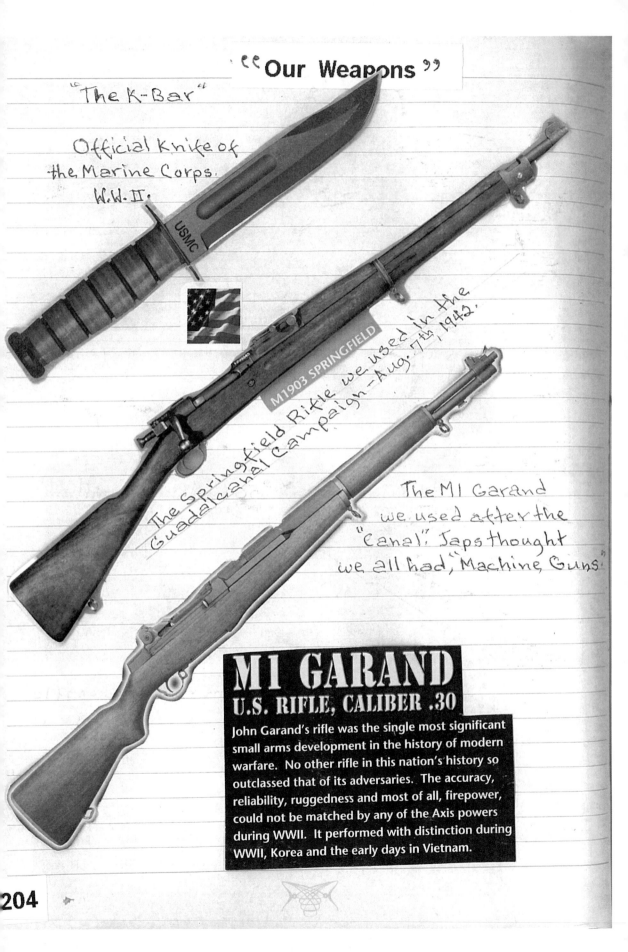

"The K-Bar"

Official Knife of
the Marine Corps.
W.W. II.

USMC

M1903 SPRINGFIELD

The Springfield Rifle we used in the
Guadalcanal Campaign—Aug. 7th, 1942.

The M1 Garand
we used after the
"Canal". Japs thought
we all had, "Machine Guns".

M1 GARAND
U.S. RIFLE, CALIBER .30

John Garand's rifle was the single most significant
small arms development in the history of modern
warfare. No other rifle in this nation's history so
outclassed that of its adversaries. The accuracy,
reliability, ruggedness and most of all, firepower,
could not be matched by any of the Axis powers
during WWII. It performed with distinction during
WWII, Korea and the early days in Vietnam.

"Gung-Ho"

Remembering American Sacrifices for Freedom and Country

"There is no greater honor than duty done." -Robert E. Lee

"Atomic Warfare Is Here"

A lone B-29 Superfortress drops a single bomb and change the world forever!

"Best of Their Breed"

The USS Missouri cruises Tokyo Bay at the time of the Japanese surrender, 1945.

Japanese Surrender

On the morning of September 2, 1945, more than two weeks after accepting the Allies' terms, Japan formally surrendered. This black-and-white photograph shows the signing that took place on the USS Missouri.

Surrender signing on Sept. 2nd, 1945 to end the War

VJ Day Newspaper

This reproduction of Washington D.C.'s *The Evening Star* from August 14, 1945, presents the heavily-anticipated news of Japan's surrender.

EXTRA **The Evening Star** 5 Cents

WHITE HOUSE ANNOUNCES THE WAR IS OVER

MacArthur to Receive Surrender of Japanese

"Thank God"
&
"The Armed Forces"

SEMPER FI

MARINES

We Did It Together!!

"Army"

"Navy"

"Air Force"

"Marine Corps"

"Coast Guard"

and -

The Merchant Marine

"Prisoners of War & Missing In Action Flag:"--

    This is the only flag ever displayed in the U.S. Capitol Rotunda where it stands as a powerful symbol of national commitment to America's POW/MIAs.

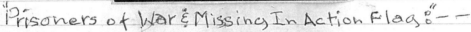

"Taps"

Day is done,
  gone the sun,
From the hills,
  from the lake,
From the sky,
  All is well,
  Safely rest,
   God is nigh.

GOD
BLESS
AMERICA

What is a Veteran?

He is the cop on the beat who spent two months in Saudi Arabia sweating two gallons a day making sure the armored personnel carriers didn't run out of fuel.

He is the barroom loudmouth, dumber than five wooden planks, whose overgrown frat-boy behavior is outweighed a hundred times in the cosmic scales by four hours of exquisite bravery near the 38th parallel.

She (or he) is the nurse who fought against futility and went to sleep sobbing every night for two solid years in Da Nang.

He is the POW who went away one person and came back another – or didn't come back AT ALL.

He is the Parris Island drill instructor who has never seen combat – but has saved countless lives by turning slouchy, no-account rednecks and gang members into Marines and teaching them to watch each other's backs.

He is the parade-riding Legionnaire who pins on his ribbons and medals with a prosthetic hand.

He is the career quartermaster who watches the ribbons and medals pass him by.

He is the three anonymous heroes in the Tomb of the Unknowns, whose presence at the Arlington National Cemetery must forever preserve the memory of all anonymous heroes whose valor dies unrecognized with them on the battlefield or in the ocean's sunless deep.

He is the old guy bagging groceries at the supermarket -- palsied now and aggravatingly slow -- who helped liberate a Nazi death camp and who wishes all day long that his wife were still alive to hold him when the nightmares come.

He is an ordinary and yet and extraordinary human being – a person who offered some of his life's most vital years in the service of his country, and who sacrificed his ambitions so others would not have to sacrifice theirs.

He is a soldier and a savior and a sword against the darkness, and he is nothing more than the finest, greatest testimony on behalf of the finest, greatest nation ever known.

So remember, each time you see someone who has served our country, just lean over and say, "Thank You." That's all most people need, and in most cases it will mean more than any medals they could have been awarded or were awarded.

Two little words that mean a lot, "THANK YOU."

It's the soldier, not the reporter, who gave us our freedom of the press.
It's the soldier, not the poet, who gave us our freedom of speech.
It's the soldier, not the campus organizer, who gave us our freedom to demonstrate.
It's the soldier, who salutes the flag, who serves others with respect for the flag, and whose coffin is draped by the flag, who allows the protester to burn the flag.

Of all the gifts you could give a U. S. service member, prayer is the very best one.

Prayer for our service members:
Lord, hold our troops in your loving hands. Protect them as they protect us. Bless them and their families for the selfless acts they perform for us in our time of need.
Amen

Author unknown: Originated in "An American Veteran"

209

A Letter From AMVETS Executive,

Joseph T. Piening.

"It is while men talk of the lessons of history----
----they ignore, them."

Dear Fellow American,

Over sixty-five years ago, as the Holiday
Season approached, our nation suffered a
devastating surprise attack. While Americans
enjoyed Sunday dinners the U.S. Pacific Fleet,
lying at anchor in Pearl Harbor, Hawaii, was
all but destroyed.

Worse, early estimates indicated more
than two thousand military personel and
civilians had been killed by the Japanese
air strikes over Oahu. Grim news reports of
enemy damage were eased somewhat by
the many inspiring accounts of extraoror-
dinary American heroism.

Amidst the ruins of our nation's resolve
to avoid war, outraged Americans vowed never
again to let down our, "eternal vigilance...."

Forward sixty years however, with oil
still rising from the sunken U.S.S. Arizona as
a reminder,- the brutal wake-up call of Dec.
7th, 1941 had lost much of its hue and cry. On
September 11th, 2001, our nation's mutual pledge
to, "eternal vigilance", once again wavered.

Within hours though, reminiscent of our
nation's original, "Day of Infamy", the -

United States of America mustered its proud few. Still another generation of extraordinary patriots was mobilized to, "bear the battle".

Four years hence, more than two thousand American fighting men and women have given their lives voluntarily to safeguard each of us from a repeat of 9/11. Nevertheless, on the home front, our best efforts toward, "eternal vigilance",— are under attack daily in what appears seditious debate.

Some Americans insist terrorism amounts to aggression. Others cry, "bring the troops home, we can't win." Fortunately for America, the President of the United States isn't listening.

And gratefully, neither are America's GIs. Young as most of them are, each boasts a common sense bond,— faith of their fathers in America's commitment to freedom,— Patrick Henry said it best, "Give me liberty or give me death."

In Arling National Cemetery, thousands of American heroes lie at parade rest beneath solemn courses of bleak white stone. Each of them, in their season, nurtured Thomas Jefferson's, "tree of freedom", and now lie in eternal close order.

Amidst such honored silence, one imagines the strange murmur of battle. And above its anguish, the assurance of Armageddon if we again fail the lessons of history.

""A Speech by Abraham Lincoln""

We have been the recipients of the choicest bounties of Heaven. We have been preserved these many years in peace and prosperity. We have grown in numbers, wealth, and power as no other nation has grown. But we have forgotten God. We have forgotten the gracious hand which preserved us in peace, and multiplied and enriched and strengthened us; and we have vainly imagined, in the deceitfulness of our hearts, that all these blessings were produced by some superior wisdom and virtue of our own.

Intoxicated with unbroken success, we have become too self sufficient to feel the necessity of redeeming and preserving grace, too proud to pray to the God that made us!

It behooves us, to humble ourselves before the offended Power to confess our national sins, and to pray for clemency and forgiveness.

— Abraham Lincoln

FORT SUMTER

Pay tribute to the first battle of the Civil War

On the morning of April 12, 1861, Confederate forces surrounded Fort Sumter - then controlled by a small Union force commanded by Major Robert Anderson - in the Charleston Harbor. Unprepared for the siege that followed, Anderson was forced to surrender the fort to the Confederates the next afternoon. The 34-hour bombardment of Fort Sumter marked the beginning of the American Civil War.

Exerts From A Letter by James C. Roberts, President of the World War Two Veterans Comm.

The World War II Veterans Committee has been deignated as an official WWII oral history biographer.

They need our help to record the stories of America's aging World War Two Veterans before they pass on and their stories are lost forever.

Over Sixty-Five years ago the largest battle in this history of the world took place – Jun 6th, 1944, – the D-Day landing at Normandy.

Years of planning and training led up to the June 6th landings. The allies used, 5,300 ships and landing craft, 1,500 tanks & 12,000 airplanes. But in the end, it all came down to this:

150,000 scared Kids, – – most not yet 20 years old, – – who entered a nightmare so they could save the world!

Sadly, though, many young people today have forgotten the brave deeds of our troops around the world.

That's because many of our nation's schools don't teach about the heroism and the sacrifices made for our freedom.

Then there are things to remember like, Bill Clinton cancelling the postage stamp that would have commemorated the bombing of Hiroshima, – – an act that saved the lives of thousands of U.S. troops.

And Clinton denounced the term, "V-J Day" as insensitive to the Japanese.

And he also shunned our European allies by celebrating the 50th anniversary of "V-E Day" with Boris Yeltsin in Russia.

Don't forget the national news media's attacks on General Eisenhower and our U.S. forces who won the War in the Pacific.

Journalists, like Peter Jennings depicted our troops as, "bullies", for dropping the A-bomb on Hiroshima and Nagasaki.

The Smithsonian Museum in Washington, D.C., gladly joined in with a display that portrayed America as the aggressor and Japan as a small nation valiantly trying to preserve its culture.

You and I know that's not the true story!

Isn't honoring and preserving the true history of WWII heroism, and sacrifice worth your best support!

Or are we going to allow the likes of Peter Jennings shape what our young people think of our Veterans?

I hope you'll choose to help keep the truth about America's WWII Veterans with your true stories.

James C. Roberts

A Must Read Story...!!

In September of 2005, on the first day of school, Martha Cothren, a social studies school teacher at Robinson High School in Little Rock, did something without permission of the school superintendent, the principal or the building supervisor, - she took all of the desks out of the classroom.

The kids came for the first period, they walked in, there were no desks. They obviously looked around and said, - "Miss Cothren, where are our desks?" And she said, - "You can't have a desk until you tell me how you earn them."

They thought, "Well, maybe it's our grades."
"No," she said.
"Maybe it's our behavior,"
And she told them, "No, it's not even your behavior."

And so they came and went, - the first, second and third periods and still no desks. By early afternoon television news crews had gathered in Miss. Cothren's class to find out about this crazy teacher who had taken all the desks out of the classroom. The last period of the day, Martha Cothren gathered her class. They were at this time sitting on the floor around the sides of the room. And she says, - "Throughout the day no one has really understood how you earn the desks that sit in this classroom ordinarily." She said, "Now I'm going to tell you."

Martha Cothren went over to the door of her classroom and opened it, and as she did 27 U.S. Veterans, wearing their uniforms, walked into that classroom, each one carrying a school desk. And they placed those school desks in rows, and then they stood along the wall. By the time they had finished placing those desks, those kids for the first time, - I think perhaps in their lives, understood how they earned those desks.

Martha said, "you don't have to earn those desks. These guys did it for you. They put them out there for you, - but it's up to you to sit here responsibly to learn, to be good students and good citizens, because they paid a price for you to have those desks, - and don't ever forget it!!"

My friends, I think sometimes we forget that the freedoms that we have are freedoms not because of celebrities, - but freedoms are because of ordinay people who did extraordinary things, who loved this Country more than life itself, who not only earned a desk for a kid at the Robinson High School in Little Rock, but who earned a seat for you and me to enjoy this great land we call home. This wonderful nation that we better love enough to protect and preserve with the kind of conservative, solid values and principles that made us a great nation.

"We live in the Land of the Free because of the Brave." ⭐ ⭐

rmies Don t Fight Wars, Countries Fight WARS

by Mark Shields

In his landmark book on the American infantryman, respeted military journalist George Wilson quoted Col. Steve Siegfried, a combat veteran, on why the U.S. must, - in a time of war, - have a military draft of civilians: "Armies don't fight wars, Countries fight wars, I hope to hell we learned that in Vietnam.... A country fights a war. If it doesn't, then we shouldn't send an Army."

Sadly, we have failed to learn what, - Siegfried sought to teach us!

The depersonalized, detached mind set of policy makers and think-tank commandos toward American Soldiers and Marines outraged Jim Webb: "Their attitude strikes me as: You volunteered, - you took the money, - shut-up and die."

The strength of a nation, we know from the pain of history, is measured by that nation's will and resolve to stand together for the common good through individual sac- rifice.

If the goals of our Nation are worth fighting for, - then we ought not hesitate to ask all Americans to share the risk and -

sacrifice of fighting!!

Do Americans, in 2007 believe that a country, — not just an army, — fights a war?

Exerts from article written by, — Mark Shields.

THINKING of YOU

In Support Of Our Troops

"Notes, Quotes, and More"

"It doesn't take a Hero to order men into battle, it takes a Hero to be one of those men who goes into battle".

Norman Schwarzkof

Soldier, - above all other men, is required to practice the greatest act of religious training - sacrifice.

In battle and in the face of danger and death, He discloses those divine attributes which His maker gave when He created man in His own image. No physical courage and no brute instinct can take the place of the divine help wich alone can sustain him.

General Douglas MacArthur.

"Wars maybe fought with weapons, but they are won by men. It is the spirit of the men who follow and of the man who leads that gains the victory."

General George S. Patton

"Yesterday is history, tomorrow is a mystery, and today is a gift;

that's why they call it the present."

ELEANOR ROOSEVELT (1884-1962)

219

"The Soldier's Creed"

I am an American soldier,
I am a Warrior and a member of a team,
I serve the people of the United States
and live the Army Values.
I will always place the mission first,
I will never accept defeat,
I will never quit.
I will never leave a fallen comrade,
I am disciplined physically and mentally
tough, trained and proficient in my
warrior tasks and drills.
I always maintain my arms, my equipment
and myself,
I am an expert and I am a professional,
I stand ready to deploy, engage, and destroy
the enemies of the United States of
America in close combat.
I am a guardian of freedom and the
American way of life.
I am an American soldier!!

"Their story is known to all of you. It
is the story of the American man at arms. My
estimate of him was formed on the battlefields
many, many years ago, and has never changed.
I regarded him then, as I regard him now, - as
one of the world's noblest figures."

General Douglas MacArthur.

"Eleanor Roosevelt In New Zealand"

While in Wellington, New Zealand, 1943, Mrs. Roosevelt came for a visit and on this one day we were on our way back to Camp from a work detail. We didn't know at the time that she was there until we were told by the M.P.'s to slow down,— Eleanor was just ahead. We concocted a greeting for her and I was to give the signal at the time we were even or just passing her very slowly. I was sitting on the, "tailgate", of the truck and had a good view of our approch,— I was ready! I gave the signal and all together we sounded off,— "yoo-ho Eleanor."

The next day the newspaper headline was a statement by,— Eleanor Roosevelt,—"We, the Marines, should be rehabilitated before being allowed back in the States",— or words to that effect.

by Charles Wysocki, Jr.

Each soldier's eye shall brightly turn to where thy sky-born glories burn…

-Joseph Randolph Drake

U.S. Marine Corps... The Marines of **World War II** never faltered in their relentless drive to clear the Pacific of Imperial Japanese invasion forces. Island after island, wave after wave, the Marines exhibited great valor and selfless service. They smashed Japanese stronghold after Japanese stronghold, returning home victorious in 1945,

Korean War Marine veterans have endured the same problems. The ROK War Service Medal and Combat Action ribbon was not approved until just recently for Korean veterans. Today our experts can make sure Korean veterans are properly recognized and know all their awards.

In **Vietnam**, the Marines stopped the NVA from the DMZ to the coastal plains. Their courage and sacrifice was never properly acknowledged. Today our country recognizes and respects their valiant efforts in Vietnam. The Vietnam era Marines deserve to have their military honors displayed as a tribute to their devotion to duty and country.

During the **Cold War**, Marines served afloat on every ocean as well as in almost every country in the world. Long tours of difficult and sometimes very dangerous service have received little acknowledgment. Cold War Marine veterans need to be recognized for their enormous contributions in defeating worldwide communism and the collapse of the Soviet empire.

The **Liberation of Kuwait** saw a brilliant Marine attack after long, difficult training in the desert heat. Marine professionalism in this baking desert war earned honors and respect.

The **Liberation of Afghanistan** and **Iraq** in the **Global war on Terror** shows again how tough and decisive today's Marines are. Their new honors are well earned.

History provides us with defining moments from which we judge where we are with where we have been. The Civil War provides the United States with one of its critical defining moments that continues to play a vital role in defining ourselves as a Nation. Fort Sumter is the place where it began.

America's most tragic conflict ignited at Fort Sumter on April 12, 1861, when a chain reaction of social, economic and political events exploded into civil war. At the heart of these events was the issue of states rights versus federal authority flowing over the underlying issue of slavery.

We have staked the whole furture of American civilization, not upon the power of government, far from it. We have staked the future of all of our political institutions upon the capacity of mankind for self-government; upon the capacity of each and all of us to govern ourselves, to control ourselves, to sustain ourselves according to the Ten

<u>Commandments of God."</u>

James Madison
The Father of the U.S. Constitution

US Army Air Force

The Army Air Force, fighting on 3 fronts, swept the sky clear of all foes but not without sacrifice. At times, their losses were second only to the Infantry. Fighters, bombers & transports flew from Berlin to Burma and back. No country, no Air Force had ever met such a challenge as World War II and no other deserved the awards more than the Army Air Corps. From the beginning at Pearl Harbor to the finish of the Japanese Empire with the Atomic bombs, America's airmen were patriots.

The Army Air Force and US Air Force has defeated every foe our country has sent them against. At times their losses have been second only to the Infantry but they never wavier only triumphed. Their valor and dedication is legend.

World War II... From the very first few days, Marines spearheaded the recapture of the Pacific, storming every Japanese stronghold and crushing the enemy.

Korea... From the Pusan perimeter to the landings at Inchon, Marines smashed the enemy. The surprise Chinese attack followed by frozen Chosin evolved into bitter hilltop fighting where Marines chewed up Chinese Division after Division. Today South Korea remains free and prosperous due, in large part, to Marines.

Vietnam...500,000 Marines served in Vietnam from 1962 to 1975. From the DMZ and Khe Sanh to the battle of Hue and Dong Ha the largest field Marine Command ever employed stopped the VC and NVA cold.

Kuwait... In the famous 100 hour war ending in the Liberation of Kuwait and the destruction of the Iraqi army, the Marines led the assault right up the middle.

The task force would cross and recross the International Date Line as it zigzagged its way toward the Gilberts. One Marine said, "This is the damndest week we ever lived through. Two Sundays and no Thursdays. What in the hell will they think of next?"

" U. S. Air Power "

World War Two is the defining event of modern history. Its huge economic and human cost is unparalleled. Its aftermath has touched the lives of every person alive today and it will continue to do so for generations to come.

US Air Power was the deciding factor that determined the outcome of that mammoth conflict. Nearly 13 million young Americans went off to war

during 1941-45, while the remainder of the nation worked together for the common goal of victory.

The progression of time has only enhanced the relevance and significance of Air Power upon the

course of contemporary world events. To be able to learn from the past better prepares us for the challenges of the future.

The land of the free and the home of the brave.

From the National Anthem
of the United States of America

In times like these, it's worth remembering what our military fights for, and dies for. And acknowledge the huge debt owed them for defending America from those who would take freedom and justice from us. We hope you'll find a place for this decal, to honor your role in keeping America safe.

Marine Corps

U.S.S. President Hayes

The *U.S.S. President Hayes* AP-39 was laid down by the Newport News Shipbuilding and Dry Dock Co. on December 26, 1939 and launched October 4, 1940, Mrs. Cordell Hull sponsoring. The ship was turned over to the American President Lines in February, acquired by the U.S. Navy July 7, 1941, and commissioned December 15, 1941 with Comdr. F. W. Benson in command.

January 6, 1942 *President Hayes* sailed for San Diego via the Panama Canal. During February and March she evacuated civilians and dependents from Pearl Harbor. On July 1 she embarked for the Tonga Islands loaded with Marines. On the evening of August 7 *President Hayes* landed units of the 2nd Marine Regiment on Guadalcanal and spent the next several months shuttling supplies and reinforcements from Tonga, Noumea, and New Zealand. The ship was re-designated APA-20 effective February 1, 1943. *President Hayes* also participated in the Rendova landings at the end of June, shooting down 7 enemy planes. *President Hayes, President Adams, President Jackson,* and *Crescent City* were nicknamed the "Unholy Four."

The rest of the war *President Hayes* continued to move troops and supplies from island to island in the Pacific. At Manus, November 1944, she witnessed the explosion of the ammunition ship *Mount Hood* and dispatched fire and rescue parties to the stricken ships. At the end of the war *President Hayes* served with the "Magic Carpet," returning 1400 discharged soldiers to Los Angeles on each of two round trips. She earned 7 battles stars for World War II service.

President Hayes continued to serve with the Pacific Fleet until decommissioned June 30, 1949. She was assigned to the Pacific Reserve Fleet in 1950 and her name was struck from the Navy List and transferred to the Maritime Commission October 1, 1958

This is one of the four ships that took the 2nd Marine Division to Guadalcanal for the first offence against the Japanese. The Hayes was my ship and the first ship I had ever been on. It was a real experience!!

The four ships, named the "Unholy Four", made it through wartime missions and earned many combat ribbons.

"Guadalcanal – Tulagi"

"Night Action"   U.S. National Archives

This is what we saw on the night of Aug. 8th
1942 from Tulagi during the battle of "Savo
Island". It was a night I'll never forget!!

Heavey Cruiser
HMAS Canberra with
American Warships
Iron Bottom Bay,
Aug. 7, 1942

The Canberra was an Australian ship –
and sunk by the Japs the night of Aug. 8th, 1942.

"One of our light tank on the "Canal"

"A foxhole on Tulagi for defense"

Top - "Beautiful Mt. Cook."

Bottom - Chateau Tongarira
National Park.

Top - Natives of New Zealand, - the Maori,
    In a typical Maori village.

Bottom - Original inhabitants of
    New Zealand were the Maori's.

They were very nice people and I did have a
date with one of the young ladies, - - - - .

231

Top: Baker, Simon, Vollmer, Perry
Bottom: Glazer & Cable

† They didn't make it at "Tarawa"!

New Zealand

Don Stoffer
Corp. Joe Sobolewski

Jack Dubuque
Chuck Wysocki
Floyd Schouviller

My Buddies
of
D-2-18
2nd Marine Div.

New Zealand

1st Row-Frye, Jackman, Tomaszewski, Glasser.
2nd Row-Costa, Duffy, Kinder, Woods, Schouviller,
Robinson.

New Zealand

Carmen Yonke
Ang Copla
Harry Turner

Duane Strinden
Harry Turner

The "China Gal" Assists In Burials

D-2-18 landed on Red Beach 2. We were in Higgins boats. They ran aground about 600 yards off shore. We walked ashore from there. Since the island was only 4' above sea level, the Japs could not miss their targets. A lot of our dead Marines went out with the tide.

PFC Charles Wysocki, Jr.

What is left of D-2-18 assembles by the graves of their dead comrades.

After four days, we gathered up our dead men—at least the ones who had dog tags. There were 17 in all. Corporal Joe Sabal (or Sobol) was in charge of the burial.

A tank with the name "China Gal" buried the Japs and what Marines who did not have dog tags in shell holes. A friend of mine, from Columbus, Kansas, was one of the Marines killed and buried originally with the 17 Marines mentioned above. I brought his personal things to a meeting with his family. Later, they brought his body back home, and we buried him there.

Doyle Robinson

D-2-18, "We Buried Our Buddies"

A Sight I'll Never Forget

I read your comments about the battle of Tarawa and the mystery of the location where our dead were put to rest. I can not answer the question for sure. I can only tell you what I saw.

After the island was secured, our Gun Section, 75mm Pack Howitzers, was told to move out to the beach and wait to be loaded aboard a small boat for movement to a transport. As we left our position, we walked single file behind a service that was being conducted for our dead. I glanced to the right as we passed. Our dead were all lying in a shallow trench-like area, side by side. I did note that the body of the man on the extreme right was a Lieutenant Colonel. I also noted that our flag was flying on a make shift pole. I will never forget that day.

Ed Gamble

This was the main Japanese Command Center on Betio, - Red Beach 3. It was destroyed by putting fuel down the air intakes* and then ignighting it, - woosh, - fried Japs!

1st Lt. Alexander Bonneyman was awarded the, "Medal of Honor," posthumously, for his "Heroic Action", in taking this Command Center.

Staff. Sgt. William J. Bordelon was also awarded the, "Medal of Honor," posthumously, for his, "Heroic Action", for destroying several Jap pillboxes in the initial assault on Betio.

Both of these Marines were members of the 18th Marines.

"Rest In Peace"

The 6th Wave

I landed with the 6th wave. As has been said, we had so many dead on the beach we had to watch where we stepped, as we had lost so many men there. I was a corpsman, and I was busy with the wounded. But, when things settled down, there was a caterpillar digging a long trench. The bodies were laid in it like rows of corn and then covered up. That was why, in later years, when mothers would talk about bringing their sons' bodies home from Tarawa, I knew that it would be impossible.

It sounds pretty bad when we talk of it today, but the heat was so bad it had to be done. I also think that a lot of the men lost there went down with their landing craft, or drowned in the sea when their boats got caught on the coral reefs.

I served with D-1-2 on Guadalcanal. We hit on Florida Island August 7, 1942, before the First Marines hit Guadalcanal. We were told to take provisions to last for 72 hours, after which we would be relieved to regroup. That did not happen. We were relieved in February 1943.

I am proud that I was able to serve with the U.S. Marines.

Milton H. Searle

"Tarawa". Sitting on a Jap Tank.
Leo Pakula, ?, Floyd Schouviller, ?, Don Stoffer, ?, Joe Sobol, Chuck Wysocki, Jimmey May, Emory Ashurst

That's me way on top X of the tank, with some of my "buddies". This Jap tank was knocked out on the beach.

Amtracks, like the one I was in, headed for the Betio beach. I was in the 3rd wave and we made it to the beach OK.

Some of our Amtracks hung up on the seawall. There weren't enough Amtracks for this operation.

Knocked out Jap tank.

Not much
protection on
Betio,-just
the Jap made
fortifications.

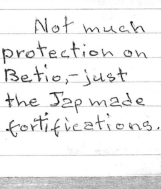

Amtrack hung up on
the seawall during the
assault on "Tarawa Atoll.

Marines charge in-
land from the seawall,-
under intense enemy fire.

"The Three Red Beaches"

Red Beach #1 - ★

    Landing - 9:13 A.M.

    Officer - Maj. John F. Schoettel

      Maj. Schoettel did not show up so Maj.
Michael P. Ryan took over and was
instrumental in clearing, "Green Beach",
so the 6th Marines could come in
and help finish and destroy the Japs.

      In my opinian Maj. Ryan should
have received the, "Medal of Honor", for
his, "Heroic Action", on Red Beach #1.

Red Beach #2 - ★

    Landing - 9:22 A.M.

    Officer - Colonel Herbert Amey

      Col. Amey was killed in the assault on
Red #2. Lt. Col. Walter I. Jordan, who was
an observer for the 4th Marine Div., took
over, — although unprepared he felt it
was his responsibility to carry on.

Red Beach #3 - ★

    Landing - 9:17 AM.

    Officer - Major Henry, (Jim), Crowe

      Only one of the three assault-battalion
Comanders reached the beach on D-Day.
Major Crowe with some difficulty did.

      I landed on Red #3 from an Amtrack in
the 3rd wave under heavy enemy fire!

239

Souvenirs of Tarawa.   Corp. Joe Sobolewski
That's me holding the flag.   (Sobol)

This P.O.W Camp was used by the U.S.
Military to hold Jap prisoners. When we
took over it was used as our base camp
in Hilo, Hawaii, - D.-2-18.

We came to Hilo after we took Tarawa
to rest, get replacements, and train for our
next objective, - Saipan and Tinian in the
Marianas, Islands.

After the Marianas Campaign I would
be sent back to the good ol' U.S.A..

"The Home Front"

Rosie
the
Riveter

Rosie the Riveter – who inspired thousands to contribute to the war effort and join the work force.

God
Bless
America

LIMITED EDITION

Wartime Worker
In this Lockheed factory in Burbank, California – as in thousands of factories across the nation – "Rosie the Riveter" filled in for the men who went off to fight in WWII.

Fortress Factory
Of the more than 12,000 B-17 Flying Fortresses built during WWII, 2,750 of them came from this converted Lockheed Vega factory in Burbank, California.

LIMITED EDITION

To all the "Defense Workers," who helped us, the military, to defeat the enemies of our Country and the World we say ---

 Thank You!

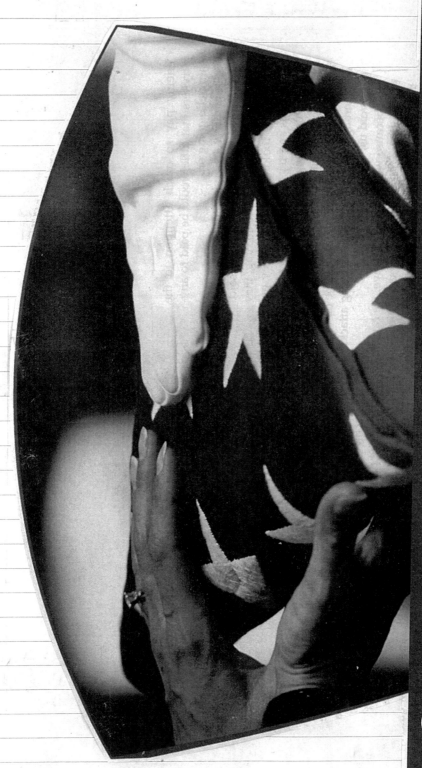

OUR COLORS SHOULD FLY... NOT FOLD

First Reunion of Co. "D":
Roy Hulse, June Sandow, Joe & Beth Sobol, Floyd Schouviller,
Duane & LaDonna Strinden, Frank Smith, Pat & Harry Turner,
Chuck & Bernice Wysocki, Phillip Shields, Gus Gustafson,
Solly and J.J. Woods.   Summer of 1947,-Minneapolis, Minn.

243

"A Visit With My Buddie, Floyd"

CHUCK & FLOYD

Floyd was my partner in the assault on the Island of Betio- Tarawa Atoll,- Nov. 20th, 1943

He asked me, if I remembered the bullet that missed my head, by half an inch. I do!

MOLLY & BERNICE

Floyd and Molly Schouviller lived in St. Paul, Minnesota.

Flag returned after 39 years

by Sandra Samples
Green Valley News

MEMENTOS - Charles Wysocki, of Green Valley, displays memorabilia from his days with the U.S. Marine Corps. His experience included the 76-hour battle for Tarawa Island in 1943 which claimed more than 5,000 Japanese and American lives. (News photo by Judy Jacobi, 12-28-82, G.V. News)

(News photo by Judy Jacobi, 12-28-82, G.V. News)

Nearly 40 years ago, a young Marine wandered restlessly over Tarawa Island in the Pacific awaiting orders and transportation to move onto the next battle.

Walking aimlessly around the island that covered less than a square mile, he came across one of the gun emplacements torn apart during the 76-hour battle that claimed more than 5,000 American and Japanese lives.

A Japanese flag caught his eye and he picked it up as a "souvenir" of his short stay on Tarawa, the only souvenir he would collect during his stay overseas.

"Being in the front line troops, you don't have time to pick up souvenirs like the second and third waves," the Mrine said, now 60-year-old Charles Wysocki of Green Valley.

He kept the flag he found Nov. 25, 1943, until about six or seven months ago when he came across it while cleaning and decided he had no reason for keeping it.

"I sent the flag to the Japanese embassy in Washington, D.C. hoping they could do something with it," Wysocki said.

The embassy wrote back to him in August thanking him and informed him the original owner had been identified and a relative found.

"The person is identified as the late Mr. Tatsuo Kawano, who was drafted from the suburb of Tokyo, served in the Japanese Navy and died on Tarawa Island Nov. 25, 1943," the letter said.

The letter described the flag as "a gift for a departing sailor from family members, relatives and friends, to wish his well-being," one that the soldiers carried on their persons throughout the fighting.

Kawano's brother, Yuichi, now living in Tokyo, was sent the flag by the embassy and Wysocki was commended for his action in returning the flag.

Thinking the matter was closed, Wysocki was surprised to answer the door the morning of Dec. 6 and find a registered letter from Yuichi Kawano (Kouno) - complete with photos and a check for $100.

The letter, typed in stilted English, told the story of a young Japanese sailor whose family and friends had sent him off with wishes of good luch written on a flag.

"After the war of 39 years (ago), to see my dead elder's article, I'm now shedding tears of gratitude," the letter said.

It went on to explain how the 39th anniversary of the defeat of the Japanese army Nov. 25, 1943, was observed with the erection of a memorial tombstone on Tawara Island.

The flag and its owner were reunited after 39 years to complete the memorial, as Wysocki learned that the Japanese believe the soul will not rest until all belongings are gathered together.

February 1983

245

July 15, 2004

Hi Chuck!

Ran out of correction tape for my electric typewriter so will give writing a chance.

Received your "lost memoirs" - guess you finally got all off your chest like I did. Great job, and something your family will cherish for posterity and may be your family will realize what we had to go through during WWII.

I don't know if a few of my family and relatives have taken time to read my book - guess all they care about is cars these days anyway. My only living sister (she is 84 and failing) did read the book and doesn't believe that her brother did or say some of the things I wrote about - and she was a sgt. in the WAC.

My grandson who lives just under a mile from me is so involved with a woman who is divorced and has two teen-age boys that he doesn't bother calling me - doesn't say much anyway - its been 3 months since we last talked (short phone call - was very busy he says) - thats why I tell people I have a dysfunctional family, good thing I can still take care of me.

So much for "Dear Abby" - Marines move forward! I'm mailing (2) pkgs - one with some articles (may have mailed some of the before), the other package is a Marine book I won at a chapter reunion - enjoy, and you don't have to return any of it.

— Off to the Post Office - - -

Semper Fi, and God Bless!!

Cobber - Mike Masters

246

"I Remember - 65 Years Later"

Yes, I remember many, many incidents of my World War Two experiences, that seem like they happened yesterday. -

I was 19 years old when I enlisted in the United States Marine Corps,– Feb. 5th, 1942,– I am now 84 and this is the year, 2007.

I remember the day I left home, Feb. 5th, after saying good-bye to my sisters and especially my Mother. As I was walking away from our house I turned around for one last look and I saw my Mother in the kitchen window waving good-bye to me,– I waved back,– not knowing it would be almost 4 years before I would see her again. Every time I think of that day I get a lump in my throat,– just as I did that day,– long ago.

A couple of days later I would arrive in San Diego, Cal., by train and taken to the Marine Corps. Recruit Depot by bus,– for, "Boot Camp." I remember the bus driving through the main gate and seeing a great big replica of the Marine Corps insignia above the entrance, to the base. This was to be the start of my Marine Corps experience,– a vivid remembrance that would last for the rest of my life.

The days of training, marching and the rifle range were all memorable,– but the day we were to board our first ship,– the U.S.S. President Hayes. I'll always remember because it was my first ship that I had ever seen and also the biggest. For weeks, I and other Marines, would learn the art of disembarking a troop ship, going over the rail and down the cargo nets and into the Higgins landing boats and then the long ride into the beaches for a sim- ulated assault. It also included getting sea-sick, which I handled very well!!

One day, in the afternoon, after another day of ship to shore practice landings we returned to our ships, - not knowing we had made our last practice landing, - we went about our usual chores of squaring away our gear, going to the evening chow, relaxing for a bit and then hitting the sack. The next morning we were awakened about 5:AM., and told to assemble topside for roll call. When we got topside to take a look around, - there was no sight of land anywhere. I had a very pec- uliar feeling and wondered, - "are we on our" - we would soon find out! After roll call we were told that we were on our way to the first assault against the Japanese Empire, - but we were not told where until later in the trip. When we were told it was a place we never heard of. It was in the Solomon Islands called, - Guadalcanal. The other islands in the group that had to be taken were, - Tulagi, the one I landed on, Gavutu, Florida, and Tanambogo. I'll never forget the news we got that morning, - we were to meet the enemy!

The Second Marine Division had four ships that were used all during our ship to shore train- ing and now would be taking us to our first engagement against the Japs. The ships were the, U.S.S. President Hayes, - my ship, Pres. Adams, Pres. Jackson and the Crecent City. They were nicknamed the, "Unholy Four", and as far as

I know they survived the war.

While on these ships and on our way to the, "Canal", we ran into a three day storm! Talk about scary times, - this was one time I thought we weren't going to make it! you have to remember this was my first time aboard a sea going ship and my first time to experience a storm at sea. Being on a ship that is tossed around like a toy is not for the weak of heart. One minute you'd be on top of a wave, - the next minute you'd be in the hollow of a wave with a wall of ugly looking water all around you! Scared, - you bet I was and to this day I can see that wall of water, - scary! Yes, I remember.

The next indelible memory came on the second night of our landing on Tulagi. It happened around midnight, - unexpected! The Jap Navy had come down the, "slot", undetected and opened up with a barrage that shook the whole island. Every time they fired their guns the night would light up like daylight and you could hear the rumble of the shells coming in, - but where they would land and explode was everyones guess. I know I prayed they would miss me! I dove into the closest foxhole, - they were never deep enough, - and I shivered, sweat and prayed some more! Believe it or not but it was over 100 degrees plus and I was as cold as I would be in a Wisconsin winter. The explosions were tremendous, earth shaking, deafening with hot shrapnel flying all over the place. The explosions would shake your whole body and the concussions would rattle your teeth!! I was a hell of a, "Welcome", to the Pacific Theater of War! It was a very, very harrowing experience which we would endure several more times during the battle for the, "Canal". The fear and the anxiety of those days will always be with me.

The next island we would take was one of beauty, wonderful and friendly people, plus a lot of lonely women. It was a place, that none of us would never forget. It was a place we would like to go back to, — as some of our Marines did. I know I thought about it many times, — but it would never happen. I'll always have the memories of the wonderful Country of, — New Zealand, — the Country we all fell in love with.

The most penetrating event that has so deeply embedded itself in my memory would take place on Nov. 20th, 1943, — the assault on Tarawa Atoll in the Gilbert Islands. The effects of that bloody, "76 Hour Battle", would last for the rest of my life, — they just won't go away.

The first three waves of the assault would be made in, "Amtracks", — tracked vehicles that could cross the Coral Reef very easily, — the, "Higgins Boat", could not. We could have used a lot more of the "Amtracks". The, "Higgins Boats", coxswains would have to drop their Marines off in the water, — 300 to 500 yards from the, "beachead", — it was a slaughter, — but the Marines never stopped trying to get to the beach. What kept these Marines driving forward under the most devastating wall of enemy firepower!! They were the real heroes, they gave their lives so others would live to continue the assault on "Betio", to it's conclusion, — it would be a very costly assault!!

I was in the third wave, — in an "Amtrack", and we made it to the beach O.K. We went over the side, like we were taught, — didn't even get my feet wet, — and raced to the sea-wall, — the only protection there was; "Thank God" for that sea-wall!! The carnage that greeted me was devestating, — dead and wounded were all over the beach, — wrecked Amtracks and Tanks were hung up on the sea-wall, — some burning others completly destroyed. The noise was unbelievable, — the smell of gun powder, smoke & fuel was devastating and it would get worse when the bodies of the dead would start to decompose. The vapors would choke you and burn your eyes, — you would have to be there to understand what I am trying to tell you!!

Seconds after I reached the the seawall I had a vision of my Mother, for only a second or two, — I knew then that I was going to make it.

Just as I moved to another position, at the sea-wall, I heard a terrific "BANG", — a bullet had hit a fraction of an inch above my head into the sea-wall, — that one I heard! I'll remember that sound forever! The Nips were firing at us from a partialy sunken Jap ship in the harbor. That ship was

was taken care of by our Navy and Marine dive bombers. I, with my partner, Floyd, were part of the, "Beach Party",- so when we could we did whatever we could for the wounded. It wasn't until late afternoon of the second day that we were able, with help, to move them to an, Aid Station,- I hope they all made it!!

After the battle we all looked like a bunch of, "Zombies",- eyes starring into no place,- lips parched and cracked,- clothing so dirty and filthy that they could stand up by themselves,- and we didn't smell to good.

I tried eating some, "C-Rations", but it wouldn't stay down,- nothing would, not even water. It would be about eight days before I could eat again and during that time I lost, 30 pounds,- with the help of Navy, "Chow", I did regain them.

Very vividly I remember and will for all the days of my life the burying of our, "Buddies", on Betio. I know that I cried as we all did,- it was hard to say,- "Good-Bye!!" May they rest in, Peace".

I have, "Thanked God", every day of my life for watching over me and protecting me all the days of my life through war and peace. Yes, I'll remember the battle for Tarawa Atoll, my buddies, the horror of war,- that will result in my having nightmares, dreams and drinking. Certain smells and noises will trigger my memory of my wartime experiences to this day - July 2007,- and the days to come. Tarawa,- we were happy to leave it!

If ever we wanted to leave a place it was, – "Tarawa"; but it would never be forgotten!

After leaving Tarawa we went to the Hawaiian Islands, – what a beautiful place to rest and regroup. While there we had some good times, but what I remember most is the young lady I met, she was about 13 or 14 and very pretty. She was a native Hawaiian and lived near the town of Hilo. Sorry, but I don't remember her name, – she invited me to come to her home, which I accepted, and met her parents, – wonderful people, who invited me to have dinner with them, – it was great. During the evening I spotted a pair of skies behind a partialy open door and that got me, – "where would you go skiing in Hawaii," – I asked. I was taken to the door and they pointed to the top of a mountain, – guess what, – there was snow at the top. We had a good laugh; but I learned, – there is skiing in Hawaii! I met some wonderful people and I will remember.

The next date in my book of memories would occur on June 20th, 1944. About 3 or 4 days after the assault on Saipan, in the Marianas Islands we were working our way inland going through a wooded area loaded with drums of fuel. All of a sudden the Japs opened up with an artillery barrage, – we scattered for cover, – I dove for the cover of a tree that was partially hollowed out, – I was going to try and get in the hollow, – but someone had already gotten there before

me,– a dead Jap and I didn't bother to move
him! While I was diving for cover a shell exploded
and some of the shrapnel tore into both of my
arms,–it stung a bit and I was bleeding pretty
good. A Corpman, (medic), was called and he
patched me up while we were still under fire.
I was taken to a rear area for a couple of days
rest and then returned to my outfit. The wound
turned out not to be serious and healed up O.K,–
except to this day there are little slivers of
shrapnel floating around in the elbow area and
every once in awhile they'll hit a nerve and it will
hurt until they work loose and move on till the
next time. It is a reminder for me.
          The next stop would still be in the Marianas,
an island just a couple of miles from Saipan
called Tinian. We would assault Tinian on July
26th, 1944 and the one memory I have happens
the first couple of hours of the landing. We
went in on the left side of the "beachead", and
we had to go through a very rugged area of
coral and rock. This area,–prior to our landing,
was bombed and liquid fire dropped. As we
advanced through this area a most horrible
sight greeted us,–bodies of many Japs burned
to a crisp and still smoldering. It was gruesome
and the stench made your eyes and nose burn.
There wasn't much to identify them,–maybe a
buckle or uniform button or what was left of
a rifle. We got out of there as fast as we could,–
but I'll always remember that horrible destruction of a human being,–but that's war!!

My next memory is one I don't mind
having and remembering. After returning to
Saipan from Tinian we set up camp to await
our next move. It was a couple of days after
we moved in that at a morning roll-call was
held a bunch of names were called, mine
was one of them. We were told to step forward
as our names were called, it was then announced, "the names of those called will prepare
to leave Saipan, your being sent Stateside!!"
WOW, I almost had a heart attack!! We hugged
each other in joy at the news, but we felt
sorry for the ones who would not be leaving,
we wished them, "good luck", and hoped they
would be going home soon. Late that afternoon
we boarded a troop transport and headed for
the good ol U.S.A.. Sorry, but I don't remember
the day or date, many times the day or time
didn't matter, it was daytime or nightime
that mattered.
    There have been many events, besides
those I have already mentioned, that have
clogged my memory all these years, so I'll
just mention them briefly starting in "Boot
Camp." To get into the Marine Corps I had to
have a Hernia repaired and while in "Boot
Camp", on the first extended field exercise,
which included, hitting the deck, I experienced a sharp pain in the incision area, it
put a scare in me, but I didn't report it although I did experience some occasional jolts.
    On Tulagi the days I suffered with, -

Malaria, Dysentery, Dingue Fever and Jungle Rot, - will not go away!

The day the Army M.P.'s raided Tulagi looking for, "Stills", - they did find a bunch but not ours.

The night on Tulagi when Mike, whose tent was above a gravel pit, - stepped out of his tent to release himself, - after having a few drinks earlier, - took one step to far, - he tumbled down the side of the pit to the bottom, - got up, climbed back up to his tent, went to sleep and didn't remember a thing in the morning.

Shortly after landing on Tulagi I and another Marine were sent to get some ammo, - we were on, "ALERT," at that time anticipating a Jap counter attack. It was early evening when we left and night when we were returning to our positions when we were stopped at a check-point and asked for the password, - what password, - we were never informed of one, - so for about an hour we were held at bay until word got to one of our Officers of our problem at the check-point. The password was given to us, "banana", by the Officer and we gave it to the guard who gave us the O.K. to proceed to our positions. The Jap attack that we expected never happened.

On our visit to New Zealand, (Wellington), where I, - at age 20, had my first legitimate date, (affair), with a female. I didn't know much about females and what to do, - but I sure learned in a hurry!

I'll always remember when we arrived in

the U.S., docking at Treasure Island, Calif..
We disembarked from the ship and were standing
around waiting for our next order when this
man approached us and asked us about his son,
Tony Lazzari, who was killed on Betio. We
told him he died charging up the beach, - cussing
the Japs as he was cut down by a burst of
machine gun fire from a Jap fortification.
I was a very difficult thing to do, - he "Thanked"
us with tears in his eyes! Having to tell someone how their son was killed was one of the
hardest things I have ever had to do. I don't
know how he knew we were coming in on that
ship, - but he did!

There are so many memories of horror,
sadness, good times, happiness, comaradie and
prayers that have been said over and over.

The most heart warming and loving
reunion was yet to be experienced. It happened Sept., 1944 while I was in the Philadelphia
Navy Hospital being treated for "Combat Fatigue" and other related conditions. While in
the Hospital my Mother wrote a letter to the
Hospital Administrator, unknown to me, asking
if I could go home for a family reunion.
The family had not been together since 1938
when my brother, "Bob's" National Guard
Unit, - 121st Field Artillery, 32nd (Red Arrow), Div.,
was called up to active duty. One day, after
receiving the letter a Doctor came to my ward
and told me about my Mother's request, - I
was quite surprised! A long discussion

followed about my condition, my ability to travel, how long I would be able to be gone and what I would have to do while traveling and while I was at home. I was finally given a total of 10 days, - if I remember correctly, - and I had to borrow money from the Red Cross because I hadn't been paid up to that time. I did finally get home and my brother had gotten home a couple of days before I did. When I walked into the living room of our home everyone was there; but I could only see my, "Mom", at that moment, - I hugged her and hugged her with tears in my eyes, - I was so happy to see her again after all these years, - that had seamed like an eternity. I then gave my sisters and brother hugs and especially welcomed my brother, "Bob", home. Bob served in the Pacific, as I did, at New Guinea, and the Phillipine Islands. When Dad got home it was another session of, "Welcome Home", and pats on the back, - he wanted to know everything, - inbetween, "shots of whisky." In the next few days there was a lot of talk, a lot of questions and my, "Dad", pulled out a pile of newspaper clippings of the, "War", and he told me he knew where I was all the time, - I was surprised at how accurate he was! When it came time leave, - it was a very sad day, but I had to get back to the Hospital. It was great seeing the family again and then I knew what we were fighting for!!!

After returning to the Hospital, - worn and tired, - which didn't make the Doctors happy,

259

I would resume my treatments and programs which included a "speech making" tour of the State of Pennsylvania for the Salvation Army which was very successful. Then I was assigned to work in a "Battery Factory", whose employees were mostly females. I didn't last very long on that job! Not with all those sex starved females! I also made a "Radio Broadcast" on a Philadelphia Radio Station called "A Salute to America" - Very proud of that one!

It was late Feb. 1945 when my Doctor came to see me to tell me I was going to be sent home; but I didn't want to go home I wanted to stay in the Corps and make a "Military Career" for myself - the Doctor said "fine, but your career just ended - your going home" - and I did. I would be discharged on March 17th, 1945 from the Philadelphia Navy Yard.

After being discharged from the Corps another chapter in my life would begin. My medical records, (copies), would be sent to the V.A. Hospital at Wood, Wisc. - 1945 and I will be cared for through July, 2007 and plus the remaining hours, days, months or years of my life, - I am 84 this date, - July 13th, 2007. The V.A. Medical Staff have cared for me all these years and they have been wonderful, - I have nothing but praise for them

I met my wife in 1946, - on a blind date, - got married on Feb. 15th, 1947. God was good to me, - and because of her, - I am here today! She stood by me through all these many years, -

I couldn't forget the War! I took to heavy drinking, - it didn't help, - I would disappear once in a while for a day or two, - I'd have nightmares, dreams and everything was reminding me of the horrors I'd been through. One night I was chocking my wife, - who I thought was a Jap, - she was able to wake me up and I neve felt so bad in my life. Although I would have these problems it would not interfere with us having a family of three wonderful children, - Patricia Ann, Paul Douglas and David Charles. In 1976 we would lose David in an auto accident, - he was 19, - we miss him very much. Pat and Paul would become very good teachers, - Pat would marry a wonderful man, - Jeff Jinkins, and give us 3 beautiful grandchildren, - Elizabeth, Ryan and Michael. We love them all.

When I enlisted in the Marine Corps I didn't drink alcaholic beverages or smoke cigaretts, - I was 19, - but when I came home I was drinking and smoking over 3 packs a day. One day the Doctors at the V.A. told me they would not be responsiple for me if I didn't quit drinking and smoking, - the warning was enough, - I quit both, - cold turkey and have not touched either for over 40 years. I'm one very happy person that I was able to quit both when I did, - you can to, - if you want to!

To this day I still have health problems, - some are war related and others as a result of growing old, - but I am still under the care of the V.A. Doctors in Tucson. I have the most

wonderful wife and family who have understood my problems and helped me through the
bad times. This year, 2007, we celebrated
our 60th, Wedding Anniversary with our family
and friends. I thank the, "Lord", everyday
for all of His blessings and ask Him to watch
over us all the days of our lives.
        Abraham Lincoln said of the United States:
"To care for him who shall have borne the battle
and for his widow and his orphan . . . "

I have been cared for,- and I remember!!

"A day does not go by that I don't think of
        my, "Buddies".

I AM THE FLAG OF THE UNITED STATES OF AMERICA

My name is Old Glory. I fly atop the world's tallest buildings. I stand watch in America's halls of justice. I fly majestically over institutions of learning. I stand guard with power in the world.

Look up and see me. I stand for peace, honor, truth and justice. I stand for freedom. I am confident. I am arrogant. I am proud. When I am flown with my fellow banners, my head is a little higher, my colors a little truer. I bow to no one!

I am recognized all over the world. I am worshiped – I am saluted. I am loved – I am revered. I am respected – and I am feared.

I have fought in every battle of every war for more than 200 years. I was flown at Valley Forge, Gettysburg, Shiloh and Appomatox. I was there at San Juan Hill, the trenches of France, in the Argonne Forest, Anzio, Rome and the beaches of Normandy. Guam, Okinawa, Korea and KheSan, Saigon, Vietnam know me; I was there.

I led my troops, I was dirty, battle worn and tired, but my soldiers cheered me, and I was proud. I have been burned, torn and trampled on the streets of countries I have helped set free. It does not hurt, for I am invincible.

I have been soiled upon, burned torn and trampled in the streets of my country. And when it's done by those whom I've served in battle – it hurts. But I shall overcome – for I am strong. I have slipped the bonds of Earth and stood watch over the uncharted frontiers of space from my vantage point on the Moon. I have borne silent witness to all of America's finest hours. But my finest hours are yet to come.

When I am torn into strips and used as bandages for my wounded comrades on the battlefield; when I am flown at half-mast to honor my soldier; or when I lie in the trembling arms of a grieving parent at the grave of a fallen son or daughter: I am proud.

"A dramatic and uplifting way to honor the United States flag."

The flag-folding ceremony represents the same religious principles on which our country was founded.

The portion of the flag denoting honor is the canton of blue containing the stars representing the states our veterans served in uniform.

The canton field of blue dresses from left to right and is inverted when draped as a pall on a casket of a veteran who has served our country in uniform.

In the Armed Forces of the United States, at the ceremony of retreat the flag is lowered, folded in a triangle fold and kept under watch throughout the night as a tribute to our nation's honored dead.

The next morning it is brought out and, at the ceremony of reveille, run aloft as a symbol of our belief in the resurrection of the body.

"Recruiting and War Bond Posters"

U.S. Navy Recruiting Poster

McClelland Barclay. Painted in 1942 by one of the most famous illustrators of the day, the original oil painting used for this recruiting poster now resides in the U.S. Navy art collection.

Now All Together

C.C. Beall. Based on Joe Rosenthal's famous photograph of the flag raising on Iwo Jima, this poster was created in 1945 for the 7th War Loan bond drive, which raised over $26 billion in just six weeks.

All Service Women's World War II Recruitment Poster

This reproduction of a recruitment poster seeking women for all service branches in World War II.

Heritage

Lou Nolan. This reproduction of a U.S. Navy recruiting poster shows the history and longevity of the Navy with a proud young petty officer showing a little boy – perhaps a sailor of the future – "Old Ironsides," the USS Constitution.

Buy War Bonds

N.C. Wyeth. Based on an original poster created in 1942 as part of a U.S. government effort to encourage Americans to provide financial support for the war effort,

Keep Him Flying! Buy War Bonds

Georges Schreiber. Created in 1942 as part of the home front war effort, this poster was adopted for official use throughout the country.

Armed Services Recruiting Trucks

A: U.S. Army.
B: U.S. Marine Corps.

Replicating 1941 Chevrolet pick-ups used by U.S. armed services for recruiting during World War II,

U.S. Navy Recruiting Poster

McClelland Barclay. Painted in 1942 by one of the most famous illustrators of the day, the original oil painting used for this recruiting poster now resides in the U.S. Navy art collection.

Follow the Flag
Based on the poster painted by James Henry Daugherty in 1917 to aid U.S. Navy recruiting efforts.

Ready – Join U.S. Marines Metal Sign

Based on the poster – featuring a square-jawed sergeant in his famous Marine Blue Dress uniform – painted by Haddon Sundblom to aid U.S. Marine Corps recruiting efforts during World War II,

NEW!

Join – U.S. Army Air Corps

NEW!

Recruiting posters such as this were instrumental in increasing the size of the U.S. Army Air Corps from 51,000 airmen in 1940 to more than 152,000 in 1941.

Coming Right Up!
Based on the famous poster painted by James Montgomery Flagg to aid U.S. Army Air Force recruiting efforts during World War II....

LIMITED EDITION

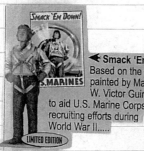

Smack 'Em Down!
Based on the poster painted by Maj. W. Victor Guinness to aid U.S. Marine Corps recruiting efforts during World War II.....

LIMITED EDITION

"Memorable Events"

PT-109
Commanded by John F. Kennedy, PT-109 – one of the many sleek and deadly motor torpedo boats serving in the Pacific – was sliced in half by the Japanese destroyer Amagiri in the Solomon Islands on August 2, 1943, but due to the heroic efforts of her commander, all but two crew members survived.

The Magnificent Fight ▶
John Shaw. Against terrible odds in late 1941, U.S. Marines, aided by their few remaining F4F Wildcats, defended Wake Island on land and in the air for more than two weeks, inspiring a nation and establishing fame for the U.S. Marine Corps.

Avengers of the Philippines ▶
John Shaw. Flying his TBM Avenger, Lt. (JG) George H.W. Bush leads a formation of Avengers and Hellcats from Air Group 51 back to the USS San Jacinto after bombing enemy ships in Manila Bay on November 14, 1944.

The Turning Point
Midway, June 1942
R.G. Smith. The Japanese carriers Akagi, Kaga, and Soryu are devastated during the Battle of Midway in a defeat from which the Japanese navy will never fully recover.

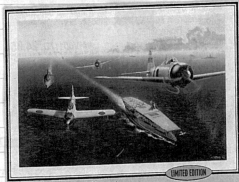

Awakening the Giant
C.S. Bailey. Japanese Zeros from the Imperial Japanese Navy's flagship carrier Akagi proceed to the opening strike at Pearl Harbor, December 7, 1941.

The Black Sheep Squadron

This World War II photograph captures the members of VMF-214 during a respite between missions when, as a publicity stunt, they were given a St. Louis Cardinals baseball cap for every Japanese plane shot down.

Yamamoto's Last Flight

Stan Stokes. In 1943, this squadron of P-38s made an incredible long-distance flight to intercept Admiral Yamamoto, the mastermind of the attack on Pearl Harbor.

LIMITED EDITION

P-38 Lightning

P-38 Lightning

Features the famous Pudgy V markings of Maj. Thomas McGuire, the number two U.S. ace of World War II who achieved 38 kills while flying with the 475th Fighter Group in the Pacific theater.

The Doolittle Raiders

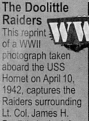

This reprint of a WWII photograph taken aboard the USS Hornet on April 10, 1942, captures the Raiders surrounding Lt. Col. James H. Doolittle in the left front of the group just eight days before their mission.

LIMITED EDITION

Yamato's Final Voyage

Tom Freeman. In April, 1945, the Japanese battleship Yamato, surrounded by the rest of her Task Force II, heads south toward Okinawa on the mission from which she will never return.

WWII

LIMITED EDITION

Valor in the Pacific

Robert Taylor. B-29 Superfortresses of the 499th Bomb Group, 20th Air Force, return home after a daylight raid on Tokyo.

Fortress Under Attack

Robert Taylor. 43rd Bomb Group B-17s fend off Japanese fighters high over the Pacific.

WWII

Wildcat Fury

David Gray. Flying his F4F Wildcat, 1st Lt. James E. Swett of VMF-221 roars past one of the seven D3A2 Val bombers – which were en route to attack Tulagi Harbor – he shot down on his first combat mission on April 7, 1943.

Trial by Fire

Tom Freeman. Despite being struck by four bombs and five kamikazes off the coast of Okinawa on April 16, 1945, the Sumner-class destroyer USS Laffey (DD-724) refused to die, and is still afloat as a museum ship in South Carolina.

LIMITED EDITION

LIMITED EDITION

First to Fire

Don Stivers. On December 8, 1941, at Clark Field in the Philippines, the 200th Coast Artillery found itself at war. The Japanese would later march them off to the death camps, but always in their minds they would know that they were the first to fire on the enemy.

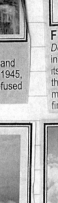

LIMITED EDITION

Marianas Turkey Shoot

Roy Grinnell. Lt. Alexander Vraciu – in a period of only eight minutes – splashes six Japanese "Judy" dive bombers during the air battle that became known as The Marianas Turkey Shoot.

NEW

World War II Naval Fighters

The U.S Navy's three legendary World War II carrier-borne fighters – the F4U Corsair, the F6F Hellcat and the F4F Wildcat – fly in magnificent formation

B-17 "Memphis Belle" Die Cast Model

Memphis Belle of the 91st Bomb Group, piloted by Capt. Robert K. Morgan and noteworthy for surviving 25 missions.

Off to the Turkey Shoot

WWII

Stan Stokes. F6F Hellcat pilot and Medal of Honor recipient Capt. David McCampbell departs the USS Essex during the Marianas Turkey Shoot.

LIMITED EDITION

Dick Bong
America's Ace of Aces

Bong & O'Conner. Through the firsthand accounts of those who knew him best, you'll examine Maj. Richard Bong's fascinating life and military career, from his childhood to his World War II exploits – he became America's all-time leading ace with 40 victories in the Pacific theater – and his ill-fated final flight as a test pilot flying a P-80 Shooting Star in 1945.

"Famous Flyers"

A Pair of Famous Nines

Stan Stokes. Ted Williams, the Hall of Fame baseball player, was recalled to active duty for the Korean conflict and assigned to an F9F Panther jet. On this mission, Williams' Panther was hit, causing an engine fire. Rather than bailing out, he made a crash landing at over 200 mph with no landing gear, escaping just as the plane burst into flames.

F9F PANTHER

Ted Williams at War

Nowlin. Ted Williams was the only Hall of Fame ballplayer who saw military service in two wars – he was a flight instructor with the U.S. Marine Corps in World War II and he flew thirty-nine combat missions in the Korean War. This definitive account of Williams' military service, based on extensive interviews and detailed examinations of his military records, covers it all – including the time he was shot down and barely escaped with his life.

Charles Lindbergh Newspaper

This reproduction of the *Brooklyn Daily Eagle* from May 22, 1927, takes you back to the frenzied day when Charles Lindbergh became the first person to fly solo across the Atlantic Ocean. You'll read contemporaneous accounts of the throngs who met him in France, comments from President Coolidge, of Clarence Chamberlin's dashed hopes to be first, and more. And, as if that weren't enough, this newspaper is also filled with other stories of the day – even original advertisements!

Spirit of St. Louis

Amelia Earhart Newspaper

This reproduction of the *Chicago Herald and Examiner* from July 5, 1937, takes you back to the fateful time when Amelia Earhart was lost during her round-the-world flight attempt and searchers were rushing to the scene. And, as if the fascinating contemporaneous account were not enough, this newspaper is also filled with other stories of the day – even original advertisements – that make reading it an experience like few others.

Amelia Earhart

Amelia Earhart – the first woman to fly solo across the Atlantic Ocean and the first civilian to receive the Distinguished Flying Cross –

Spirit of St. Louis

Ted Williams. Charles Lindbergh's Ryan NYP – the Spirit of St. Louis – battles the elements just above wave top, its J-5 Whirlwind power plant keeping up the drumbeat that got the plane and its pilot from New York to Paris.

269

"Headlines and Signs"

D-Day Newspaper
This reproduction of the *Cincinnati Times-Star* from June 6, 1944, takes you back to the day when the Allies hit the beaches to begin their nearly year-long fight to Berlin. You'll see the first photograph to be transmitted by Signal Corps radio from England to Washington and, as if the fascinating contemporaneous accounts were not enough, you'll also see other stories of the day – even original radio broadcast schedules

December 8, 1941 Newspaper
This reproduction of *The Baltimore News-Post* from December 8, 1941, takes you back to the day after Japan attacked Pearl Harbor and the Philippines – the day when the war that Adolf Hitler started by invading Poland became a worldwide conflict. And, as if the fascinating contemporaneous accounts were not enough, this newspaper is also filled with other stories of the day – even original advertisements and cartoons.

Berlin Cold War Metal Sign
The crossing point between East and West Berlin during the Cold War was marked with warning signs that informed people of the approaching border.

V-E Day Newspaper
This reproduction of the *Norfolk Ledger-Dispatch* from May 7, 1945, takes you back to that glorious day when Germany surrendered unconditionally. You'll see a photograph of German generals surrendering to Field Marshall Montgomery, enjoy a special section on Vice Admiral Mitscher leading the ongoing charge in the Pacific, and even see a page on "Battle Trophies" brought home by victorious Americans. And, as if the fascinating contemporaneous accounts were not enough, you'll also see many other stories of the day – even classified ads and comics.

Hughes H-4 Hercules "The Spruce Goose"
This shot of the HFB taxiing in Long Beach Harbor was taken by Arthur Forest in 1947.

Howard Hughes

Air Raid Shelter Metal Sign
A replica of the World War II signs that directed people to take cover from enemy air raids

The Stonewall Brigade
Larry Selman. The 29th Division's 116th Regiment, officially nicknamed the "Stonewall Brigade," landed on Omaha Beach on June 6, 1944, spearheading the Allied invasion of Nazi-occupied France.

Rangers At the Point
Larry Selman. Soaked, bloodied and exhausted, Army Rangers breach the German defenses at Pointe du Hoc in search of five 155mm cannons that threaten the invasion beaches. 1st Sgt. Leonard Lomell, who is seen here returning fire, later found and disabled the cannons, an action for which he was awarded the Distinguished Service Cross.

Fury of Assault
The Blitz of London
Robert Taylor. During the London Blitz of December, 1941, Heinkel He 111 bombers from KG 55 are engaged by a lone Royal Air Force Hurricane night-fighter from 85 Squadron.

The Struggle Begins
Pete Brothers
Roy Grinnell. Flying his Hurricane through the flak defenses of Dover Harbor, Pete Brothers downs a German Me 109 of JG 51 to earn his first victory of the Battle of Britain.

Rommel
The Desert Fox
James Dietz. At the forward edge of a relentless advance, Field Marshal Erwin Rommel surveys the desert before him, seeking yet another opportunity to defeat a beleaguered opponent with ingenuity, audacity and the striking power of the vaunted Afrika Korps.

Arnhem Drop
Simon Smith. Presenting the largest airborne operation in history, when more than 20,000 men were dropped into Holland on September 17, 1944.

271

Hang Tough, Bastogne 1944

John Shaw. On December 24, 1944, north of Bastogne, Belgium, Easy Company, 506ᵗʰ P.I.R., 101ˢᵗ Airborne, "hang tough" and hold their line, ultimately helping to turn the tide in the Battle of the Bulge.

LIMITED EDITION

Bill Mauldin's Army

Greatest World War II Cartoons

Mauldin. Mauldin's "Willie and Joe" characters suffered through World War II like a million other GIs and kept us smiling through the pain. Follow them through boot camp, to North Africa, Europe, and finally home. This was the "classic" story of G.I. Joe in World War II. *"Great stuff"*

Up Front

Mauldin. This is a classic portrait in text and cartoon of the American combat soldier in Europe during World War II. Willie and Joe epitomize the dogfaces who slopped thru the mud, fought in the rain and cold... all with gallows humor. So insightful, you are there with them.

CELEBRATING VICTORY

U.S. soldiers in Germany hold up news of the Nazis' surrender in May 1945, *above*, while at the same time, euphoria over victory in Europe breaks out in Times Square in New York City, *left*.

The S.S. Jeremiah O'Brien, known as "The Lucky O'Brien," is one of two fully-restored operating survivors of the 2,710 World War II Liberty Ships.

WWII Liberty Ship

"Couldn't do with out"

Arctic Encounter ➤

Robert Bailey. Flying a Ju 88, Oberst. Hajo Herrmann leads his Luftwaffe combat group, KG 30, into attack against the Allied ships of convoy PQ-17 on July 5, 1942, in the high arctic. Twenty-three of the 34 PQ-17 vessels were sunk in the Allies' worst arctic defeat of World War II.

LIMITED EDITION

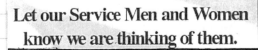

Let our Service Men and Women know we are thinking of them.

"War Mongers"

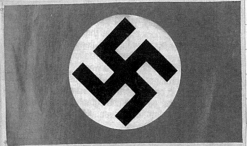

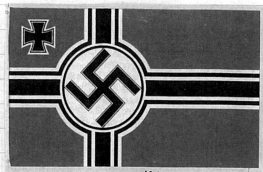

German WWII Party and State Flag
The Nazi Party formally adopted the swastika, or Hakenkreuz, in 1920 and used it on the party's flag, badge and armband.

Kriegsmarine Flag
A replica of the flag used by the German Navy during the Second World War,

German SS Runes Flag ▶
The SS Sig Runes design was created in 1931 when Walter Heck, a Sturmfuhrer in the SS, drew two Sig Runes side by side and noticed the similarity to the initials of the SS. For 2½ Reichsmarks, Heck sold the rights to the SS and it quickly became one of the most commonly used forms of SS unit insignia.

| | ITALIAN

Hitler and Mussolini Photograph
Two of the most notorious dictators of the 20th century together claimed the lives of more than 30 million people – all the while achieving nothing for their respective countries except destruction and chaos. This photograph captures Hitler and Mussolini in Munich, Germany, in 1940.

When? It's Up to You!
This replica of a Canadian poster created during WWII to raise money through the sale of war bonds

God Bless America

| | RUMANIAN

God is With Us! Sign
Replicating the Nazi propaganda slogan that was even worn on the belt buckles of German army soldiers during WWII.

War Bonds Sign
Replicating an advertisement used to raise funds through the sale of war bonds,

"They Belived"

Bedtime Stories
Replicating vintage art from the cover of *Bedtime Stories*, a pulp magazine popular with American soldiers in the 1930s,

Canvas Print!

Come and Get It
Gil Elvgren. Painted in 1959, this cowgirl is reminiscent of the cheesecake pin-ups that inspired American pilots' World War II aircraft nose art.

LIMITED EDITION

Alberto Vargas
Works From the Max Vargas Collection
Austin. This, the first book on the works of Vargas in more than a decade, is also the first to include a generous selection of his vivid original drawings

ALBERTO VARGAS

A Tasty Treat
Gil Elvgren. Painted in 1965 by the great Gil Elvgren, this is the style of pin-up that provided American pilots of World War II and beyond with the inspiration for much of their aircraft nose art.

LIMITED EDITION

Army Air Force Pin-Up Girl
Saluting the troops of the Army Air Force, this pin-up girl was an inspiration to the servicemen of World War II.

LIMITED EDITION

Pin Me Up!
This wall calendar commemorates one of the most celebrated of all modern American icons – the illustrated pin-up girl. In these beautifully printed pages, you get 13 full-color illustrations from classic artists Gil Elvgren, Earl Moran and Zöe Mozert, each of which recalls the golden age of pin-up mania in all its provocative glory.

PIN ME up!

Pin-ups were and still are very popular with the troops around the world and will be for a long time. Great moral builder!

"World War One"

SPAD XIII

Replicating the legendary bi-plane of Eddie Rickenbacker, the American hero who shot down 26 enemy aircraft flying for the "Hat in the Ring" Squadron.

LIMITED EDITION

The Black Rattlers
Don Stivers. Because it was against the law for white and black troops to serve together, the African-American men of the 369th Infantry Regiment were given a choice: return home or be reassigned to the French army. They chose the latter, and became the first regiment in U.S. history to serve with a foreign army. This print shows the 369th, a.k.a. the Harlem Hell Fighters, in Sechault, France, on September 29, 1917.

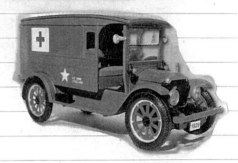

NEW

LIMITED EDITION

Mark of Distinction
Russell Smith. With his squadron's lion cub mascot, "Whiskey," resting in the shade of a Nieuport fighter, William Thaw – a founding member of World War I's famed Lafayette Escadrille – presents the new Indian Head squadron insignia to Capitaine Georges Thenault.

THEY KEPT THE SEA LANES OPEN

INVEST IN THE VICTORY LIBERTY LOAN

Invest in the Victory Liberty Loan
They Kept the Sea Lanes Open
Leon Shafer. Designed to instill patriotism, confidence and a positive outlook, posters were used extensively during WWI to assist the military and persuade all Americans to help with the war effort.

Army Ambulance.

World War One was supposed to end all "Wars," – but it seems that Hitler and his cohorts didn't get the word. They paid the price!

Fly Our Flag
With Pride!

" Why We Fight "

We fight for the love of our country and its Constitution that guarantees us our, Rights, Freedom and the Pursuit of Happiness,

We fight for our loved ones, family and friends,

We fight for every one of you and all, Freedom loving people,

We fight for, "Peace".

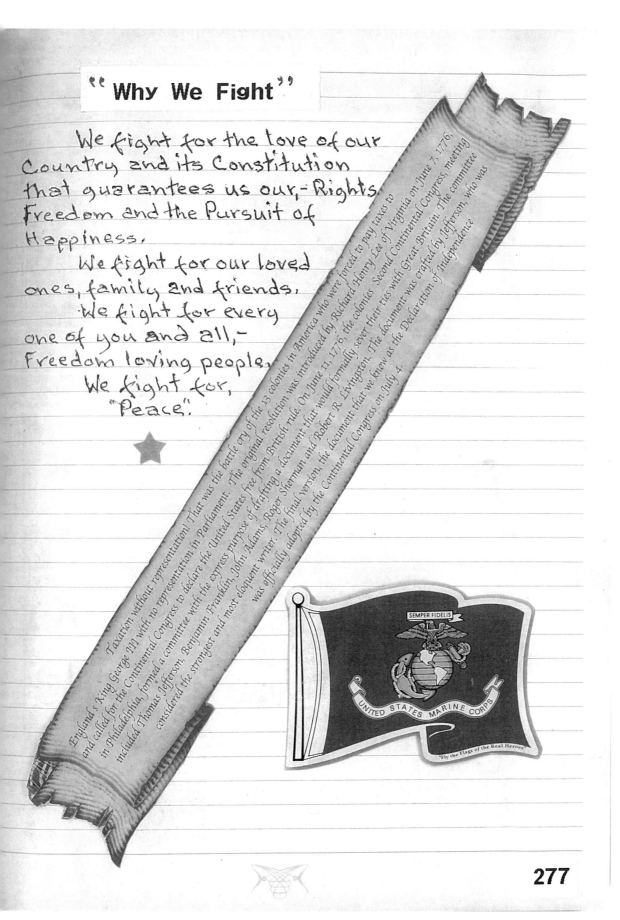

Taxation without representation! That was the battle cry of the 13 colonies in America who were forced to pay taxes to England's King George III with no representation in Parliament. The original resolution was introduced by Richard Henry Lee of Virginia on June 7, 1776, and called for the Continental Congress to declare the United States free from British rule. On June 11, 1776, the colonies Second Continental Congress, meeting in Philadelphia, formed a committee with the express purpose of drafting a document that would formally sever their ties with Great Britain. The committee included Thomas Jefferson, Benjamin Franklin, John Adams, Roger Sherman and Robert R. Livingston. The document was crafted by Jefferson, who was considered the strongest and most eloquent writer. The final version, the document that we know as the Declaration of Independence was officially adopted by the Continental Congress on July 4.

SEMPER FIDELIS

UNITED STATES MARINE CORPS

"Fly the Flags of the Real Heroes"

The Declaration of Independence

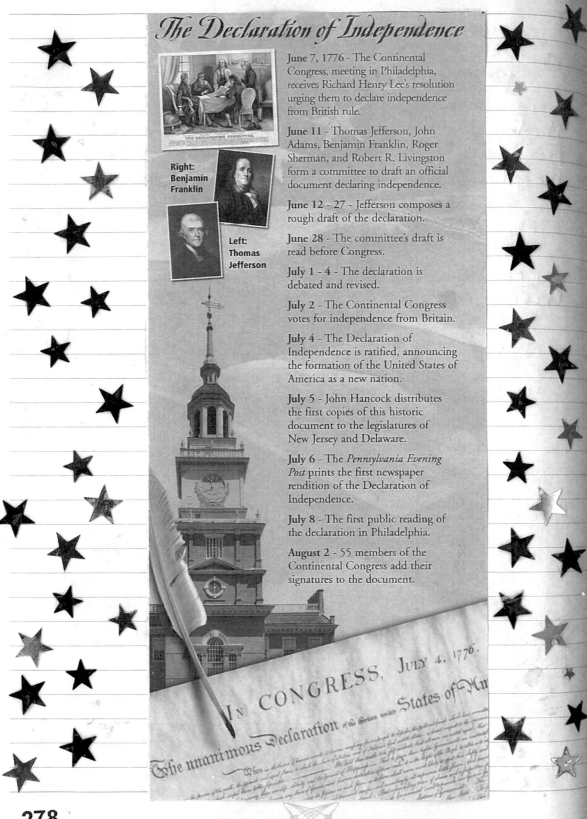

June 7, 1776 - The Continental Congress, meeting in Philadelphia, receives Richard Henry Lee's resolution urging them to declare independence from British rule.

June 11 - Thomas Jefferson, John Adams, Benjamin Franklin, Roger Sherman, and Robert R. Livingston form a committee to draft an official document declaring independence.

June 12 - 27 - Jefferson composes a rough draft of the declaration.

June 28 - The committee's draft is read before Congress.

July 1 - 4 - The declaration is debated and revised.

July 2 - The Continental Congress votes for independence from Britain.

July 4 - The Declaration of Independence is ratified, announcing the formation of the United States of America as a new nation.

July 5 - John Hancock distributes the first copies of this historic document to the legislatures of New Jersey and Delaware.

July 6 - The *Pennsylvania Evening Post* prints the first newspaper rendition of the Declaration of Independence.

July 8 - The first public reading of the declaration in Philadelphia.

August 2 - 55 members of the Continental Congress add their signatures to the document.

Right: Benjamin Franklin

Left: Thomas Jefferson

"We hold these truths to be self-evident, that all men are created equal, that they are endowed by their Creator with certain unalienable Rights, that among these are Life, Liberty, and the pursuit of Happiness..."

The Declaration of Independence

The summer of 1776 was a defining time for the British colonies in America. Unfair taxation and intolerable acts of oppression at the hand of the English monarch, King George III, had led to increased clashes with the British forces. The fuse of revolution was lit.

In the midst of this tense and uncertain time, the Continental Congress met at Independence Hall in Philadelphia to act on Richard Henry Lee's motion to declare independence from England. In preparation for this vote, the Congress selected a committee to draft a declaration of independence. The committee, composed of John Adams, Benjamin Franklin, Thomas Jefferson, Robert R. Livingston, and Roger Sherman, chose Jefferson to write the document because he was considered the most eloquent writer.

Jefferson began his work in seclusion on June 11, 1776, and after a series of revisions by the committee, submitted the document to the Continental Congress on June 28. On July 4th, the Declaration of Independence announced to the King and the world that the colonies were now free and independent states. The United States of America was born.

To this day, Jefferson's powerful message of freedom is considered the benchmark of democracy worldwide.

Life

Liberty

Freedom

"Memorial Day-The Past To The Present"

What has happened to, "Memorial Day", and the, "Honor", and, "Respect", it deserves. Yes,-"Memorial Day", is a Holiday,- a day of fun, golfing, picnics, or going to a Mall for the Memorial Day Sales. It's a weekend that everyone looks forward to,- but they forget, "Memorial Day", is a time to, "Honor", and show our appreciation for our Country's fallen wartime heroes. From the American Revolution to the Persian Gulf War and all inbetween and after,- hundreds of thousands of American men and women in uniform have selflessly given their lives protecting our, "Freedom", and the, "Freedom", of all, "Peace", loving Countries.

When I was a young teenager, many years ago in the 1930's,- I am now, 84,- 2007,- people showed more interest and respect for our War Dead. I remember all the places of business would close their doors and hang a sign on it,- "Closed for Memorial Day in Honor of Our Veterans,- Will Open At 12:00 Noon". In those days you could see the U.S. Flag flying from almost every home and business place. People were proud to fly, "O'l Glory", and participate in the Memorial Day programs in the City of Milwaukee Parks. U.S. Flags were given to the children and placed at the gravesites of all the Veterans at all the cemeteries to, "Honor", them. It was a day of rememberance and prayer for our, "Fallen Heroes", of all the Wars past to present.

What I'd like to see is our places of business pick up the traditions that I was a part of when I was a teenager. Close your stores and malls for a half a day to Honor those who gave their all for us for the "Freedom" we enjoy today. I'd also like to see our schools develope a program of "Rememberance" to enlighten the students about the purpose of "Memorial Day". Invite Veterans from the local Veterans Organizations to come to their schools to talk to them about their "Wartime" experiences. They must be told year after year that War is not the answer to world problems, - diplomacy is. They must be told of the sacrifices of our "Fallen Warriors" and the service they rendered for the U.S.A..

Memorial Day Program, - Am. Leg. Post #66 ..

Have your Memorial Day Sales,—but wait until twelve noon and wait until the U.S. Flag has been raised to the top of the mast after flying at half-mast all morning in,"Honor", of all who,"Gave Their All", for theirs and ours Country. I ask all of our Citizens, students and Veterans to take an hour of your time,—in the morning,— to attend a Memorial Day Program in your Community in,"Rememberance", of those who didn't come back! That's not to much to ask,—is it!!

I Know there are some who cannot attend these programs because they are ill or handi-capped,—but they can still participate by saying a prayer asking the,"Lord", to watch over our, "Fallen Heroes".

When the,"Fallen Troops", reach the,"Golden Gates", they'll say to St. Peter,—"Let us pass we have spent our time in,—"Hell",—and he will pass them through the,"Golden Gates".

Today the Armed Forces of the United States are deployed around the world keep-ing the,"Peace", and fighting those who would destroy the U.S.. We must support our troops wherever they may be serving. They all will have their,"Memorial Days", in the future and those who will be here,—the Citizens of this great Country must never forget those who put their,"lives on the line", so that the bene-fits of,"Freedom and Democracy", will always be here.

Memorial Day is meant to honor and pay our respects to those Americans who have given their lives in service to our nation, who stand in an unbroken line from Lexington's rude bridge to Cemetery Ridge to the Argonne Forest to the beaches of Normandy to the blood drenched beaches of Tarawa to the frozen Chosin Reservoir to the Ia Drang Valley to the sands of Kuwait to the streets of Baghdad.

We must never forget, "Memorial Day", and those gallant defenders of Democracy who gave their all so that we may live in a land that's, – "Free".
"God Bless America."

Memorial Day Tribute

"They answered their country's
call to arms,
into battle they did go,
Where their final destination was,
No one will ever know.

May their final resting place,
Under some unknown sod,
Be forever hallowed,
For it is known
only unto God."

TMP

Arlington National Cemetery

285

"The History of Arlington National Cemetery"

For more than 140 years Arlington National Cemetery has been the final resting place for America's war heroes. Yet it was not always the Nations most hallowed shrine. Before being used as a cemetery the land was owned by the wife of General Robert E. Lee, Mary Ann Randolph Custis. Lt. and Mrs. Lee were married on the estate, and it is here they raised their seven children. In April 1861, Lt. Col. Robert E. Lee resigned his commission in the U.S. Army and shortly thereafter left Arlington.

Immediately, the hills of Arlington and the Custis Lee mansion were used for the defenses of Washington. The hillsides served as a campsite for Federal Forces, and a Freedman's Village, to house former slaves, was established on the land.

In it's earliest beginnings as a cemetery, Arlington was a potter's field, where two types of soldiers were buried, - those who were unknown and those whose families did not have the resources to have their loved ones returned to their home towns. Army Hospitals were established in the Nations Capitol, and soon were receiving the sick and wounded from the battlefields of Virginia. Burial space in the local church and private cemeteries was soon exhausted and finding appropriate grounds to inter the war dead became a serious problem. On

May 13th, 1864, Pvt. William H. Christman, a laborer
with the 67th Pennsylvania Infantry Regiment,
was interred in the Arlington estate. A hapless
recruit whose career in the Army spanned just
90 days, he was the first soldier interred in this
National Shrine.

As America grew, so did Arlington Cemetery.
It became the final resting place for soldiers
and patriots, and events would be memorialized
here that would change the potter's field into
the preeminent burial ground in the world.

"U.S. Casualties"

War	Killed	Serving
Revolutionary War - 1775-1783	4,435	Unk.
War of 1812 - 1812-1815	2,260	287,000
Mexican War - 1846-1848	13,000	79,000
Civil War - 1861-1865	365,000	2,200,000
Spanish Am. War - 1898	2,400	307,400
World War One - 1917-1918	117,000	4,800,000
World War Two - 1941-1946	405,000	16,000,000
Korean War - 1950-1953	37,000	5,700,000
Vietnam War - 1964-1973	58,000	8,744,000
War on Terror - 2001-Jun. '07*	3,555	(Ongoing)

*Not final.

From the July/August 2007 Purple Heart Mag.

 "Some Gave All - All Gave Some"

First in War, First in Peace,
First in the Hearts of His Countrymen

George Washington
The Father of Our Country

When it came time for the fledgling country of the United States to elect its first leader, there was only one man for the job: George Washington. The brilliant Commander who led them through the great battle for independence was unanimously elected President in 1789. The fierce determination of a warrior, combined with the manners and morality of a fine southern gentleman, made him perfectly suited to set the precedents for the office of President. His leadership on the battlefield won America its independence, but it was his leadership in office that created the mold from which the United States was cast.

Facts about George Washington

- The only President to be elected unanimously — not once but twice.

- Was the only President inaugurated in two cities: New York and Philadelphia.

- Wore poorly fitted false teeth that gave him a very stern appearance. Contrary to legend, they were not made of wood.

- Never had children, but helped raise Martha's 2 children from a previous marriage.

288

George Washington

February 22, 1732- George Washington is born in Pope's Creek, Virginia.

March 1748- Begins career as a surveyor at the age of 16.

November 16, 1752- Enters Virginia Militia and becomes a major.

1754-1759- Serves as lieutenant colonel in the British army during the French and Indian War. Builds Fort Necessity in Great Meadows, PA.

January 6, 1759- Marries Martha Dandridge Custis (1731-1802), a widow with 2 children.

1759-1775- Manages Mount Vernon Plantation and serves in Virginia House of Burgesses.

April 19, 1775- Battles at Lexington and Concord.

May 1775- Serves as Virginia delegate to the Second Continental Congress. Elected Commander in Chief of the Continental Army.

July 4, 1776- The Declaration of Independence is signed.

December 25, 1776- Leads surprise attack on Hessian troops by crossing frozen Delaware River at night.

1777-1778- Remains with his weary and hungry troops through the harsh winter at Valley Forge.

October 1781- British surrender at Yorktowne ending Revolutionary War.

December 23, 1783- Retires to his Mount Vernon Plantation.

July 2, 1788- The U.S. Constitution is ratified.

February 4, 1789- Unanimously elected as the first President of the United States.

March 4, 1793- Sworn in as President for a second term.

March 4, 1797- Declines third term and retires to Mount Vernon.

December 14, 1799- George Washington dies from a severe throat infection.

Early survey map by a young Washington

Full size replica of Fort Necessity

Valley Forge, Pennsylvania 1777

"Let There Be Peace On Earth"

Let there be peace on earth,
    and let it begin with me!
Let there be peace on earth,
    the peace that was meant to be.
With God as our father,
    brothers all are we.
Let me walk with my brothers
    in perfect harmony.

Let peace begin with me,
    let this be the moment now,
With ev'ry breath I take,
    let this be my solemn vow,
To take each moment and live each
    moment in peace, eternally.
Let there be peace on earth,
    and let it begin with me.

What beautiful words to live by!

★ ★ ★

"God who gave us life gave us liberty. And
can the liberties of a nation be thought secure
when we have removed their only firm basis,
a conviction in the minds of the people that
these liberties are a gift of God? That they
are not to be violated but with His wrath. Indeed
I tremble for my country when I reflect that
God is just, that His justice cannot sleep forever."
        Thomas Jefferson, 1781."

THE UNITED STATES MARINE CORPS

Nothing epitomizes the legendary fighting spirit of the Corps more than the battle for Iwo Jima, the costliest 36 days of fighting for Marines in World War II. When five leathernecks raised the Stars and Stripes on Mount Suribachi, they created the enduring symbol of Marine courage and sacrifice. In their struggle to raise the flag, the whole world witnessed the esprit de corps that drives each Marine to do the impossible.

We Salute Our Flag, Our Veterans, & Our Armed Forces

"Iwo Jima - The Two Flag Raisings"

Iwo Jima, The First Flag
Ron Stark. On February 23, 1945, atop Mt. Suribachi, Marines of the 5th Division hoist the first American flag over Iwo Jima. As Old Glory breaks the skyline, a tremendous roar of shouts and whistles emerges from the Marines on the beaches and the sailors at sea. Later, this flag will be lowered and a replacement raised, and though a photo of the second flag would be cherished back home, this first flag belonged to the heroes of Iwo Jima.

FLAG RAISING ON IWO JIMA, FEBRUARY 23, 1945

Flag Raising on Iwo Jima
The flag raising on Iwo Jima's Mt. Suribachi will forever symbolize the valor and sacrifice of the U.S. Marines.

COMMEMORATING IWO JIMA 1945

Top photo by -
    Charles Lindberg
Bottom photo by -
    Joe Rosenthal

"The Corps"

**FOUNDING
OF THE CORPS
1775**

**SEMPER FIDELIS
OFFICIAL MOTTO
ADOPTED 1883**

**AVIATION DIVISION
FOUNDED
1913**

**COMMEMORATING
THE KOREAN CONFLICT
1950**

**IRAQI
FREEDOM
2003**

In Honor of Courage . . .

"War In The Air and At Sea"

Sub Base Pearl Harbor
Tom Freeman. Though U.S. battleships were the main target of the December 7, 1941, Japanese attack on Pearl Harbor, it was the USS Tautog, a submarine, that was the first to bring down an enemy aircraft.

Ordeal in Vitiaz Strait
Jack Fellows. On December 27, 1943, 28 aircraft of the Imperial Japanese Navy surprised PT-190 and PT-191 as they crossed the Vitiaz Strait between New Britain and New Guinea. In the ensuing battle, the PT skippers successfully eluded their tormentors as they ran at forty-plus knots toward the cover of a heavy rainsquall.

Trial by Fire
Tom Freeman. Despite being struck by four bombs and five kamikazes off the coast of Okinawa on April 16, 1945, the Sumner-class destroyer USS Laffey (DD-724) refused to die, and is still afloat as a museum ship in South Carolina.

Dauntless Courage
David Gray. At the Battle of Midway, Lt. (jg) Norman "Dusty" Kleiss pulls his SBD skyward as he inspects the devastation inflicted by his bombs on the Japanese aircraft carrier Kaga.

Sixth on the Sixth
Russell Smith. Major George Preddy in his famous P-51, Cripes A' Mighty 3rd, claims his 6th and final kill of the day on August 6th, 1944

The USS South Dakota (BB57), a South Dakota Class Battleship, received 13 battle stars for service during World War II.

"The Infantry"

The Greatest Generation
Robert Sargent. Taken by a photographer for the U.S. Coast Guard, this photograph shows the view from a Coast Guard landing boat of U.S. troops wading to shore on Omaha Beach while under heavy Nazi machine gun fire during the D-Day invasion of Nazi-occupied France.

THE GREATEST GENERATION
D-DAY LANDING • OMAHA BEACH • JUNE 6, 1944

LIMITED EDITION

The Desperate Hours
Don Stivers. Obeying the last order – to "hold at all costs" – they received before their communications were cut, Sgt. Lamoine "Frank" Olsen and his company hold for 2½ days without reinforcement or re-supply, buying precious time against the surprise German offensive known as "The Battle of the Bulge."

LIMITED EDITION

◀ Down to Earth
Larry Selman. Although scattered and forced to land in flooded fields, the 507th Parachute Infantry Regiment, 82nd Airborne, held key positions along the Merderet river during the D-Day Invasion of Normandy.

LIMITED EDITION

Arnhem Drop
Simon Smith. Presenting the largest airborne operation in history, when more than 20,000 men were dropped into Holland on September 17, 1944.

LIMITED EDITION

Cold Steel
Don Stiver. Captain Lewis Millett leads Easy Company, 27th Infantry Regiment, in its bayonet assault on Hill 180 in Soam-Ni, Korea, on a cold winter day in February, 1951.

Brothers in Battle

Don Stivers. In the cold darkness of early morning on March 2nd 2002, the 10th Mountain Division – along with the 101st Airborne, Afghan, and other coalition forces – initiates Operation Anaconda, assaulting a large pocket of Taliban and Al-Qaeda terrorists that had taken refuge in the valleys, villages and caves of the Shah-E-Kot Valley in Eastern Afghanistan.

Easy Company Captain

After suffering nearly 50% casualties during the summer of 1944's Normandy campaign, the men of Easy Company, 506th Parachute Infantry Regiment, 101st Airborne Division, were dropped into Nazi-occupied Holland to capture key bridges over the Rhine.

U.S. Army Ranger

Courage Under Fire

One battle is forever associated with the U.S. Marine Corps: Iwo Jima. Honoring the heroic memory of the men who paid the supreme sacrifice,

Soviet Infantry Scout with Dog

Depicting a Soviet infantry scout with his dog during Operation Bagration – the Soviet Belrorussian Offensive – in 1944,

U.S. Army "Buffalo Soldier" Bazookaman Figure

Depicting a U.S. Army bazookaman from the 92nd Infantry Division, the "Buffalo Soldiers," which became the only African-American infantry division to see combat in World War II when it fought in Italy in 1944,

If there is a job to do, these guys will do it!

"Iwo Jima -The First Flag Raised"

On Feb. 23rd, 1945 atop Mt. Suribachi, Marines of the 5th Division hoist the first American flag over Iwo Jima.

As Old Glory breaks the skyline, - a tremendous roar of shouts and whistles emerges from the Marines and the sailors all over Iwo.

Later, this flag will be lowered and then replaced by a larger one.

This first flag belongs to the Heroes of Iwo Jima!

This photo was taken by Charles Lindberg - a, "Combat Photographer."

P.S. - I, the Author of this book, feel that, - Mr. Lindberg, has never received the publicity, the honor and the glory he deserves. This photo of the first flag to be raised on Iwo was the flag the Marines first saw. The sight of Old Glory is what inspired and encouraged the Marines to continue the fight to victory. "Thanks", - to all who participated in this historic flag raising and, "Thank you", Mr. Lindberg, for a great photo.

Charles Wysocki, Jr.

"Worth Repeating"

Short memories are the most conven-
ient and, obviously, a large number of people
have forgotten these words;—
"Let every nation know whether it wishes
us well or ill, that we shall pay any price, bear any
burden, meet any hardship, support any friend,
oppose any foe, to assure the survival and the
survival and the success of liberty."

Who said it,— President John F. Kennedy
in his 1961 inaugural address.
M.O. Seymour—Tucson Citizen

Flag of the brave!
thy folds shall fly
the sign of hope
and triumph
high...

300

With malice toward none;
With charity for all;
With firmness in the right,
As God gives us to see the right,
Let us strive on to finish
The work we are in;
To bind up the nation's wounds;
To care for him who shall have
Borne the battle,
And for his widow,
And his orphan –
To do all which may achieve and
Cherish a just and lasting peace
Among ourselves,
And with all nations.

Abraham Lincoln

From his second Inaugural Address
March 4, 1865

The New Colossus

...Here at our sea-washed, sunset gates shall stand
A mighty woman with a torch, whose flame
Is the imprisoned lightning, and her name
Mother of Exiles. From her beacon-hand
Glows world-wide welcome; her mild eyes command
The air-bridged harbor that twin cities frame.

"Keep, ancient lands, your storied pomp!" cries she
With silent lips. "Give me your tired, your poor,
Your huddled masses yearning to breathe free,
The wretched refuse of your teeming shore.
Send these, the homeless, tempest-tost to me,
I lift my lamp beside the golden door!"

Emma Lazarus

"Did You Know"

As you walk up the steps to the building which houses the U.S. Supreme Court you can see, near the top of the building, a row of the world's law givers, - each one is facing the one in the middle who is facing forward with a full frontal view, - -- it is Moses and he is holding the, "Ten Commandments!

As you enter the Supreme Court courtroom- -- the two huge oak doors have the, "Ten Commandments engraved on each lower portion of each door.

As you sit inside the Courtroom, you can see the wall, right above where the Supreme Court Judges sit, --- a display of the, "Ten Commandments!

There are Bible verses etched in stone all over the Federal Buildings and Monuments in Washington, D.C..

James Madison, the Fourth President, known as, "The Father of Our Constitution", made the following statement, "We have staked the whole of all our political institutions upon the capacity of each and all of us to govern ourselves, to control ourselves, to sustain ourselves according to the, "Ten Commandments of God."

Patrick Henry, that Patriot and Founding Father of our Country said, "It cannot be emphasized too strongly or too often that this great nation was founded not by religionists, but by Christians, - not on religions, - but on the Gospel of

303

Jesus Christ."

Every session of Congress begins with a prayer by a paid preacher, whose salary has been paid by the taxpayer since 1777.

Fifty-two of the 55 founders of the Constitution were members of the established Orthodox Churches in the colonies.

Thomas Jefferson worried that the Courts would overstep their authority and instead of interpreting the law would begin making law, ---- an oligarchy, - the rule of few over many.

The very first Supreme Court Justice, - John Jay, said, - "Americans should select and prefer Christians as their rulers."

How, then, have we gotten to the point that everything done for over 220 years in this Country is now suddenly wrong, and, --- Unconstitutional?

Please, copy and forward this to every - one you can. Lets put it around the world and let the world see and remember what this, "Great Country", was built on. ★

From my Son, Paul - 2004

HONOR THE SACRIFICES
OF OUR VETERANS
BY PROUDLY FLYING
THE AMERICAN FLAG!

The following are, "Food For Thought", - →

304

"The Law Is The Law"

So if the U.S. Government determines that it is against the law for the words, "Under God," to be on our money, then, so be it.

And if that same government decides that the "Ten Commandments," are not to be used in or on a government installation, then, so be it.

And since they already have prohibited any prayer in the schools, - on which they deem their authority, then, so be it.

I say, "so be it", because I would like to be a law abiding U.S. Citizen.

I say, "so be it", because I would like to think that smarter people then I are in positions to make good decisions.

I would like to think that those people have the American Publics' best interests at heart.

But, you know What Else I'd Like !!

Since we can't pray to God, can't Trust in God and cannot Post His Commandments in Government buildings, - I don't believe the Government and it's employees should participate in the Easter and Christmas celebrations which honor the God that our Government is eliminating from many facets of American life.

I'd like my mail delivered on Christmas, Good Friday, Thanksgiving and Easter, - after

305

all, it's just another day.

I'd like the U.S. Supreme Court to be in session on Christmas, Good Friday, Thanksgiving, Easter, - as well as Sundays. After all, it's just another day.

I'd like the Senate and the House of Representatives to not have to worry about getting home for the "Christmas Break,"- After all, it's just another day.

I'm thinking that a lot of my taxpayer dollars could be saved, if all Government offices and services would work on Christmas, Good Friday, Easter and Thanksgiving.

It shouldn't cost any overtime since those would be just like any other day of the week to a Government that is trying to be, "politically correct."

In fact, --- I think that our Government should work on Sundays, - (initially set aside for worshipping God ---), because, after all, our Government says that it should be just another day ---.

What do you all think?? If this idea gets to enough people, - maybe our elected officials will stop giving into minority. opinions and begin to represent the majority of, - All of the American People. So Be It, ---.

Please Dear Lord, - Give us the help needed to keep you in our Country. ★

From a friend, - Charlotte Collins, Phoenix, AZ

306

"What and Who Do We Believe"

For hundreds and hundreds of years the question has been asked, - "How was the universe formed and what was its beginning?" Some say it was an explosion, - or by evolution, - still others say it was by a super being. We must all determine for ourselves through our own beliefs. We can read all the History books about the origin of the world, - including the Bible and we'll still have questions.

Most of us were brought up in religious families and went to religious schools and we believed what we were taught about a super being called, - "God", "Allah", "Jesus", "Our Savior, and others according to our individual religion. As we grew up our religious beliefs grew stronger, - for others there were to many unanswered questions about their religion and they fell by the wayside. It is very hard to believe in a "God", and the here after when no one has come back after they have died to tell of the wonders of life after death.

As for myself, - I believe the creation of the universe was by my, "God", - but none of us will know until we meet our maker.

If it was by an explosion, - as some say, - who supplied the material, - the gases and the ignition. If it was by evolution, - why isn't it continuing today!

I also believe that all of us were put on this earth for a reason and that is to see what each one of us will do with our lives. What we do with our lives will determine our reward or punishment in the hereafter.

Ask yourself,—"If there is no God"... Who choreographed the waltz of the planets? Who commands the wildflowers to bloom? And why are human beings equipped with a conscience? Who is in the center of the earth controlling the rotation of the earth? Who created all of the different animals? Who created the clouds, rain, snow, lightening, sand, ground and much more? The creation of a baby is a miracle of "God". Take time to look at yourself in a mirror and ask yourself,— who gave me eyes to see the beauty of the world,— who gave me a nose to breath the life giving air,— who gave me a mouth to talk with and eat the foods of life,— who gave me ears to hear with,— who gave me hands, fingers, legs, feet, a body with so many organs with a heart for life. Who did all these things,— not a scientist,— so it must be by the one I call, "God",— our Creator and Savior.

Another convincer as to the presence of a, "God", or a supreme being was during World War Two while I was in the U.S. Marine Corps and a participant in four D-Day landings in the Pacific. No matter where we were,— at a Marine Base, aboard a Troop Transport or in Combat on a, "God Forsaken Island", most of us attended a religious service whenever we could or we said our own prayers. Before every battle the Chaplain, aboard ship, would give us a blessing before we disembarked from the ship to engage the enemy. The Chaplains, of all the religions, were always there for us, – they would have their services whenever and wherever they could.

I remember one incident very vividly, – it was the day we buried our, "Buddies", after the bloody battle for, "Tarawa Atoll". It was a very sad time for those who survived. We buried 15 of our, "Buddies", and we all prayed to, "God", to have mercy on their souls. We also thanked the, "Lord", for our survival. I know that I prayed and asked for, "Gods", protection, – just as I do today. Even to this day, – 65 years since I enlisted in the Marine Corps and went away to War, – I correspond with the few, "Buddies", remaining and we always end our phone calls and letters with a, "God Bless you", – "Be With God", – "May the Good Lord Be With You", or "Stay With God". There has always been a strong belief in a, "Supreme Being", amongest my Marine Buddies, – just as there is today with my family, relatives and friends.

Here is a very interesting fact, – America's founders did not intend for there to be a separation of God and state, as shown by the fact that all 50 states acknowledge God in their state Constitutions. After reviewing acknowledgements of God from all 50 state

Constitutions, - one is faced with the prospect that maybe, - just maybe, - the ACLU and the out-of-control Federal Courts are wrong!!

William Penn said, - "Those people who will not be governed by God will be ruled by tyrants."

If you are a believer in a, "Supreme Being", as are millions of people around the world, - keep looking up for, --- "We Trust In God".

If you found this to be, "Food For Thought",.. send to as many that you think will be touched by it also.

I am a Catholic and a believer in, "God", our Creator and Savior. I live by the, "Ten Commandments", of God, - and if everyone did, - what a wonderful world this would be!
"God Be With You"

Charles Wysocki, Jr.

" BECAUSE OF WHAT AMERICA IS AND WHAT AMERICA HAS DONE,

A HIGHER HOPE, INSPIRES THE HEART OF ALL HUMANITY."

Here we mark the price of freedom

Victory in Europe Day, May 8, 1945

The United States entered the Second World War in 1941 not to conquer, but to liberate a world fast falling to the forces of tyranny. The World War II Memorial honors the 16 million who served in uniform, of whom more than 400,000 gave their lives. It also honors the many millions who supported the war effort on the home front and celebrates the American spirit, national unity, and victory. It recognizes the price paid by families. The blue star signifying a son or daughter in service *(flag above)* was proudly displayed in windows nationwide. It was all too often replaced by a gold star signifying another casualty of war.

The war that changed the world also changed life at home. After 1945 education expanded through the G.I. Bill. Technology surged as industries retooled for peace. Women's rights and civil rights made new strides toward that great goal: liberty and justice for all.

Aboard U.S.S. *Missouri*, Gen. Douglas A. MacArthur, Commander of the Allied Powers in the Pacific, signs documents ending the war on September 2, 1945.

• Dec. 7, 1941 Japan attacks Pearl Harbor • Dec. 11, 1941 Germany declares war on

Aug. 6 & 9, 1945 U.S. drops atomic bombs on Japan •

WWII

Freedom is not Free

Here's to you, America,
The battle rages on
For we're one nation under God
And no one stands alone.
Our Fathers' faith abides in us
And God still lights the way.
Here's to you, America…
God bless the U.S.A.!

Clay Harrison

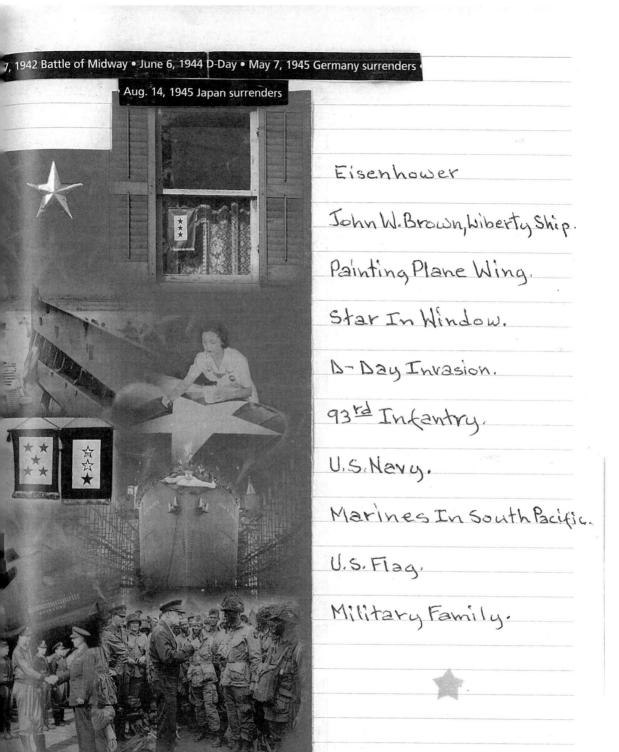

4,000 gold stars on the Memorial's Freedom Wall commemorate the more than 400,000 Americans who gave their lives.

Eisenhower

John W. Brown, Liberty Ship.

Painting Plane Wing.

Star In Window.

D- Day Invasion.

93rd Infantry.

U.S. Navy.

Marines In South Pacific.

U.S. Flag.

Military Family.

"We pledge allegiance○○○○○○ —

Our future is in their hands!!

"...symbolic of all that's great about the U.S.A."

For our nation's combat soldiers who survive, the war never ends. Those who don't end up *"a dog tag on a cross of wood,"* have lived fear as none should ever have to.

They march into the breach trained to be killing machines, but unlike the weapons they carry each can think and feel. More often than not, the carnage they experience brings on a lifetime of nightmares and guilt.

Their exclusive brotherhood, forged through a kinship of misery, has been and is shared by generations of *"ordinary"* countrymen who put aside hopes and dreams to fight and die for each other and America.

This letter from a World War II marine attempts to help his mother understand what he has been through on Okinawa:

"Never was there a finer group of men anywhere in the world. The hardships, suffering and heroic acts ... are much too unbelievable to ever be recorded, but as long as I live, their names and valorous deeds will be imbedded in a memory that's not soon forgotten."

Riddick Kelly's letter defines the timeless character of the American combat soldier who fights on, in Afghanistan and Iraq.

Here's to You, America!

Here's to you, America,
You've stood the test of time
Although there were obstacles
And many hills to climb.
Here's to you, America,
One nation under God!
You stayed the course and boldly walked
The path the pilgrims trod.
Here's to you, America,
Old Glory waving high;
We pledge allegiance to you yet
For the brave still "Do or die!"
And the Lady in the Harbor
Still stands at freedom's door
And lifts her torch to light the way
For the masses evermore.

"The American's creed"

"I believe in the United States of America as a Government of the people, by the people, for the people; whose just powers are derived from the consent of the governed; a democracy in a Republic; a sovereign Nation of many sovereign States; a perfect Union, one and inseparable; established upon those principles of freedom, equality, justice, and humanity for which American patriots sacrificed their lives and fortunes. I therefore believe it is my duty to my Country to love it; to support its Constitution; to obey its laws, to respect its flag; and to defend it against all enemies."

William Tyler Page, 1918

"Land of the free and home of the brave."

"No arsenal or no weapon in the arsenals of the world is so formidable as the will and moral courage of free men and women."

Pres. Ronald Reagan

"A man who is good enough to shed his blood for his Country is good enough to be given a square deal afterwards."

Pres. Theodore Roosevelt
July 4, 1903

"The stories of past courage can define that ingredient – But they cannot supply courage itself. For this each man must look into his own soul."

John F. Kennedy

HOME OF THE BRAVE

Walk a mile in my shoes?
If you'd like to meet bonafide heroes, true friends who offered "life and limb" for your freedom and mine, drop into a Department of Veterans Affairs Regional Hospital ward. **You won't be sorry you did.**

"Our dept to the heroic men and valiant women in the service of our Country can never be repaid. They have earned our undying gratitude; America will never forget their sacrifices.

President Harry S. Truman

"Memories"

    —   My enlistment in the United States Marine Corps,—Feb. 5th, 1942, at Milwaukee, Wisconsin,—my home town.

    —   That same day, late afternoon, as I was leaving home for the Northwestern Railroad Depot, I turned around to look back at the house and I saw my Mother,—in the kitchen window, waving, "Good Bye", to me,—I waved back to her. It would be a long time, before I would see, "Mom", again.

    —   At the railroad station, my Dad, who worked for the Railway Express Company, took time off from his job,—so he could come down to the Depot to say, "Good Bye", and wish me, "Good Luck."

    —   A couple of days after arriving at the Marine Corps Recruit Depot, San Diego, Calif., we had to remove our civilian clothing which would be sent back to our homes. I had a beautiful pullover sweater that I didn't want to part with,—but the officer in charge said,—"It had to go", and it went,—I never saw it again!

    —   The first couple of weeks of, "Boot Camp", were the toughest I have ever had to go through. Every muscle and bone in my body ached,—but I survived! One time during field drills I had to hit the deck and my hernia incession gave me a real good jolt,—I thought I had torn the incession wide open,—but lucky

318

me, — I didn't! I didn't report it and it seemed to be O.K. from then on.

— My first time aboard a ship, — ever, was the U.S.S. President Hayes, a combat troop ship. I never saw such a big ship. It was one of the four ships that would take us to the "Canal", — they were nick-named the, "Unholy Four". They were the Hayes, the Adams, the Jackson, and the Crescent City.

— The 3 day storm we ran into on the way to the, "Canal". It was a terrifying experience, and, "yes", I was scared, very scared!! At times there was a wall of water around our ship, — I'd swear it was going to bury us. We'd rise to the top of a wave and sometimes we could see several water spouts in the distance, — like tor-nados, — only on the water. Almost everyone got seasick and were puking all over the ship, — what a mess! We survived the storm which was the only real bad storm we experienced in the better than three years in the Pacific Theatre, — one was enough! There were several casualties amongest the ships, — washed overboard as a result of the storm.

— "Chaplains", — couldn't get along without them, — they were always there when they were needed, — on board the ships, in camps, and on the battlefields. I'll always remember attending mass on the, "Hayes", and the Chaplain blessing us and the words of encouragement the day before the assault on the, "Canal" and Tulagi. The Chaplain who held services on Tulagi had two pistols on a gun belt and at the end of the services he'd whip out the pistols and said, "Let's go get some Japs." I remember the, "Rabbi", who invited us to come to the Jewish Services by saying, "Whatever your religion may be, - come, - close your eyes and make believe your at your own religious service," - we did and the service was wonderful. Why can't we get along with each other today the way we did then?

—   "Malaria", - I never thought I'd get it, - but I did, - on the island of Tulagi. If the Japs had known how depleted our troops were at that time, - they could have walked in with little opposition. We were very sick and the Doctors and the Corpsman had their hands full taking care of us and staying well themselves. The only thing they had to treat us with was, "Quinine", - in powder form. They would take a piece of toilet paper, put some Quinine on it, roll it up in a ball, tell you to open your mouth, then throw the ball of Quinine in as far as they could and say, - "Swallow It", - we did, but most times the ball would break before we could get it down. I was the most awful tasting medicine I had ever experienced in my life, - but we got well!

—   On Tulagi, this character would keep showing up almost every evening in our area, - and no one knew who he was or where he came from, - he wasn't from our outfit. Every time he showed up he'd be wearing the same uniform, - a U.S. Navy, "whites", uniform. We soon found out what he was up to and he was told to go peddle his wares elsewhere, - but he did not. One night when he was again in our area, doing his thing or trying to, - some of the guys grabbed him and took him down to the beach and gave him a "sand bath" - scrub brush and sand! We never saw "the very nice fella" again. - The guy who said our first combat experience would separate the men from the boys, - it did, he was the first one to be sent back to the States, - "unfit for combat." Every time there was a, - "Condition Red", on Tulagi he'd run up to the C.P., - Comand Post for safety and protection. This could happen to anyone, - some could take it, some could not. The breaking point for each person would and was different. Maybe he wasn't as stupid as we thought he was. I don't know how I lasted, - in combat, as long as I did!!

Robert Montgomery, - the Actor and a P.T. Boat Squadron Commander was stationed at Tulagi. They would usually go out at night to patrol the slot and intercept enemy ships, and they would come back in the morning with their engines wide open. What a terrific noise they would make! This one morning they came roaring in and this one P.T. was riding with its bow high above the water with the head, - toilet, exposed, - it had been hit. It wasn't funny, but it sure looked funny with a toilet fully exposed and still in one piece. One afternoon I west down to the P.T. Base to visit with the guys and swap sea stories. I was introduced to their skipper as, "Commander Robert Montgomery. I really couldn't tell if it was him or not, - he had grown a big black beard that covered most of his face, - but when I heard his voice I was sure it was Mr. Montgomery. His crew members said it was him, - I believed them.

We left Tulagi, - Feb. 9th 1943, and I had just turned 20, Jan. 10th, - and now we were on our way to New Zealand, - a Country I'll never forget. It was a beautiful Country and full of wonderful people, - very caring and thankfull to us for stopping the Japs who were on their doorstep. Up until this time I had never been out with a female, - this was to change very abruptly. I knew some young ladies back home but never dated them, - it seemed I was more interested in sports. In New Zealand there were very few available young men, - they were all in the Armed Forces of New Zealand serving on the battle-fields of the world. When we arrived we were starved for female companionship just as they were for the male, - we obliged each other. I met many very wonderful young ladies, - some did, - and some didn't. Many of the relationships ended up in marriage. I had hoped to return to New Zealand to marry a wonderful young lady I had met, - but that was never to happen. I'll always have fond memories of New Zealand for the rest of my life, and I'll remember what we were fighting for and why.

Footnote: During wartime, combat troops, like us, - will live life to the hilt, - and we did. We did everything we could think of, - drink all the booze we could, make all the women we could and have as much fun as we could! We didn't know what the next assault would bring, - life or death, so we lived for the moment!!
—   There were four guys in our outfit, who in civilian life were railroad men, - and one day they decided to go for a train ride, - they did! They borrowed an engine from a railroad yard near the city of Wellington. Wherever the tracks went they went, - eventually they were stopped and arrested by M.P.'s, (Military Police), and brought back to camp. When they arrived they were in sad, sad shape, - they were, "bombed", out of their minds. One was brought back on a stretcher, - out like a light and his complexion was green, - he was a sick Marine, but he survived, - only to die on Tarawa. Their punishment was to be confined to the camp for a couple of weeks with a severe reprimand, - they were lucky it could have been a lot worse! Hope they enjoyed their, "train ride".
—   "Tarawa", - the memory of my landing on "bloody red beach 3", will always be with me as will the vision of my Mother. What will take a permanent place in my memory is the burial of our 15, "buddies", who gave their all for you

and me. I'll remember the look of horror in the eyes of those who survived the, "76", hours of the, "Hell", that was, Tarawa. The memories are like indelible ink, - they cannot be erased, - ever!

— "Saipan", - just another island but it to holds many memories. The most important happened on the third day of the assault as we were advancing inland from the beach. All of a sudden the Japs opened up with an artillery barrage that was exploding all around us and as I was diving for cover a shell exploded spewing shrapnel all over, - that's when a piece hit me in both arms, around the elbow area and to this day slivers of shrapnel are floating around and once in awhile they'll hit a nerve and it will hurt until it moves on. Yes, - I remember!!

— When I got hit a call for a, "Corpman", was called out and still under enemy fire a Corpman came to my side to tend to the wound and stop the bleeding. I didn't know the Corpman, but I sure want to, "Thank", him for being there!

— After we had returned to Saipan, after taking Tinian, we had set up a camp site and one morning after roll-call a few names were called, including mine and we were told we were being sent back to the States. We were going, "home", - "home", what a wonderful word! It was hard to believe we were going, "home, - but it was true.

— The day we landed at "Treasure Island", Tony's Dad met us, – he worked on the dock and how he knew we were coming in on that ship we'll never know! He asked us how his son died, – this was a hard thing to do, – but he had the right to know. We were behind the sea-wall and to our left was an open area strung with barbed-wire, – all of a sudden, Tony, got up and started running up the open space into the barbed wire where he got hung up and a Jap machine gunner cut him down. All the time he was running up the beach you could hear him yelling and cussing out the Japs. Tony died, fighting on Tarawa, for his Country and his loved ones. Tony's Dad, with tears in eyes, – "Thanked us", and left.

— I ended up in the Navy Hospital, Phil., Pa. for better than four months. I was being treated for Combat Fatigue, Nervous Stomach, Jungle Rot and Rehabilitation. After awhile I volunteered to help out taking patients to their appointments, – like the blind and the handicapped. I'd line them up, – like a congo line, and I would lead them through the halls to wherever they had to go and back again. Sometimes we'd sing as we went through the halls, – we were pretty good!

— Another time there was this young Marine, who had lost a leg in combat, and was refusing all help for the fitting of an artificial limb. I visited him a couple of times trying to help him change his mind. He was very stubborn until

325

this one day when I went to visit him, - he was standing on his crutches by his bed, - still refusing to get fitted. I felt that I had to do something to change his mind, - so I Kicked the crutches out from under him and he fell to the floor. I asked him if he wanted to go through the rest of his life falling down or be in a wheelchair. I helped him up, - he went for the fitting, and the last time I saw him he was smiling and getting around real good on his new leg.
  -      The day I was told I was going to be discharged from the Hospital and sent home, - the Doctor came in one morning and gave me the news, - I told him I wanted to stay in the Corps and make a career in the military. He said, "your career just ended, - your going home", - and I did!
  -      "V.J." Day: When I came home I had to get a new wardrobe, - all the clothes I left behind were gone and none of the family could tell me what happened to them, - but I did notice my Dad wearing a pair of pants that looked like mine. On this day I was doing some shopping, - in downtown Milwaukee when it came over the radio that Japan had surrendered, - "Thank God". In minutes the streets were loaded with people celebrating the end of World War Two. If you were in a uniform, as I was, you were swept up by the crowd and went with the flow. What a "Glorious" day! I finaly got home. but my shopping would have to wait until

another day. That night I gave "Thanks", to the Lord!

— One day after I came home from the war, Bob, who lived in Madison, Wisc., came down to Milwaukee for a visit and we ended up at my favorite watering hole, "The Stables." While we were there this defense worker came in bragging about all the money he was making and hoped the WAR, would continue for a while longer,— Bob didn't care to much for that remark and told him so,— then decked him! The other customers in the bar gave him a standing ovation!

P.S,— He was asked to leave,— immediately!

Memories,— I have many; some good and some I wish I could forget, but I can't!

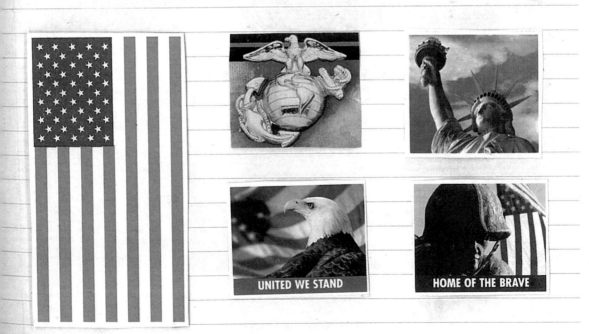

UNITED WE STAND   HOME OF THE BRAVE

"You Don't Know"

You don't know what war is until you
have walked in the shoes of a, "Combat Soldier!

> THE POSITIVE SIDE OF LIFE:
>
>
>
> Living on Earth is expensive, but it does include a free trip round the sun every year.
>
>
>
> Birthdays are good for you; the more you have, the longer you live.
>
>
>
> Happiness comes through doors you didn't even know you left open.
>
>
>
> Ever notice that the people who are late are often much jollier than the people who have
to wait for them?
>
> Most of us go to our grave with our music still inside of us.

> You may be only one person in the world, but you may also be the world to one person.
>
>
>
> Some mistakes are too much fun to only make once.
>
>
>
> Don't cry because it's over; smile because it happened.
>
>
>
> We could learn a lot from crayons: some are sharp, some are pretty, some are dull,
some have weird names, and all are different colors....but they all exist very nicely in the
same box.
>
>
>
> A truly happy person is one who can enjoy the scenery on a detour.
>
>
>
> Have an awesome day, and know that someone who thinks you're great has thought
about you today!..

Dear God, we pray to You
For people in all the world,
For other nations,
For other races,
For people who think differently
And live differently.
Help us to respect, understand,
And love each other.
Let there be no hate among nations.
Forgive all injustice.
Let wars end.
Let Your message be
Proclaimed everywhere.
Give us peace.

– Amen

Let Freedom Ring

Let freedom ring across the land
Today and every day.
Oh, guard it with a passion,
Lest it quickly slip away.
For freedom is a precious thing
For which many fought and died,
And we must guard it feverishly
Throughout each day and night.

Let freedom ring across this land,
Across this land of ours,
This glorious land, America,
Embraced with stripes and stars.
Oh, let it be a beacon bright,
A light to share with others;
Let freedom's ring inspire hope
That all might live as brothers.

Loise Pinkerton Fritz

"I Don't Believe - by Samuel Thompson"

Samuel Thompson wrote: I don't believe in Santa Claus, but I'm not going to sue somebody for singing a Ho-Ho-Ho song in December.

I don't agree with Darwin, but I didn't go out and hire a lawyer when my high school teacher taught his theory of evolution.

Life, liberty or your pursuit of happiness will not be endangered because someone says a 30-second prayer before a football game. So what's the big deal? It's not like somebody is up there reading the entire book of Acts. They're just talking to a God they believe in and asking him to grant safety to the players on the field and the fans going home from the game. "But it's a Christian prayer," some will argue. Yes, and this is the United States of America, a country founded on Christian principles. And we are in the Bible Belt. According to our very own phone book, Christian churches outnumber all others bett er than 200-to-1. So what would you expect-somebody chanting Hare Krishna?

If I went to a football game in Jerusalem, I would expect to hear a Jewish prayer.

If I went to a soccer game in Baghdad, I would expect to hear a Muslim prayer.

If I went to a ping pong match in China, I would expect to hear someone pray to Buddha.

And I wouldn't be offended. It wouldn't bother me one bit. When in Rome...

"But what about the atheists?" is another argument. What about them? Nobody is asking them to be baptized. We're not going to pass the collection plate. Just humor us for 30 seconds. If that's asking too much, bring a Walkman or a pair of ear plugs. Go to the bathroom. Visit the concession stand. Call your lawyer. Unfortunately, one or two will make that call. One or two will tell thousands what they can and cannot do. I don't think a short prayer at a football game is going to shake the world's foundations.

Christians are just sick and tired of turning the other cheek while our courts strip us of all our rights.. Our parents and grandparents taught us to pray before eating, to pray before we go to sleep. Our Bible tells us just to pray without ceasing. Now a handful of people and their lawyers are telling us to cease praying. God, help us. And if that last sentence offends you, well.........just sue me.

The silent majority has been silent too long.. it's time we let that one or two who scream loud enough to be heard, that the vast majority don't care what they want.. it is time the majority rules!

It's time we tell them, you don't have to pray.. you don't have to say the pledge of allegiance, you don't have to believe in God or attend services that honor Him. That is your right, and we will honor your right.. but by golly you are no longer going to take our rights away .. we are fighting back.. and we WILL WIN! After all the God you have the right to denounce is on our side!

God bless us one and all, especially those who denounce Him...

God bless America, despite all her faults.. still the greatest nation of all.....

God bless our service men who are fighting to protect our right to pray and worship God....

May 2008 be the year the silent majority is heard and we put God back as the foundation of our families and institutions.

Keep looking up...... In God WE Trust

Keep this moving, goodstuff speaks for itself.

Given to me by my son, Paul. —

Obituary for Common Sense

Today we mourn the passing of an old friend by the
name of Common Sense. Common Sense lived a
long life but died from heart failure at the brink of the
millennium. No one really knows how old he was since
his birth records were long ago lost in bureaucratic red tape.

Common Sense selflessly devoted his life to service
in schools, hospitals, homes, factories and offices, helping
folks get jobs done without fanfare and foolishness.

For decades, petty rules, silly laws and frivolous lawsuits
held no power over Common Sense. He was credited with
cultivating such valued lessons as to know when to come in
out of the rain, the early bird gets the worm, and life isn't
always fair.

Common Sense lived by simple, sound financial
policies (don't spend more than you earn), reliable
parenting strategies (adults are in charge, not kids),
and it's okay to come in second.

A veteran of the Industrial Revolution, the Great
Depression, and the Technological Revolution,
Common Sense survived cultural and educational trends
including feminism, body piercing, whole language and
"new math."

But his health declined when he became infected with the
"If-it-only-helps-one-person-it's-worth-it" virus. In recent
decades his waning strength proved no match for the
ravages of overbearing federal regulation.

He watched in pain as good people became ruled by
self-seeking lawyers and enlightened auditors. His health
rapidly deteriorated when schools endlessly implemented
zero tolerance policies, reports of six year old boys
charged with sexual harassment for kissing a classmate,
a teen suspended for taking a swig of mouth-wash after
lunch, and a teacher fired for reprimanding an unruly
student. It declined even further when schools had to get
parental consent to administer aspirin to a student but
cannot inform the parent when the female student is pregnant
or wants an abortion.

Finally, Common Sense lost his will to live as Lifetime Values became contraband, churches became businesses, criminals received better treatment than victims, and federal judges stuck their noses in everything from the Boy Scouts to professional sports.

As the end neared, Common Sense drifted in and out of logic but was kept informed of developments, regarding questionable regulations for asbestos, low flow toilets, "smart" guns, the nurturing of Prohibition Laws and mandatory air bags.

Finally when told that the homeowners association restricted exterior furniture only to that which enhanced property values, he breathed his last.

Common Sense was preceded in death by his parents Truth and Trust; his wife, Discretion; his daughter, Responsibility; and his son, Reason. He is survived by three stepbrothers: Rights, Tolerance and Whiner.

Not many attended his funeral because so few realized he was gone.

Now we have Beetle Bailey

BEETLE BAILEY/Mort Walker

335

" Beetle Bailey - by Mort Walker "

In World War Two we had Bill Mauldin's, "Willie & Joe", of the U.S. Army. His characters suffered through the war like a million other GI's and kept us smiling through the pain. This was the, "classic", story of G.I. Joe in the war.

Today we have, "Beetle Bailey", of the U.S. Army and their present day, 2007, episodes in the Army. Samples are shown here of the, Daily and Sunday cartoon strip. —

BEETLE BAILEY/Mort Walker

BEETLE BAILEY/Mort Walker

These were taken from the Tucson Citizen, a daily newspaper, - Weekend Plus section.

BEETLE BAILEY/Mort Walker

BEETLE BAILEY/Mort Walker

BEETLE BAILEY/Mort Walker

BEETLE BAILEY/Mort Walker

These are from the Tucson Sunday Newspaper- the Comic section.

HE OVER-DRINKS

HE OVER-REACTS

"The Men and Women of W. W. Two."

World War II U.S. Marines

portraying the courageous U.S. Marines who fought so valiantly in the Pacific

U.S. Navy Signalman

This 1/6 scale, next generation figure brings to life a U.S. Navy Signalman who landed at Omaha Beach on D-Day. You

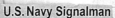

Battleship Row Crewman

Representing a Battleship Row crewman aboard ship in Pearl Harbor on December 7, 1941

Women of World War II

These fully articulated collectible figures include authentic uniforms with details such as caps, jackets, blouses, neck-ties, skirts and uniform pumps.

A: WASP...
B: WAVES.
C: WAAC...

USMC Heavy Machine Gunner

Wake Island, December 1941

Representing the handful of brave U.S. Marines that held off the Japanese invasion of Wake Island for weeks.

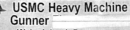

342

P-40 Warhawk Pilot
This highly
dressed and equipped in the style of Pearl
Harbor P-40 heroes Ken Taylor and George
Welch features triple-jointed arms and legs;

George W. Bush Pilot
This intricately detailed, articulated and highly collectible 12" figure depicts President Bush as he appeared on May 1, 2003, when he landed on the USS Abraham Lincoln (CVN-72). While at the controls of an S-3B Viking aircraft – designated "Navy 1" – from the "Blue Sea Wolves" of VS-35, he overflew the carrier before handing it over to the pilot for landing.

USMC Gunner
This highly collectible,
figure brings to life a USMC gunner who
fought in the bloody conflict at Okinawa

U.S. Marine

MITED EDITION

Rosie the Riveter Figure
This fully articulated collectible
figure replicates Rosie right
down to her denim work suit,
bandana, saddle shoes, factory hardhat,
welder's mask and gloves.

World War II Nurse
One of the most prominent roles played by
women in times of war is that of the nurse –
a role requiring both skill and courage, especially during World War II with its modern
weaponry and extended battlefronts

Thousands of men and women, like those pictured on these two pages, answered the call to defend their country in the military and the defense plants. They did what they had to do and, "Victory", was their reward.

The New Rising Sun
Don Kloetzke. The orange glow of the first atomic bomb to be exploded in combat lights the skies of Hiroshima as its deliverer, the B-29 "Enola Gay," banks to avoid the deadly shock wave.

It starts with the first picture on the left, - the dropping of the first atomic bomb on the city of Hiroshima by the B-29, - "Enola Gay".

Triumph and Peace
Tom W. Freeman. This dramatic print portrays the battleship USS Missouri (BB-63) and the USS Nicholas (DD-449) entering Tokyo Bay for the formal surrender ceremony of the Imperial Japanese forces, September 2, 1945.

Next is the battleship U.S.S. Missouri entering Tokyo Bay for the surrender of the Imperial Japanese Forces.

V.J. Day - Time Square.

We are civilians -

Kissing the War Goodbye
As Times Square erupts with excitement on VJ Day, this sailor celebrates with an impromptu kiss.

The Spirit of '46
N.C. Wyeth. Originally painted as the theme for a Hercules, Inc. calendar, this poster features WWII veterans ready to go back to the factories after serving their country abroad.

" SO SORRY "

Action in the Slot
Tom Freeman. The Japanese destroyer Makigumo goes down at the hands of PT-124 in 1943.

Last Voyage of the Yamato
Stan Stokes. The huge Japanese battleship Yamato, on a suicide mission to Okinawa late in the war, is attacked by hundreds of aircraft, including these Avengers from the USS Yorktown.

Japanese Aircraft Carrier Hiryu
Depicting the Soryu-class aircraft carrier Hiryu (Flying Dragon), which took part in the attack on Pearl Harbor and was sunk by air attack during the Battle of Midway on June 5, 1942,

Japanese ships that didn't make it, - and many, many more. So sorry!

Pawn Takes Castle
Tom Freeman. SBD Dauntlesses attack and sink the Japanese carrier Akagi (see kit on page 21), helping to secure the American victory at Midway.

The Last Mooring
Tom W. Freeman. On December 5, 1941, two days before her appointment with destiny, the USS Arizona berths at quay F-7, Pearl Harbor, Hawaii.

D-Day Normandy Landings
Robert Taylor. Under bombardment from German shore batteries, a large Allied transport ship lowers her landing craft during the D-Day Normandy landings on June 6, 1944.

The last day of the Arizona. Beginning of the end.

"Here and There"

Cold War Crossing Sign

Berlin Cold War Metal Sign
The crossing point between East and West Berlin during the Cold War was marked with warning signs that informed people of the approaching border.

YOU ARE LEAVING THE AMERICAN SECTOR
ВЫ ВЫЕ ЗЖАЕТЕ ИЗ АМЕРИКАНСКОГО СЕКТОРА
VOUS SORTEZ DU SECTEUR AMERICAIN
SIE VERLASSEN DEN AMERIKANISCHEN SEKTOR

Known Around the World.

SNAFU Metal Sign
Featuring a popular acronym – SNAFU – used by U.S. troops in World War II and an equally famous WWII image of Kilroy peering over a wall.

Never Been In One

BRIG Metal Sign
Now you can really be admiral of the ship... with your own brig!

Been a passenger many times.

U.S. Navy LCM(3) Landing Craft
Depicting a Landing Craft Mechanized (LCM) that could carry 60 troops or an M4 Sherman tank

World Famous

"Jeep"

Flying Tigers Blood Chit
This 8"x 10" leather reproduction of the chit worn by the Flying Tigers during World War II states in several Chinese dialects to take care of the wearer and return him safely to U.S. forces – and offers a reward for doing so.

Westbound
A Date with the General
William S. Phillips. Having bombed its targets in Kobe, Japan, during the Doolittle Raid of April 18, 1942, the B-25B Mitchell – No. 15 – flown by Lt. Donald G. Smith heads toward the Chinese coast.

WWII

LIMITED EDITION

Production Wins Wars Metal Sign
Replicating a vintage advertisement used to motivate factory workers to do their part during World War II.

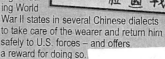

KEEP 'EM FIGHTING
MORE PRODUCTION
PRODUCTION WINS WARS

346

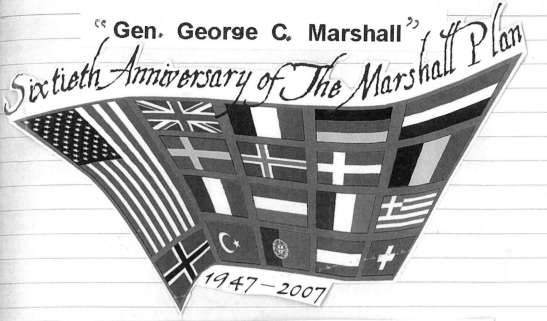

"Gen. George C. Marshall"

Sixtieth Anniversary of The Marshall Plan

1947 – 2007

June 5, 2007 marks the 60th Anniversary of Marshall's Speech at Harvard initially proposing the European Recovery Program, which became known as "The Marshall Plan."

George Catlett Marshall has been referred to as "the greatest American of the 20th century;" both the organizer of victory in World War II and the architect of peace for the postwar period. His 1947 plan to rescue Europe from the brink of political and economic collapse earned him the Nobel Peace Prize in 1953.

Yet Marshall and his many accomplishments, the quality of his character, and his selfless devotion to duty remain unknown to many younger Americans. The George C. Marshall Foundation is dedicated to changing that.

For more than forty years, the Foundation, located on the campus of Marshall's alma mater, Virginia Military Institute, in Lexington, Virginia, has promoted the principles that made George C. Marshall one of the great American leaders of the twentieth century. The Foundation, with its museum and library, is a living memorial for all who study and draw inspiration from the life and career of General Marshall

GEORGE C. MARSHALL
FOUNDATION
LEXINGTON • VIRGINIA

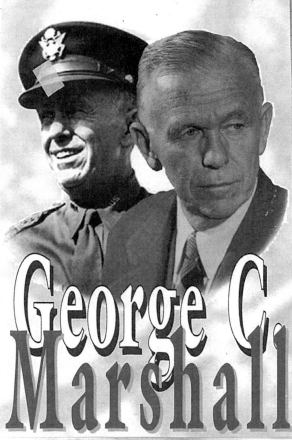

George C. Marshall

Flowers For The General

General Marshall is greeted by a small child bearing flowers while on an inspection trip of the western front, October 1944.

Photo is from the Frank McCarthy Collection of the George C. Marshall Foundation's Archives.

Winston Churchill, in an eloquent tribute, said: "He has always fought victoriously against defeatism, discouragement and disillusion. Succeeding generations must not be allowed to forget his achievements and his example."

349

"Gen. Georage C. Marshall"

I am including, Gen. George C. Marshall, in my book, because I feel he is one of our great, "statesmen", of World War Two. Probably many of our adults and for sure the youth of our Country have never heard or remember him. He never did get a lot of publicity but he quietly worked behind the scenes to bring an end to World War Two. He saved Europe from brink of collapse with his, — "Marshall Plan". General Marshall should be remembered for his accomplishments and his devotion to duty. Remember him as the architect of, "Peace". ——
Remember, — General George C. Marshall.

Charles Wysocki, jr.

GEORGE C. MARSHALL FOUNDATION
MUSEUM ❖ RESEARCH LIBRARY ❖ ARCHIVES
P. O. Drawer 1600, VMI Parade, Lexington, Virginia 24450

GOD BLESS AMERICA

German Mauser from WWII

K98 Sniper from WWII

Mauser Bayonet
Replicating
the S84/98 III
bayonet used on the
famous Mauser K98 bolt-action rifle,
which was adopted as the standard infantry rifle of
the Werhmacht in 1935, this bayonet features metal
grooved grips, a blood grove and a blue metal scabbard.

This was the official rifle of
the German Army in W.W.II.

★

"If we allow a mother to kill her own child, how
can we tell people not to kill each other?"

Mother Teresa

WWII

Union Jack Flag
This replica of the United Kingdom flag

U.S. Navy Recruiting Poster
McClelland Barclay. Painted in 1942 by one of the most famous illustrators of the day, the original oil painting used for this recruiting poster now resides in the U.S. Navy art collection.

To Victory
U.S. Army Air Force
This nostalgic artwork is a reproduction of a classic World War II USAAF recruiting poster. Posters such as this motivated young men to join and inspired the nation to support the war effort.

U.S. Navy Recruiting Poster
This replica World War II recruiting poster features a brave young sailor (with a PBY Catalina flying past!) encouraging us to join him in the fight.

Want Action? Join U.S. Marine Corps
James Montgomery Flagg. This colorful poster replicating a 1942 recruiting advertisement features an image of a Marine reaching out his hand for new recruits to join the fight in the Pacific.

Back the Attack!
Georges Schreiber. Featuring an image of a determined U.S. Army paratrooper who just put his boots on the ground.

1941 Willys Army Jeep

The first sports utility vehicle.

353

Doolittle Raid On Tokyo

    Sixty-five years ago, the Doolittle Raiders launched their suprise attack against Japan in response to the attack on Pearl Harbor. The daring operation helped boost America's morale in the early days of World War Two.

    On April 18th, 1942, 16 B-25 Mitchell bombers, led by then, Lt. Col. James Doolittle, launched a strike against Tokyo from the deck of the U.S.S. Hornet. The Raiders had to take off early when their task force was spotted by the Japanese and they did bomb Tokyo. They were to ditch or bail out somewhere along the Chinese coast when they ran out of fuel. Still only 7 of the 80 men died as a result of the Raid. Lt. Col. James Doolittle was awarded the Medal of Honor for planning & leading the Raid.

"Quotations On Patriotism and Prayer"

Peace is the highest aspiration of the American People. We will negotiate for it, sacrifice for it, we will never surrender for it, now or ever.

Ronald W. Reagan.

This massive attack was intended to break our spirit.
It has not done that.
It has made us stronger, more determined and more resolved.

Rudolph Giuliani

Responding to challenge is one of democracy's greatest strengths.

Neil Armstrong

Liberty is a thing of the spirit —
to be free, to worship, to think, to hold opinions, and to speak without fear, — free to challenge wrong and oppression with surety of justice.

Herbert Hoover

The cement of this union is the heart — blood of every American.

Thomas Jefferson.

There are those, I know, who will say
that the liberation of humanity, the freedom
of man and mind, is nothing but a dream. They
are right, - it is the American Dream.

Archibald MacLeish

Those who won our Independence
believed Liberty to be the secret of
happiness, and courage to be the secret
of Liberty.

Louis D. Brandeis.

Our Country is not the only thing to
which we owe our Allegiance. It is also owed
to justice and humanity. Patriotism
consists not in waving the Flag, but in
striving that our Country shall be
righteous as well as strong

James Bryce

Ask not what your Country can do
for you, but what you can do for your Country.

John F. Kennedy

I have never advocated war, -
except as a means of Peace.

Ulysses S. Grant.

356

Patriotism is easy to understand in America, — it means looking out for yourself by looking out for your country.

Calvin Coolidge

If you are ashamed to stand by your colors, you had better seek another flag.

Author Unknown

My God! How little do my countrymen know what precious blessings they are in possession of, and which no other people on earth enjoy!

Thomas Jefferson

The things that the flag stands for were created by the experiences of a great peoples. Everything that it stands for was written by their lives. The flag is the embodiment, not of sentiment, but of history.

Woodrow Wilson

So let me assert my firm belief that the only thing we have to fear is fear itself.

Franklin D. Roosevelt

Those who deny freedm to others deserve it not for themselves, and under a just God, cannot long retain it.

Abraham Lincoln.

The true test of civilization is — not the census, not the size of the cities, nor the crops. — no, but the kind of man the country turns out.

Ralph Waldo Emerson.

This must always be protected.

" COMING HOME – a dream we all had "

That's my dad! This picture was taken when the *USS South Carolina* returned, the emotion of the moment captured as a boy is reunited with his father after deployment. Submitted by Lt. Col. Robert H. Willis, AUS-Ret.

" My Thoughts "

About the War Movies,---- there are none that truly depict the horrors of War and they never will. It's impossible to show what goes on in the mind of a combat soldier, sailor, pilot or marine. Is it fear, anxiety, your insides jumping and shaking all over,- you can't stop it! It is very difficult to describe the feelings and the thoughts of men under intense enemy fire. I know that when I went in I was thinking of my Mother, but mostly of the job I had to do once I got on the beach. War does not solve the problems nations have between them- selves,- War just destroys everything! The one movie that, I think, comes the closest to the mind set and emotions of combat is,- "The Story of G.I. Joe,"- a black and white movie that I saw late in 1945. To many movies show the glory of War, when they should be showing the horrors, the pain and the gruesomeness that War is. We, the Veterans of,- War, want the World to be, at,- Peace,- for ever and ever,- No More Wars!!

We, the U.S.A., must alway have a strong and powerful military,- one that no other country would want to challenge. To do this I propose that when our, "Kids," reach the age of 18 they will be given 2 years of military training,- branch of service would be theirs to choose. For their service they would be guaranteed two years of college,- paid for

360

by, "Uncle Sam". There would be no exceptions as far as to who their parents are, – it is everyones duty to do what they can for their Country. It's everyones duty to be prepared to do what they can for their Country.

There are many advantages to this program, – it would prepare our youth for future, – descipline, obedience, responsibility, and love of Country. It would give our Country a trained, standing civilian Army ready for any emergency. Some would like the Military life and make a career of it, – but most of all it would help everyone in their civilian life by knowing what their responsibilities are. I think my proposal would help cure many of the problems we now have in our Cities.

If you agree, – let your people in Washington know.

Charles Wysocki, Jr

DO YOU REMEMBER WHEN...

- You'd reach into a muddy gutter for a penny?
- Nobody owned a purebred dog?
- No one ever asked where the car keys were because they were always in the car, in the ignition, and the doors were never locked?
- Stuff from the store came without safety caps and hermetic seals because no one had yet tried to poison a perfect stranger?
- Kids played baseball with no adults to help them?

" The Laws Of War "

What laws, – as far as I'm concerned there were none when I was overseas during World War Two. I know the Japs didn't play by any rules and they felt they didn't have to, – because they did not sign the papers at the Geneva Convention after World War One. We have heard of the many atrocities by the Japs including the Bataan Death March and the of Nanking. History has proven the Japs did not play by the rules, – but neither did we. I know of times when we could have taken some prisoners, – but we had no place to keep them or extra men to guard them, – so, they were taken care of. War is a battle for survival and how we did it was not always by the book. Wars are not fought by rules, but by any way possible to survive. If I would have had a choice I'd do whatever I had to do to save my life, – so, as far as I'm concerned there are no rules in War. You do what has to be done to win a battle.

Charles Wysocki, jr.
9-21-07

362

Yellow Ribbons

Yellow ribbons everywhere
Yellow ribbons show we care
For our soldiers overseas
We ask the Lord to bless them, please.

To walk beside them all the way
And bring them safely back, we pray.
And let all violence finally cease
Through God's grace, may we have peace.

Many nations suffer loss
Still we're clinging to the cross
Lord, fill our minds with streams of love
Let Thy light shine from above.

May all leaders guide the way,
Lord, hear our prayers as we display
Yellow ribbons everywhere
Yellow ribbons show we care.

Edna Massimilla

Perfect Peace

I sought peace... that's what I longed for most,
And yet, it always seemed to vanish like a ghost.
And so, I prayed for peace...
I knew on God I could depend
That this turmoil in my heart
Would soon come to an end.

Then God in His wisdom directed my gaze
Through the morning mist and early dawn's haze
To my garden wherein there gracefully grows
One yet remaining red, red rose;
Its petals dripping, drenched with dew.
Ah! This was peace... I knew... I knew!

Then, I spoke peace to my fellowman,
Lest he should fall from God's own plan.
That he could live a life so free
If given peace like that given me.
That he need not search throughout the lands,
For God holds peace within His hands.

Lou Ella Cullipher

America the Beautiful

O beautiful for spacious skies,
For amber waves of grain,
For purple mountains majesties
Above the fruited plain!
America! America!
God shed His grace on thee
And crown thy good with brotherhood
From sea to shining sea!

O beautiful for pilgrim feet
Whose stern, impassioned stress
A thoroughfare for freedom beat
Across the wilderness!
America! America!
God mend thine every flaw,
Confirm thy soul in self-control,
Thy liberty in law!

The Author,–Charles Wysocki, Jr. formerly of Milwaukee, Wisc. now a resident of Green Valley, Ariz. since 1976. I am 84 and this is my first attempt at writing a book,–hope you like it.

The Author, – at his desk working on his book.
Notice, – there is no type writer or
computer in th e picture The book is completly
hand printed.

Father, We Thank Thee

Father, we thank Thee:
For peace within our favored land,
For plenty from Thy bounteous hand,
For means to give to those in need,
For faith to walk, our hands in Thine,
For truth to know Thy law divine,
For strength to work with voice and pen,
For love to serve our fellow men,
For light the goal ahead to see,
For life to use alone for Thee,
Father, we thank Thee.

Grenville Kleiser

Yes,—it is time for me to say, "Thank you".
to all who have helped me put this book together.

I, "Thank", the good Lord for giving me the
time and the energy to write this book. I also
ask Him to give to the world,—PEACE,—for ever &
ever. Please,—no more WARS!!

Charles Wysocki, Jr.

JASMINE, the last addition to our home, she is a very nice cat and very smart

OUR MILITARY FAMILIES NEED YOUR HELP

Remember the families of our GI's, they to are at WAR.

Thank You!
Please know that, wherever you are,
what you're doing for America —
and for the World — is greatly appreciated.

All of us here at home are with you
in spirit. Your courage keeps us safe.
Your sacrifices make others free.

May God keep you safe, and
bring you home to a grateful nation.

Prayer for Our Service Men and Women

Lord, Hold these loved ones in your loving hands. Protect them as they protect us. Bless them and their families for the selfless acts they perform for us in our time of need. Give them courage, hope and strength. May they ever experience your firm support, gentle love and compassionate healing. We ask this in the name of Jesus, our Lord and Savior.

– Amen

Hold fast to God's hand and He will lead you safely through all trials. Whenever you cannot stand, He will carry you lovingly in His arms.

St. Francis de Sales

THE LAST SALUTE TO MY BUDDIES AND ALL WHO HAVE PAID THE PRICE FOR ALL OF US – FOR FREEDOM.

"Source and Contributors."

373

U.S. MARINE CORPS photo

Marine private **Ira Hayes** points to the figure of himself in the now-famous photo of leathernecks raising the Stars and Stripes atop Iwo Jima's Mount Suribachi.

THE BALLAD OF IRA HAYES

"There they battled up Iwo Jima's hill,
Two hundred and fifty men
But only twenty-seven lived to walk back down again

And when the fight was over
And when Old Glory raised
Among the men who held it high
Was the Indian, Ira Hayes"

"The Ballad of Ira Hayes," by Peter La Farge, was a Billboard hit for singer Johnny Cash, and was recorded by Bob Dylan, Kris Kristofferson and Townes van Zandt.

Ira Hayes was born in 1923 on the Gila River Indian Reservation. On Jan. 24th, 1955 he was found dead, near his home in Sacaton, Ariz.. He suffered from post-trumatic stress.

377

HERITAGE ALBUM
by Wendy Silva

Black and white photos aged with
Time now cover the pages before you.
These pictures are a reminder of a moment
In time and give us a past to hold onto.

The hardest of times our loved ones
Endured as they steadily paved the way
Gratitude and respect they have earned and
Their legacy of love we can never repay

Each photo has a story of personal
Happiness, heartaches, blood and sweat.
But for their individual journeys and their
Legacies to live, the sacrifices we must not forget.

Hold onto the history stored within these
Precious pages and allow these stories to live.
For these memories of trial and triumph are
The most priceless treasure that one can give.

Vietnam Memorial Poster
Peter Marlow. Completed on November 1, 1982, the Vietnam Memorial was built to acknowledge and recognize the service and sacrifice of all who served in the Vietnam conflict.

Magazines:
Military Officers Magazine.
D.A.V. Magazine - (Disabled American Veteran).
Purple Heart Magazine.
Time Magazine.
U.S. Army Magazine.
A.M.V.E.T.S. Magazine.
V.F.W. Magazine - (Veteran's of Foreign Wars).
The American Legion.

Brochures:
A.M.V.E.T.S. - American Mint. —
In Honor of Courage - National Park Service -
World War Two Memorial —
Long Beach Air Museum —

Letters:
James C. Roberts -
Sgt. Mike Masters -
Loise Pinkerton Fritz -
Abraham Lincoln -
Joseph L. Galloway -
Joseph T. Plening -

Bulletin:
Church Bulletin, (Our Lady of the Valley Catholic Church)
Knights of Columbus,   "   "   "   "   "   "

Newspapers:
Tucson Citizen -
Green Valley News

Catalogs:
Military Issue –
Historic Aviation –

Booklets:
Salesian Missions, –
The American Battle Monuments Comm. –
Quotations On Patriotism and Prayer. –

Newspaper Articles:
Mark Shields –
Samuel Thompson –

Poem:
A. Lawrence Vaincourt. –

Comic:
Mort Walker –

Others:
My Buddies, – Corp. Joe Sobol, Sgt. Mike Masters,
    and P.F.C. Duane Strinden.

Friends and Relatives:
Charlotte Collins, Phoenix, Arizona
Lillian Czarnecki, Green Valley, Ariz.
Paul Wysocki, Flagstaff, Ariz.

Other Contributors:
Clay Harrison – Tom McLeod
Grenville Kleiser – Jack Bernabucci.

"True Stories of World War Two and Dates Written"
by Charles Wysocki, Jr.

Titles: Written:

1.- "How I Became A U.S. Marine"-   2000
2.- "What Stills"-   2001
3.- "Shaving Lotion and Cologne"-   2001
4.- "When The Lights Come On Again"-   2001
5.- "The Vision"-   2001
6.- "Liberty In Hilo"-   2001
7.- "My Buddies"-   2001
8.- "Day of Infamy"-   2001
9.- "My Career As A Public Speaker"-   2001
10.- "War Is Hell"-   2001
11.- "The Doughnut Makers"-   2001
12.- "Assaulting The Beaches"-   2002
13.- "I'll Remember"-   2002
14.- "Embarrassing Moment"-   2002
15.- "WOW-Real Food"-   2002
16.- "The Merchant Marine"-   2002
17.- "My Life,- (If anyone is interested")- 2003
18.- "I Remember,(65 years later)-   2004
19.- "I Want Them To Know"-   2004
20.- "Memorial Day, (The Past To The Present")-2005
21.- "Deck Courtmartial"   2006
22.- "Pioneers"-   2006
23.- "Tarawa"-   2006
24.- "Iwo Jima, The First Flag Raised"-   2007
25.- "Memories"-   2002
26.- "My Thoughts"-   2007
27.- "The Laws of War"-   2007

" Marine Talk"

Baby Shit:- Mustard

BAM:- Female Marine

Belly Robber:- Company Cook

Blouse:- Uniform Coat

Boondockers:- Field Shoes

Boondocks:- Training Area

Brass:- Officers

Brig:-Jail

Chow Hound:- Food Maniac

Cold Cocked:- Knocked Out

Company Cluck:- Office Clerk

Cuntcap:- Garrison Cap

Dogface:- Army Soldier

Dummy Run:- Practice

Eagle Shits:- Pay Day

Ears Lowered:- Haircut

Field Scarf:- Marine Tie

Grab Ass:- Horseplay

Head:- Bathroom

Horse Cock:- Cold Cuts

Joe:- Coffee

Knock, It Off:- Stop

Liberty:- Going to town

Mess Gear:- Eating Kit

Piece:- Rifle

Pogey Bait:- Candy

PX:- Post Store

Sack:-Bed

Scuttlebutt:- Gossip

Sea Bag:- Canvas Bag, (clothing)

Shit Detail:-
        Dirty Job

Shore Party:-
        Beach Detail

Side Arms:- Pistol -
        Salt & Pepper

Skivvy:-Under wear

Slop Chute:- Bar

SNAFU:- Situation
    normal, all fouled up

S.O.S.:-Shit on a
    shingle. (creamed
    chip beef on toast)

Stateside:- U.S.A.

Survey:- Replacing
    equipment, clothing

Swab Jockey:-
        Sailor

"Navy"

Aft:-Back of ship

Bow:-Front of ship

Deck:-Floor of ship

Fan Tail:-Back of ship

Portside:-Left side

Starboard:-Right side

Bulkhead:-Wall

Ladder:-Stairway

" Notes - Notes "

Walking with Grandpa

I like to walk with *Grandpa*,
his steps are short like mine.
He doesn't say, "Now hurry up." He
always takes his time. I like to walk
with *Grandpa*, his eyes see things
like mine; a birdie bright, a funny
cloud, a penny that really shines.
Most people are in a hurry,
they do not stop and see;
I'm glad that God made
Grandpa unrushed,
and almost as young
as me.

From my Grandaughter –
Elizabeth Jinkins – Algonquin, Ill.

Charles Wysocki, Jr.

"May My Buddies Rest In Peace"

Charles Wysocki
738 W Paseo Del. Prado
Green Valley, AZ 85614-2035

ISBN 142515279-1

9 781425 152796